Sounding

Issue 3

Heroes and Heroines

EDITORS
Stuart Hall
Doreen Massey
Michael Rustin

POETRY EDITOR
Carole Satyamurti

ART EDITORS
Jan Brown and Tim Davison

EDITORIAL OFFICE
Lawrence & Wishart
99a Wallis Road
London E9 5LN

MARKETING CONSULTANT
Mark Perryman

Soundings is published three
times a year, in autumn,
spring and summer by:
Soundings Ltd
c/o Lawrence & Wishart
99a Wallis Road
London E9 5LN

ADVERTISEMENTS
Write for information to Soundings,
c/o Lawrence & Wishart

SUBSCRIPTIONS
1996 subscription rates are (for three issues):
UK: Institutions £70, Individuals £35
Rest of the world: Institutions £80, Individuals £45

BOOKS FOR REVIEW
Contact Soundings Books Editor,
c/o Lawrence & Wishart

ISSN 1362 6620
ISBN 0 85315 835 5

Text setting Art Services, Norwich
Cover photograph: © Freddie Contreras from the
installation Stud 1996
Shoes supplied by Vivienne Westwood

Printed in Great Britain by Cambridge University Press,
Cambridge

CONTENTS

————————————— Continued overleaf —————————————

Part II Heroes and Heroines

NOTES ON CONTRIBUTORS

Anthony Barnett is strategy advisor to Charter 88 and editor of *Power and the Throne* (Vintage, 1994).

Mike Waite has written on young people and left politics in a number of publications, including *New Times, Socialist History* and *Renewal*.

David Donnison works at the Centre for Housing Research and Urban Studies, Glasgow University, and at the Local Government Centre, Warwick University. His books include *The Politics of Poverty* (Martin Robertson 1982) and *A Radical Agenda* (Rivers Oram 1991).

Michael Laskey co-ordinates the Aldeburgh Poetry Festival and co-edits the poetry magazine *Smiths Knoll*. His second collection of poetry, *Driving Home*, is forthcoming from Peterloo.

Bernard O'Donoghue was born in County Cork in 1945. His volumes of poetry are *The Weakness* (1991) and *Gunpowder* (1995), which was shortlisted for the TS Eliot and Whitbread prizes.

Sheenagh Pugh was born in 1950 and lives in Wales. She has published six collections of poetry and is, as far as she knows, the only poet to have been published in *Snooker Scene*.

Phil Cohen helped to set up the Centre for Adoption and Identity Studies at the University of East London. He is an adoptive parent, and started writing poetry a few years ago. He is a member of Highgate Poets.

Cynthia Cockburn is a researcher and writer based at City University, London, where she is a research professor in the Centre for Research in Gender, Ethnicity and Social Change.

Peter Tatchell is a member of the lesbian and gay direct action group OutRage! He is the author of *Safer Sexy: The Guide To Gay Sex Safely* (Freedom Editions), and *We Don't Want To March Straight : Masculinity, Queers & The Military* (Cassell).

Iain Chambers teaches at the Istituto Universitario Orientale, Naples. He is author of *Migrancy, Culture, Identity*, Routledge 1994.

John Gill is an independent curator, and curated *Boxer* and *Offside!*

Nick Hallam is a freelance publicist and writer.

Gilane Tawadros is Director of the Institute of International Visual Arts in London.

Angela McRobbie is Reader In Sociology at Loughborough University of Technology and is author of Postmodernism and Popular Culture (Routledge 1994).

Tim Lang is Professor of Food Policy at Thames Valley University. He is co-author, with Yiannis Gabriel, of *The Unmanageable Consumer* (1995), and, with Colin Hines, of *The New Protectionism* (1993).

Yiannis Gabriel is Lecturer in the School of Management, Bath University. He is the author of *Freud and Society* (1983) and *Working Lives in Catering* (1988). He is co-author of *The Unmanageable Consumer* (1995).

Barbara Taylor teaches cultural studies at the University of East London. She is author of *Eve and the New Jerusalem*, Virago 1983.

Jonathan Rutherford is the author of *Our Dead Bodies: Essays on Englishness Empire and Masculinity* (Lawrence & Wishart, forthcoming).

Graham Dawson teaches at the University of Brighton and is author of *Soldier Heroes : British Adventure, Empire and the Imagining of Masculinities* (Routledge 1994).

Becky Hall is working on a PhD at York University on the production of the West Indian Mulatto in the English cultural imagination 1790-1860.

Anna Grimshaw is a lecturer in visual anthropology at the University of Manchester. She looked after James for the last six years of his life and has edited four volumes of his writings, including *Special Delivery : The letters of C.L.R. James to Constance Webb 1939-1948*.

Simon Edge is a freelance journalist. He was the editor of the *Capital Gay* until that paper's closure in 1995.

Kirsten Notten is a PhD student at the Technical University Twente, in the Netherlands. She is working at the Department of Philosophy, as a feminist philosopher, on a dissertation on care and technology.

Susannah Radstone runs the MA in Cultural Studies: History and Theory, at the University of East London. She is the editor of *Sweet Dreams: Gender, Sexuality and Popular Fiction* (Lawrence and Wishart). She is author of *On Memory and Confession*, (Routledge, forthcoming) and editor of *Memory and Methodology*, (Berg, forthcoming).

Graham Martin is former Professor of English Literature at the Open University.

Beefing about the single currency

It has been amazing in the last few weeks to observe the Europeanisation of the British beef crisis. At first, BSE by itself was bad enough - the sad pictures of the young victims of Creuzfeld-Jacob disease, the horrifying health risks to everyone, and the evidence creeping out of the effects of deregulation, secrecy, and poorly enforced safety standards. Agribusiness seems to have been engaged in more-than-usually unnatural practices to have turned cows into carnivores.

Then the Government and its remaining allies in the press decided to blame the European Union for the ensuing crisis in the beef industry, despite the fact that mad cow disease is most prevalent in England, not on the continent, and despite the fact that it is consumers, not politicians, who have been shaping events (as Tim Lang's article explains). Continental consumers have apparently been continuing to refuse beef of all kinds, regardless of its national origins, even whilst British consumers have gone back to their home-grown burgers and joints. But there is evidence that what began its life as an absurd (if calculated) xenophobic tantrum may have found a strong echo in British public opinion. It is reported that many in Britain blame the EU for the BSE problem, and are now eating beef for Britain (though not all *Soundings* editors can bring themselves to believe this). Perhaps the very idea of mad cow disease has destabilised the public mind.

It seems that anxieties about contamination and impurity provoked by the threat to the national diet have run somewhat wild. It has been found convenient

7

to displace blame for the shambles of deregulation of the food industry on to 'Europeans' who have, after all, only been taking seriously the warnings issued by British scientists. Britain's 'rights' (to sell beef to consumers who don't want it, or to put it on President Chirac's menu at the Palace) are said have been violated. Reactions to these insults to the national dignity then became caught up in defence of a slightly more substantial idea, that of British 'sovereignty', whose endangered emblem at this point, with the EMU in the offing, is the pound. In this atmosphere, public opinion is reported to have moved against the idea of British membership of the single currency.

Thus by a strange alchemy, the foreign refusal of one British totem has been transmuted into the threat to another. In its relation to the beef crisis - in the profit-seeking of yet another deregulated industry and the Government's anxiety not to lose revenue and prospective tax cuts from this - the prime agency of money was largely repressed. When money then reappeared, as an anxiety about the preservation of 'the pound in your pocket', it was as an equally phantasmic form. It is hard to conduct rational political debate in these terms.

It is odd that British sovereignty is felt to be endangered by the fact that Continental consumers are not allowed to buy British beef, even assuming that they want to, or would be wise to do so, in present circumstances. This might seem to be more of a problem for *their* sovereignty than ours - what the British Government really seems to want is for Continental governments to be *forced* to accept British beef imports by directive from Brussels. Appeal was being made to the European Court to make a judgement to this effect, though its outcome at the time of writing is unknown.

One thing should be said from the outset, and that is that neither side in the debates about the Single Currency and the European Union uses the term sovereignty in ways which clarify very much. Sovereignty is yet another of those words, like democracy and freedom, which are regularly called upon in political debate, but whose meaning is rarely examined. Indeed, it is the contest over *which* meaning of such words is to prevail which is, or should be, the real political issue. It is, for instance, rarely pointed out that those who wax lyrical about British beef, and scorn the meddling of European bureaucrats, can often be found blithely to have given up a host of other aspects of this venerated sovereignty. They support free trade and free movement of capital (though not of non-European people) across national borders. They are willingly subservient to international bodies or foreign governments of which they approve. Michael Portillo may not be able to tolerate the idea of the British military taking orders from 'Brussels', but he can imagine its involvement in Bosnia *only* under a NATO command. Mrs Thatcher, passionate defender of the sovereignty of this nation, on arrival in 10 Downing Street promptly abolished exchange controls. In moves such as this, government ministers promote the trend towards globalisation which in the next breath they will use as an excuse for the incapacity of the national state to act in defence of its people's livelihoods. It is policies such as these which have largely undermined 'our sovereignty as a self-governing nation'. The duplicities involved in all this are bad enough. Perhaps even worse is that they so frequently remain unchallenged.

Structuring debates around binary divides, forcing them into simple formulae of either/or - when in fact the terms at issue are themselves by no means clear, or when the actual difference of interpretation of those terms never itself surfaces - is of course an endemic characteristic of party politics. It has become even more marked in an age when political communication is so dominated by the soundbite. It is not only that details and nuances are omitted, but that the whole structure of the question may be distorted.

This is one element in what is happening in the current debate about the single European currency. The question is often reduced to an either/or - are you in favour of a single currency or are you not? And here too the grounds of choice are all-too-frequently reduced to the frame of 'sovereignty' alone.

Now of course there *are* issues of sovereignty involved in the question of whether or not the United Kingdom should join in any single European currency. There is, for instance, an important argument which would link economic sovereignty and democracy. This would say that the most significant element of policy control should reside at the level of political power to which there is the greatest democratic input, and which functions under the strongest conditions of public accountability. At the moment, this might amount to an argument *against* joining a single currency, since it is at the level of the nation state rather than of 'Europe' that democratic accountability is still strongest. These are important arguments: they raise the issue of what is meant by sovereignty (sovereignty for whom - the state or the people?); they point to its non-absolute nature (power is inevitably distributed between levels); and they hold open the possibility that the most appropriate levels for different policies may change over time (the democratic input into European institutions, for instance, might one day be greater than it is now).

This, however, is still to remain within the framework of 'should we join or should we not?' - the question which any potential referendum might put. Behind that question, though, lie deeper issues, of the nature of the arrangements for the single European currency as now proposed. The EMU is one element only in the construction of the European Union. But it is a significant one, and the nature of the agreement made about it will influence the character of that broader Union.

'The particular form of national sovereignty that dominated the post-war order has been eroded'

What needs to be addressed is the character of the European social settlement to which the currency, with all its attendant convergence criteria and regulatory mechanisms - will contribute. One cannot run away from the currency issue, but it is unfortunate that it is now defining the terms of public European debate.

As things stand at present, there is a grave danger that the arrangements for a single currency would enlist member governments within a dangerously neo-liberal framework of policy-making. As Keith Middlemass has put it, 'EMU and the creation of an ECB (European Central Bank) could also lead, even in the preliminary stages, not only to increasing political power for central bankers and a regime of deflation comparable to those in Europe after 1921, and in the developed world generally after 1931, but to the entrenched dominance of giant firms.'[1]

This does not mean, however, that one must be against a single currency in principle. For what should be debated is not only *whether* a single currency, but *the terms* of any such currency. The Maastricht criteria are famous for being about 'convergence'. But it is a particular notion of convergence. Interest rates, inflation rates, current government deficit and total outstanding level of debt have to be brought into line, it is said. The criteria of convergence do not require (though the word itself might make one think otherwise) any movement towards greater economic equality. Most obviously, levels of unemployment do not figure. Moreover, once a country has joined the currency, under the proposals as they now are, it might be less able to tackle the problems of inequality. In principle, a single currency could provide an extra degree of freedom - governments wishing to increase

---

1. Keith Middlemass, *Orchestrating Europe*, Fontana, London 1995, p 554.

spending and borrowing, for instance, could spread their debt around Europe. However, it is precisely to deter such behaviour that binding rules of economic management are being defined. In principle, it is also possible for there to be a major redistribution of resources across Europe, which might address these issues. But since the departure of Delors, such a programme looks less likely. And - to return again to the nature of sovereignty - there is insufficient accountability at a European level to make the Union responsive to democratic political pressures for redistribution. Thus, the combination of fulfilling the Maastricht criteria, and of subsequently submitting to the norms of management of the European economy, would be likely to lock into the system at least the levels of inequality - both within and between nations - which currently exist. (It is interesting that a number of financial spokespeople - including Eddie George - have recently mooted the possibility of including unemployment within the criteria. Whether such musings arise from political positioning, or from bankers' judgements that the levels of inequality in the system might be unsustainable economically or socially, is itself an interesting question.)

I t is a fact of life that the particular form of national sovereignty that dominated the post-war order has been eroded. We can now recognise its particular benefits - in providing an insulating barrier within which a social settlement, including a welfare state, could be constructed - in the damage brought about by its disappearance. It was *because* the powers of the state were being deployed to some degree against capital, and on behalf of ideas of social justice, that the Thatcherite revolution was so hostile to certain aspects of national sovereignty, and so systematically dismantled the power of government to protect the people against market forces. The failure of Mitterrand's interventionist programme in 1981 was a cause for complacent celebration on the right in Britain, since it showed that the social democratic form of national sovereignty was now seemingly dead. The later difficulties experienced even by Sweden in maintaining its welfare state - the most egalitarian social settlement in Western Europe - then forced the point home.

There is no going back to what might now seem a golden age. Least of all for Britain, whose long-standing competitive weakness gives one no reason to believe in a dream of democratic socialism in one country *here*. In an international environment now so dominated by market forces, the nation state has become a less reliable shelter against economic adversity. Labour governments have rarely been courageous in their response to international market pressures, and New

Labour will begin with weaker powers at its disposal than its predecessors. Left wing nationalism does not offer a plausible economic perspective.

Nor can or should cultural identities in what are now multi-ethnic communities, consisting of increasingly widely-travelled and multi-lingual citizens, be forced back into a neo-traditional national shape. Roast beef is only one of the dishes that is now regularly on the British menu; it shares its place on a daily basis with recipes from many lands. Right-wing hostility to Europe goes, we note, with equal dislike of the plural identities and peoples that in reality comprise 'Britain'.

The European Union, in this situation, should thus be an object more of hope than of fear. It was and remains in its conception a plural, multi-national entity. Although there is certainly the possibility of a new kind of Euro-chauvinism being constructed in opposition to a non-Christian and non-white 'Other' beyond its boundaries, this need not happen. The large size of the European market might in principle make possible more effective kinds of market regulation and social protection than are now feasible for isolated national economies. The EEC and the European Union were constructed first as a customs union, then as a single market, privileging the 'level playing field' for the flow of capital, commodities and markets, over more social values. Nevertheless, the national governments most committed to the Union have not so far dismantled their welfare systems with Thatcherite zeal. There are embryonic mechanisms in the EU for social redistribution - including funding streams from which many deprived areas in Britain now benefit. The debate about the Social Chapter showed that working people's rights and entitlements *could* form part of the concept of fair competition across Europe. Britain's opt-out weakened the whole conception - and enabled others in Europe to appear more progressive than they were - but also sought to define Britain's distinctive comparative advantage as a country of low wages and weak social protection. Although it has been unfortunate that the Common Agricultural Policy has been by far the most robust form of market regulation in Europe, even this has shown that markets in the European Union need not always be sovereign.

The real argument is about what kind of Europe should be built. There is the possibility of strengthening Europe's democratic institutions - for example, its Parliament, or even through a directly elected President of the Commission. And of giving priority to economic goals of consistent growth, environmental protection, and social justice, within a mixed economy in which both markets and democratic governments have major roles. It is in this wider context that debate about the single European currency should be taking place. The crucial debate *is* about convergence criteria between member nations - but not about whether we or anyone else now meets them, but about what these should be. The convergence criteria need to be re-written, to include acceptable levels of employment, minimum incomes, and social entitlements, not merely those of rates of inflation and public debt.

Moreover, the prospective single currency is but one element in the construction of 'Europe'. The question of democratic structures should also be central. To give priority to a single currency is to promote a Central Bank as *the* dominant European institution. There are major questions to be addressed concerning the accountability of this bank itself, and there needs to be more than one locus of power in a democratic Europe.

The political left is not as powerless in this situation as it might sometimes seem. Poorer and more social democratic members, and potential members, of the European Union, have already had some leverage on policies of redistribution and the nascent social agenda. It was probably no accident that the social agenda arose when enlargement was being negotiated, and referenda had to be won (or lost) in several countries. And because the nationalist right is now so hostile to European institutions, a consensus which would support the development of such institutions needs now to include at least some of those on the left. (In Italy, for example, after the recent elections, Rifondazione Communista holds a balancing number of seats in one House, and can have a some say in Italy's European policies.) There is scope across Europe to begin the exploration of a broad social and economic agenda for a federal European Union, which would transfer power downwards to regions and cities as well as upwards to federal institutions. We shall pursue these issues further in the pages of *Soundings*.

DM & MR

The divorce

Anthony Barnett

The Windsor Spencer divorce is linked to a larger break-down. Anthony Barnett analyses the crisis of the monarchy and looks at the opposing solutions that Diana and Charles offer.

If only for trying to save the countryside and normalise AIDS, both Charles and Diana have been left-wing heroes for some. Each seeks to retain the essence of the monarchy's pre-democratic authority - its special magic - and this makes them dubious candidates for hero worship. Yet both have also sought to modernise the monarchy's appeal. Seeking to renew its support, they draw in new ways upon popular non-capitalist traditions and attempt to speak to the people 'as a whole'. Each seems to try to resist the worst divisions of British society, each seeks to offer 'hope' and reaches out, respectively, to the poor and the dying of the inner cities. It is hardly surprising that many on the left and centre prick up their ears, while many on the right roll their eyes.

The divorce between the royal couple has clarified the difference between their 'strategies' for modernising the monarchy. Perhaps stratagems is a better word, as it implies approaches that are more instinctive and personal than ones based upon instrumental intelligence. An army commander might sit down with his Chiefs of Staff to assess whether a strategy of positional or fluid confrontation is better suited to a particular war. The character of monarchy today makes this kind of choice almost impossible for members of the royal family. The collapse of their surrounding institutions and the penetrating gaze of the media intensify the personal nature of their positions. Character and personality can only be inflected so far in their relations with the public. Nonetheless, they have adopted roles and fought for their claims.

The mixture of destiny and defiance, the weight of tradition and the pull of the new, gives the fate of the monarchy a fascination, one amplified by the huge waves of popular sentiment the royals are capable of generating. Some future study of the origins and fate of 'the spectacle' at the birth of the television age is bound to take the British monarchy as its centrepiece. Illusion and disillusion, belief and disenchantment, mean that a more sussed generation ceases to be 'taken in'. The British, a people 'accustomed to success', to take a phrase from the opening sentence of Will Hutton's masterpiece, now realise that they are witnessing failure through their unique symbolic institution. It was projected as being 'above them'. This was in turn offered as a humble assurance that there was something beyond politics that could hold everything together. Then the Royal family itself fell apart.

This could hardly be just a matter of individuals. The joint failure of the heir to the throne and the future mother of the next heir to stay together as a couple (or even as an institution while living apart as many upper-class couples used to do) is not in itself a great constitutional crisis. But it is more than a little local spot of bother. The great symbol has broken open because it is part of a wider breakdown. The monarchy, we are told, represents Britain. Ironically, we salute the Royal Family for having been most faithful in this respect - well and truly representative.

In this short article I want to consider three things. First, I want to show how the breakdown of the marriage is linked to a larger breakdown. Second, I want to consider the opposing solutions that Diana and Charles offer as their ways of resolving the crisis of the monarchy - the different ways in which they think that Britain should be represented, if not ruled . The contrast brings out their shared resistance to embracing democracy. Third, I will consider how Diana has managed to fight against 'the firm's' attempt to crush her.

But first

But first, I want to start on this final aspect so as to introduce the hero of this article. This is *the relationship* between us and them. This relationship is our everyman. It is the chorus that accompanies contemporary British history. It influences the way we feel about events as it disparages mere politics. It is a source but also a distortion of the irony, satire, inventiveness, of the distance and the closeness, the humour and sentiment, of British culture.

The royal separation is a starting point for identifying our hero. It allows us to see in open air something of the relationship *between* the royal couple. And, as they argue about how to relate to us - the people - we gain a new sense of our relationship with them.

This has only been possible because of the way that Diana has argued back. Theirs is not simply the story of the collapse of a relationship. One could have imagined a Great British Sigh, a huge and maudlin regret that confirmed that our collective intentions were worthy if optimistic, as the princess retired to a separate, private life. But Diana has refused this. She will not 'go quietly'. She is in favour of a proposal for a joint announcement on television, together but separate, reassuring us that the ship of state will sail on. If she gets this it will be a triumph, as it will confirm her equality with the future monarch. If she doesn't, she has already won this status in the public eye.

> 'Her defiance punctured a centuries-old male ruling culture'

It is helpful to distinguish the way in which Diana has succeeded in claiming the right to assert herself, from the content of her assertions. Her vision for the monarchy is ludicrous. But the way she has insisted that she be heard is a victory for the forces of equality. Even if it has been fought out between the silken sheets of inheritance in multi-million pound palaces and ski-resorts, Diana's refusal to be marginalised as 'a failure' is emancipating for everyone. Her defiant unwillingness to be parked in a spare palace as the inadequate wife punctured a centuries-old male ruling culture. The fact that it was already withered and weak enough to give way does not lessen the courage it took to burst it from the inside.

Diana undertook a two-part operation. The first part was to establish the legitimacy of her own voice, to secure her own authority as a national representative or 'ambassador'. In her *Panorama* interview she described the emotional catastrophe of her marriage of convenience into a weird and uncaring family. She spoke eloquently about her oppression as a woman. She talked frankly about her own humiliating illnesses. It was more than rehearsed. She shared with 23 million people words and events that she had talked over many a time with associates and supporters. The care taken to ensure they were effective does not mean that the words were false or dishonest. Their fairness, in any case, is not the point. Her objective was to clear away the palace's charge that she is a 'sick woman'. Apparently sympathetic, if disparaging, the charge is utterly destructive: a nineteenth century obliteration that turns opinions in symptoms. She was determined not to be stigmatised as suffering illusions best suited to the asylum. Yet the pressures *had* made her ill. So she talked about her bulimia years to show they were are over. She made out that her illness was normal, like any other illness. She insists that abnormal illness is, anyway, no reason for exclusion (hence holding the hand of an AIDS victim). She proves to us that she remains hale and robust (hence the public trips to the gym).

She succeeded. The moment of her success was when, in a television discussion immediately after her *Panorama* interview, Nicholas Soames, Charles's friend and a Government minister, declared that Diana was in 'an advanced state of paranoia'. His response to her description of royal life was to escalate immediately, by dismissing it as a delusion - that instead of being grateful she is simply mental. In the past this kind of crushing rebuke might have worked. Now, it amply and instantly confirmed to viewers the truth of the Princess's claim that the other side *were* her 'enemies' and that she was up against the callous, misogynist indifference and brutality of the British upper class - the public school brutes who would not know a scruple if it hit them between the eyes.

The public decided that Diana was sane enough by any standards. Whether or not people remain supporters of Charles - and many do - no considerable body of opinion supports her being drummed out of public life as Soames would wish. It was a famous victory in which sympathy for the underdog reinforced feminist resistance. She has, triumphantly, won the right to be taken seriously. Diana must now be attended to with respect. For this she deserves seven cheers. The question that follows immediately, however, is whether what she wants for the monarchy deserves any cheers at all.

The larger breakdown

Symbolic representation by a head of state - royal or not - grows from and is rooted in society. This is why it should not just be personalised. It is often argued that the reason for the royal shambles is that they have allowed the TV cameras into their lives and that this has lifted the lid and let out the magic. It has been said that, if only Charles or Diana had behaved differently, all would have been well. Ron Davies, Labour MP and Shadow Secretary of State for Wales, gained national fame for saying that Charles was not fit to be King because he talked to plants and lived in sin - even though few men have been as faithful as Charles has been to his long-time mistress, and he has talked to far more of the poor, struggling and dispossessed, and done more for them, than has Mr Davies.

All these arguments miss the point. As Linda Colley has shown, George III became the first popular monarch in the modern sense when he was seriously deranged (he talked to *trees*) and the behaviour of his sons was notoriously appalling. His popularity was due to the success of Britain in the wars with the French. When a country does well, its representatives will have achievement projected onto them. Faults become foibles, weaknesses proof that he or she is just like us. Were Britain today creating a new world empire, Charles could talk to plants all day and would be loved for it. Today, however, he represents a social order in decline. Anyone in this position will get it in the neck *whatever they do*. To talk is self-serving, silence is arrogance, dignity is denigrated, honesty condemned as bad faith, bad faith is pilloried.

The problem, as a senior politician put it to me, is that instead of representing the constitution, the Royal Family personify it. Instead of being a symbol - a merely decorative head of state - it has become a substitute for a contemporary constitution. This has been forced upon it by compression, as the old regime has collapsed. The monarchy inherited by Britain once symbolised an enormously successful social order, that created contemporary royalty as part of its wider creation of Empire. It was a world order. The sun never set on it, even in 1946. The army, the church, the aristocracy, the empire, the City, the old-boy network and its special institutions like the BBC, these all worked, in a way that they no longer work.

It is difficult to describe the effect of the absence of Charles and Diana. Some imagination is needed, naturally enough as we are considering the monarchy. Imagine, then, that a military coup against Gorbachev had succeeded, as it might well have in 1990. Soviet troops would have mobilised and NATO would have counter-prepared. In a state of high tension, Charles and Diana, both regimental commanders-in-chief, would have visited the troops to sustain morale and *she* especially would have done so. Their marriage would have remained cold, but in the face of a determined enemy, a public breakdown would have been unthinkable *while they were needed*. Had Britain still retained its world role this would have propped up the monarchy.

The enfeebled role of the church is evidence of a different kind of hollowing out of the old props. Margaret Thatcher led a determined assault on consensus paternalism - the closed shop of the old regime - which the monarchy personifies. Her brand of Toryism, famously, seized the absolute power of 'The Crown in

Parliament' to use it for its own advantage. One of the centres of resistance was the Church of England. Even after the Falklands War it defied Thatcher and refused to baptise her triumphalism. In return, the Prime Minister used her control of patronage over the established church to weaken its leadership. She used her royal, prerogative powers to erode the confidence of one of royalty's main supports. The outcome today is the lame, inarticulate response from Lambeth to the breakdown of the royal marriage. Under confident leadership, it would have presented the Church of England with the opportunity to re-establish itself as spiritual guide at the nation's helm in a time of moral storms. Instead, the royals seem left alone, bereft of institutional support even from England's pastors.

A final example. Suppose that, when she was struggling over whether to marry the divorced Mr Townsend in the 1950s, Princess Margaret had approached the BBC and asked to give a surprise interview. The Governor would certainly have been informed, which he was not in 1995. And he would have told the Palace. It would have been simply unthinkable to do otherwise. Then it was everybody's duty to protect the monarchy. Today the BBC remains part of the governing network of the British state, but its culture is far more open and competitive, even fractured. It cannot be 'relied upon', the royal family matters much less to it as an institution that defines its ethos. So far as the media is concerned, the Royals have themselves played a direct role in eroding such deference by using the mass media to campaign against each other. By doing so, they have undermined one of their own supports. Whereas even ten years ago the Palace exercised a *de facto* monopoly over the control of royal stories, and could have stopped Diana, today its grip is broken. Without this, Diana could not have staked her claim by talking directly to the British people over the heads of the establishment.

The monarchy matters much less in the 1990s because Britain matters less in the wider world, and because the monarchy matters much less to the social order and institutions that it heads at home. In 1994, I attempted a pre-divorce description of the way the 'buttresses that supported the cathedral of royalty have crumbled... leaving it isolated and exposed'.[1] Now we can see that there is a still more direct way in which the behaviour of the royal couple could not have happened in the days when there was only one way to do things. That 'way of

---

1. 'The Empire State', in Anthony Barnett (ed), *Power and the Throne*, Vintage, London 1994, p18.

doing things' was a highly institutionalised and richly reinforced pattern of rule. Within it, Charles and Diana may well have parted on a personal basis or they might have been trained to reconcile themselves to one another. They could not have separated in the way they have. It is not that they have fallen, but that the floor gave way under them.

Their argument

Having emphasised the impersonal, external forces at work on Charles and Diana, I now want to consider their personal views. People talk about the royals endlessly, and especially share their personal feelings about them, debating who is 'at fault' etc. But they rarely take any account of what Charles and Diana actually say. The starting point should be Diana's interview, because the failure to pay attention to her aims is evidence of the perennial inability to take a woman seriously.

She declares that we must be rid of our cold, remote, unfeeling royalty. Instead she wants a monarchy that 'walks hand in hand' with the people 'as opposed to being so distant'. 'I would like a monarchy that has more contact with its people - and I don't mean by riding round on bicycles and things like that... I think the British people need someone in public life to give affection, to make them feel important, to support them, to give them light at the end of their dark tunnels.' She will offer us love. She is training her two children to understand 'people's hopes and dreams' and to resuscitate in new form the royal healing touch of old.

Diana's plan is no more extraordinary than the institution she is seeking to transform. The English were the first to overthrow the divine right of kings at the Battle of Naseby (three hundred and fifty years ago). But the subsequent restoration reinstalled the monarchy as Defender of the Faith. Public consent may be necessary, but the British monarchy reigns by the will of heaven not the rule of man. The Queen considers that the sanctity of this role requires distance not television interviews. Sense and experience tell her that she may hold court but she should not hold hands.

Confusing consent with popularity, Diana's aim is to reinvigorate the divinity of monarchy that has passed through her to her sons. She thinks this should be done by intensifying the public's love and making us feel important. To achieve this the royal family must get rid of its old-fashioned stiff upper lip superiority. In her *Panorama* interview the Princess refused to exclude the Queen from her criticism. Apparently enraged by her daughter-in-law's audacity in saying that

Elizabeth should be a *better kind* of Queen, the monarch struck back and demanded divorce.

My concern is not to take sides in this dispute, but to understand its nature. For while the Princess spoke in a popular way, her demands are not democratic (let alone republican). She explicitly disavowed the model of European royalty. But 'riding bicycles' is not what makes Euro-monarchs different from our lot. After all, how many of them drive themselves daily to a public gym? What makes them more ordinary and less important is that their role is explicitly defined by a written constitution. Across the continent from Sweden to Spain, monarchs head their nations. But unlike British royalty, they are not the unlimited embodiment of state, church and constitution. Thus, by opposing the European example, Diana makes common cause with our own pre-modern monarchy.

'When the system worked, it did not matter what they were "really" like' Her project is not an improved, democratic form of constitutional monarchy, but a modernised version of unwritten, awe-inspiring royal dominion over our hearts (and therefore minds).

Charles sees it differently. His broadcast demonstrated his traditionalist preoccupations. The long Dimbleby profile was rarely lifted by tension or argument. For me, this made the following exchange stand out - I quote from memory. When the sorry interviewer said that Charles would be King of England, he was promptly interrupted, 'King of Britain, Mr Dimbleby, King of Britain'. The last word was gently but emphatically stressed. Charles has enough sense not to see himself as the light at the end of our dark tunnels. Yet he seems more remote and peculiar than Diana. Why is this?

He stands for nostalgic pastoralism, for Victorian architecture, for the teaching of good English and preventing social breakdown in the inner cities. His holistic approach fits with the natural ideal of the monarchy. His environmentalism draws upon pre-capitalist ideals, but he has assimilated a more contemporary critique of our ills than what is on offer from most politicians. His interest in spiritualism makes him, as he put it, 'a defender of faith' rather than a defender of *the* faith. Surely this green pluralist, whose Trust has invested so much into improving life-chances for the deprived of the inner cities, should be much the more modernist of the two. But Charles is actively seeking to renew rule from above. His project thus seems more paternalist and less populist than Diana's. She has the advantage of a childhood spent watching television. She knows what it is like to enjoy shopping. The youngest sister, not the eldest brother, she 'projects' the image of having a knowledge of what it is like to be like us. And that is beyond Charles.

Public relations are political relations, which means they are more than a matter of appearances. But the reality that I am concerned with is not the reality 'behind' the appearance. It is quite possible that Diana has a Sloane contempt for 'the Tescoes' who wave at her. Even more than Charles, she is from all accounts utterly self-obsessed. Her fascination with her own publicity, we are told, will put her on cloud nine for hours when a flattering set of pictures appears, while it sends her flying into sustained rage when critical items are published. Yet arguing about *this* means being drawn into the argument about 'what they are really like', which displaces concern from what *we* are really like. When the system worked, it did not matter what they were 'really like'. As the old system shrunk, the question of their 'real life' became a substitute for the social order that was evaporating around them. The Royals went along with this, re-charging their popularity with their television re-invention of themselves as a family. It was at this point that they became more a substitute for a constitution than its symbol.

Now, we are witnessing a major conflict inside the royal family over its future role and how it should relate to the British people. Charles, a majority of the royals, and what remains of the establishment, want gradual change which they believe they can control. But it is evident that they cannot, that they are 'out of touch'. Diana, absolutely determined to be Queen Mother, wants a populist transformation. She wants to bring the sixteenth century up to date; Charles's ambitions are more modest: his sights are merely on the nineteenth century. As befits her ambition, Diana's style is far more contemporary, dealing with AIDS rather than carbuncles. Neither side seeks a democratic outcome, in which future kings would be obliged to swear allegiance to a written constitution that belonged to the people. This would emancipate us from being subjects, and make all of us - including the royals - citizens in our own country. But from their point of view they would be diminished by becoming citizens. It is not a reduction any of them have embraced. Queen Victoria once said that she *could not* and *would not* be the Queen of a *democratic monarchy*.[2] Both Charles and Diana, like Queen Elizabeth, seem committed to the same principle. They are intent on

---

2. Quoted in G.H.L. Le May, *The Victorian Constitution*, London 1979, p 93.

modernising the monarchy, as Elizabeth did in her post-war period; modernising it, that is, *for* a democracy while preserving it *from* democracy. As a result they risk pitting the monarchy against the growing forces of decentralisation. Loved and admired as they are, the royals are not going to win a long-term popularity contest with democracy itself.

Her aims

Perhaps the difference between them is that, while Charles is seeking to modernise the old monarchy for himself, Diana is using herself to do it for her son. This has pitted her directly against Charles, and in her interview she challenged his suitability for the succession. Talking about herself in the third person, she said that she 'won't go quietly' and emphasised, 'I'll fight to the end because I believe that I have a role to fulfil'.

What is this role? Her answer was unspoken, in the public interview at least. But her intention is as clear. Diana's purpose is to be The Queen Mother - the official title of the present queen of our hearts. She has invested her ambition in her elder son William (and his 'backup' as she called the younger Harry - or should one say *her* backup?). Queen Mothership is the destination she desires, the role for which she will 'fight to the end'. It is with this as her destiny that she intends to radiate her form of royal enchantment. It is the position of Queen-Mother-to-be that defines her present claim to her own royal sphere.

Even if you take the future literally (always a dangerous mistake), her desire appears absurd. For a start the present Queen could live another twenty years at least before her son ascends the throne, let alone her grandson after her. But these are people who are living in the past, a past pulled into our present by the cameras of the media. They live in the past literally, in their palaces and castles. They live there psychologically. There is a family agenda here. According to the Morton book, the fear and anger of the Spencer children with respect to the royals and the present Queen Mother suggests a conflict that would make even Oedipus shudder.

I discussed earlier in this article how the monarchy, having been the commanding representative of the expansion of British rule, is now representing its confinement. One measure of this is the way in which royal marriages are being made within the circles of those who serve the family. Diana's family is upper-class, but it was nonetheless a service Earldom. Her father was equerry to George

VI and Elizabeth II. Her grandmother on her mother's side was Woman of the Bedchamber to the Queen Mother. Doubtless this led everyone involved to think Diana would know the score: a natural enough error that may have been reinforced by the fact that Charles first met Diana when he was dating her oldest sister, while her middle sister is married to the Queen's private secretary. Long inter-twined in this helix of subordination, the two families have also shared the inevitable troubles.

Twice in her interview Diana mentioned the effect on her of her own parents' divorce. According to Morton's account, its legacy was a definite hostility to the present Queen Mother. For when the Spencers separated in the early 1960s, divorce was still a scandal to be adjudicated in court. The children's mother was deprived of custody. Quite unnaturally, this was granted to the Earl. Apparently, Diana's grandmother testified against her own daughter's suitability as a mother, and this swung the argument. The Spencer children, according to Morton, believed thereafter that it was the Queen Mother's disapproval that had decided the outcome. Believing that the children should stay with the Earl, she obliged their grandmother, her Woman of the Bedchamber, to withdraw her support from her own daughter. True or not, the Spencer children apparently thought that the Queen Mother had taken their own mother away from them. What better requital than to replace her? And what better example of the fate to be resisted, than to herself become a mother stripped of responsibility for her children, cast to the outer pale by a royal divorce?

If we put aside Diana's archaic collaboration with the presumption of the royal family, and focus simply on her achievement in making it from apparently naive waif to sophisticated ambassador, a powerful mix of forces suggests itself as combining to put her into orbit on her own.

There is the disintegration around the royal family, which deprived it of contemporary intelligence, together with their inability to understand Diana and hence control her with the necessary sympathy. But, more importantly, as I have tried to show, had the surrounding institutions that once made the monarchy - the army, the church, Britain's international role - still needed the Crown and fed their influence into it, then the manner of the royal breakdown would have been different and may not even have gone public. As it turned out, Diana's isolation within the Royal family was one of the factors that gave her room to get her own back. And her isolation within the royal family was itself an echo of the whole set-up's isolation from any network which wasn't either close to their own interests, or simply sporting. A further resource that Diana had to draw on was almost certainly provided by soaps and the general television consciousness of the need to fight back against bullying and unfeeling behaviour. And she had a lot to fight back with. Not least the adulation of the public. Charles may have shown her how to work the crowds, but it did not take her long to see that she was better at it. Then, there was the family history: Windsors attached to Spencers and taking the life out of them in repayment for many years of service. Gratitude was undoubtedly expected. 'One would have thought', one can hear the voice saying, 'that the wretched girl would have been grateful to be elevated and have fame and fortune bestowed upon her'. Revenge is more likely to have been the emotion.

It is the fate of monarchy to be hereditary and Diana is the mother of the next but one in line to the throne. When she presses for Charles to withdraw, her aim is less William's elevation than the desire to become Queen-Mother-in-Waiting, representing the future of a throne now defined overwhelmingly by women. The very instrument that she has used to stake her claim could prove her undoing. William could renounce his claim rather than be obliged to choose between his parents' conflicting claims. Whether or not this would be a modern, grown-up thing for a Royal to do, there is no doubt what the grown-up response of the British people should be. To define their country's head of state for themselves, and put an end to that relationship between them and us.

To Stanworth and beyond

Mike Waite

Mike Waite reflects on contacts with the anti-roads movement, and considers the relationships, overlaps and distances between such 'DIY' protests and more familiar concerns, agendas and approaches on the left.

I was a bystander as the eviction took place, as the old trees were felled to screams of pain and anger from protestors, as people who'd been living for months in carefully constructed treehouses - some with stained glass windows - were dragged down to earth by guards and mercenary climbers. Rolls of barbed wire marked the space in the deep valley within which the motorway flyover would be built, and scores of yellow hats stood behind it, posing bored or threatening. Every few minutes a clutch of 'tree people' would be pushed out of the battle ground and find themselves with us, on the wrong side of the wire, torn from their 'tat' (belongings), and from the site which they'd been defending and making their own. In spite of the non-violent forms of resistance they offered, many suffered injuries and arrests at the hands of police and 'security' who were psyched up and excited.

The destruction of 'the village in the sky' at Stanworth woods in Lancashire, on the route of the M65 extension between Blackburn and Preston, was at that time - May 1995 - the longest such eviction of its kind. The determination of the protestors, the stake and commitment they'd made to the cause, was a key reason. Imaginative tactics were another - the choice of a steep-sided gorge in which to make a stand ; aerial walkways of wire and rope strung between trees fifty foot

27

Tony Knox

high, allowing one individual perched up there to defend three or four trees from the axe at a time, as the contractors could see that felling any one of the trees would gravely risk the protestor's safety.

It had dawned on me gradually that something important was taking place in the woods. Conversations during a few short lifts given to 'tree people' who'd been walking along the quiet roads on my route to work made me decide to make the first trek up. More and more 'locals' lent support as the settlement grew, taking food or old clothes or money up to the woods, spending some time up there, and writing supportive letters to the local papers. By the time of the eviction I'd become convinced that the mainly young people who were central to it deserved widespread support and backing, and that their agendas and style had much to offer older radicals still in search of sources of renewal - a small part of a wider growth of support for and fascination with the DIY protest culture.

Increasing numbers of articles in the left and liberal press - from *Red Pepper* and *New Times* to *New Statesman and Society* and *The Guardian* - were pointing to and amplifying the voices of the varied new protest movements : campaigners against the Criminal Justice Act ; animal rights activists at Shoreham and Coventry ; environmental activists from Road Alert and Earth First !. Although there are differences between these strands of radicalism, there are enough similarities between them to justify the over-arching description they've attracted - this is 'Do It Yourself' protest, fuelled by a belief in the benefits and potential of people campaigning directly, using their own resources on the issues that matter to them.

The attractions were obvious. Not only did they automatically deserve to be defended, as the target of Tory and establishment vilification; but, in addition, such movements were vital, engaging and stimulating serious commitment to radical causes, and were capable of attracting wider sympathy. The way in which core anti-road campaigners committed themselves to long months of living in the treetop camps inspired respect, and a view of them as the shock-troop heroines and heroes of 1990s radical politics. Those centrally involved were most often young, from the generation which the established left has found such difficulty attracting. And their effects were direct. After years of taking the long view, of pinning restricted hopes for future change on Labour's election (perhaps the time after next), or working patiently for realignment, how refreshing it was to see actions which directly challenged government policies and exploitative, environmentally destructive industries. Even if the particular motorways which were the focus of current protests ended up being built, the actions were adding hundreds of thousands of pounds to the bill, thus creating problems for all future plans for roads, and quite possibly contributing to a real establishment rethink on the priority given to the car in transport policy.

The DIY movement has seemed exotic and new to many commentators and supporters drawn from the left. Communal meals in 'benders', and deep conversations on ecology and politics whilst sitting in tree branches high above the ground, are welcome contrasts to the thin cultures of labourism and the rule-bound aridity of the trade union movement. The location of the protests within a counter-cultural lifestyle is also attractive. It communicates a sense of total engagement, all aspects of activity being shaped by the cause - in clear contrast to the frustrating contradictions and dilemmas which shape so much of life. And there's an emphasis on fun which is the more liberating for its being irreverent. The nights just before the Stanworth eviction coincided with the time of the pagan 'beltane' celebrations, and were marked by many of the protestors by dancing naked round the woods to the sound of scores of drums being pounded to the early hours. The farmer's wife half a mile away complained to the press about the noise and was scorned by the 'tree people' - would she prefer the relentless sounds of juggernauts roaring over the flyover which they were trying to block ?

Cultural aspects of the DIY movement are many, and are important to it. Along with the reinvention of ancient rituals and interest in 'magick' (to which dismissive rationalist contempt is a lazy, inadequate and uninteresting response - especially as interests in mythology and 'new age' thinking are linked to engagements with social issues which traditional political agendas have been unable to stimulate), the scene has resourced, and is resourced by, a large variety of fanzine-style magazines and 'anti-copyright' information sheets, produced by loose collectives and anarchist groupings across the country. Musicians can be found wherever there are protests, with flutes and whistles and other folk instruments. The best known group - the Levellers - have provided the scene with tuneful anthems which have hit the charts and drawn large numbers of young people towards radical values. Others have combined such elements as protest song, and strident or humorous anti-authority messages, with folk styles or punk or improvisation. Far from 'selling out', or rising on the back of the movement, the likes of Chumbawamba and the Space Goats are an integral part of it, and the

Levellers' success has subsidised the Brighton-based organisation 'Justice?' and its widely-distributed *Schnews*.

All this hasn't come from nowhere. Some writers have traced the fragile genealogy of the movement back through the 'new age travellers' of the early 1980s, to the communities gathered around the free festivals of the 1970s and earlier, suggesting the development of largely unrecorded but resilient counter-cultures throughout these decades.[1] Often unconsciously, these counter-cultures sustained some of the values and commitments which had been part of radical left culture in the 1960s and early 1970s - and were able to do so by creating spaces outside those occupied by the organised left.

'The DIY movement is a welcome contrast to the thin cultures of labourism'

The routes taken by the 'peace convoy' and other travellers seemed, to many on the left, distractions from 'real' issues. I remember, when I was getting into activity with the Anti-Nazi League in the late 1970s, and battering my adolescent and unprepared head on the papers circulating at the annual Communist University of London, a short but intense phase of jealousy of a friend who not only had the enviable ability to grow a real beard, but dropped out of sixth form and went off with the hippy convoy, after one of the short occasional summer festivals at a site at Pickup Bank, above Hoddlesden (from which you'll soon be able to see the M65 extension). The rumours soon came back that he was living in a tipi in south Wales, and had fathered a child by a woman twice his age. (But perhaps the real shock was coming across him again a couple of years later working in an MSC-funded unemployed peoples' advice centre, more smartly groomed than I've ever been.)

Pete's journey back to the conventional and familiar locations of the left reinforced my view that 'dropping out' was copping out. But the Trades Club which housed that unemployed centre has closed down now. And now, when the hopes and alternatives nurtured by those who carried on living in the tipis and convoys have become the focus of the most currently significant anti-establishment protests by young people, I feel that maybe my choices and priorities back in the early 1980s were short-sighted.

---

1. F. Earle, A. Dearling, H. White, R. Glasse and Gabby, *A Time To Travel ? An introduction to Britain's newer travellers*, Enabler Publications, Lyme Regis 1994; G. McKay, *Senseless Acts of Beauty: cultures of resistance*, Verso, London 1996.

Lazy comrades

Unfortunately, a real appreciation of the *alternative* nature of the DIY movement hasn't been often demonstrated by its left supporters. Press commentary has often been marked by romanticisation and mythologising. Worse still, welcome attempts to celebrate, amplify and publicise the new radicalism have sometimes taken crude forms. Leftists have sought simply to aggregate its positive features to their own relatively tired organisations and traditions. This happened most explicitly in the launch document for Scargill's Socialist Labour Party, which associated itself with the 'anti-motorway and animal rights bodies', and presented itself as the answer to their needs - a 'centre' for 'co-ordinating and organising such campaigns'.[2] In so far as such calls appreciate the need for alliance, they are based on the old class-centred model, where what the Communist Party used to refer to in the 1950s as 'women, youth, the co-op etc' are simply tagged on as extra forces in a fight to be defined and led by (patronising) white male trade unionists like Comrade Scargill.

Another problem is that the meanings and motives carried by and sustaining the DIY scene are assumed to be consistent with and supportive of the already existing agendas of the left. Thus anti-roads protests are interpreted and understood simplistically as threats and movements against the Tory government, without any acknowledgement or exploration of the challenges they present to traditional left culture.

It is impossible to interpret the DIY scene in this way if the new young activists are listened to for what they actually are saying and their points valued and acknowledged on *their* terms. For most of them would reject any attempt to label them as 'left'. Resistance to political pigeonholing is just one expression of the desire by most DIY activists to lead their *own* lifestyles and not be shaped by mainstream priorities and values, whether these are about housing, jobs, consumption - or the agendas of Blair, Ashdown or whoever. Their suspicion of establishment politics covers Labour (new *and* old) as much as the Tories, and it sometimes focuses particularly on the ultra-revolutionary organisations, like the SWP and Class War, who've made crude interventions into the DIY scene and anti-CJA demos, with their mass-produced placards and incitements to confrontation. Such episodes have often caused the debates within the DIY scene over left agendas to be limited to arguments over tactics. Should demos be 'made

---

2. A. Scargill, 'Future Strategy for the Left', *Red Pepper*, January 1996, p13.

spikey' or 'kept fluffy' ?

The new DIY radicalism should be valued both for what it is, and for its potential. But the lazy, patronising and crude responses to it from parts of the left are a block to genuine alliance and inter-play. If it is assumed by people to be what they already hope and expect to find there, opportunities really to *learn* from the DIY scene are being lost. And there is much to learn from it.

This accusation of laziness also covers a failure to question and investigate the movement as fully as possible. I've come to the view that all the articles which simply *celebrate* the scene, like some appearing in *The Guardian*'s coverage of Newbury, end up patronising the people involved. All very nice, this, very unusual, very colourful clothes, and political too ... an ideal subject for a supplement article. But the movement deserves much more than this. It has established its right to be taken seriously enough to be *interrogated critically*. And here I want to begin to flag up the areas where some traditional and newer left concerns could be applied to the new radicalism.

I've wondered about my motives as I've formed these views. And I accept I might be failing to live up to the resolution I've preached above, to value and honour the movement on its own terms. But I believe that it's no disservice to a movement you've observed, supported, and even in minor ways become part of, to offer some criticisms and worries. There are many people and groupings within the movement quite robust enough to stand and respond to critique. And, in fact, many are very open to the conversations and debates now beginning about future strategies and approaches.

As well as security and police and the road-building lobby and all their political allies and apologists, some of the blocks to the effective application of the concerns being worked for through the DIY networks can be found *within* the scene. During my afternoons at Stanworth, I was shocked by the degree of cynicism, or apathy, about the value of *organisation*. I'm not proposing a Scargill-type central command here, directing and determining from a privileged leadership position. Just a bit more reaching out to the opportunities that are there to build support. (Although I've heard stories that things have moved on since Stanworth, with skills workshops being held in different parts of the country, and the protest against the Newbury by-pass involving inter-connected camps, mobile phone links, and effective lobbying of potential allies.)

Back in April 1995 in Lancashire, I remember about ten of us sitting around the communal bender talking about how 'tree people' would quite often meet or hear of 'locals' who supported them in a passive kind of way. Kind gestures like lifts up the road or a gift of money. Words of encouragement. Supportive contributions to radio phone-ins. Someone suggested going into the town centre one day to do some leafletting or get a petition signed. It was a good idea. Someone else suggested getting the press along - colourful people with drums and instruments would make a good picture. I thought I'd be able to chat to people in the council to make sure it could happen without hassle from the police or town centre security. We talked about it for an hour, but whenever the conversation got around to when would it happen, who would do it, exactly what form would it take, the conversation would go off somewhere else. I couldn't pull it back without sounding like I was back down town in a Labour Party meeting with an agenda, and the people who were really involved, living up in the trees and stringing up the aerial walkways looked at me sympathetically and offered another cup of brew. The town centre event never happened.

It was as if amateurishness was being celebrated, as if the cause would be compromised by punctuality. Opposition to 'being serious' or 'getting heavy' always struck me as odd coming from people who were, full-time, devoting their lives to protesting. Yes, part of it was about maintaining themselves emotionally, not getting drained and head-battered by things that reminded them of the mainstream world

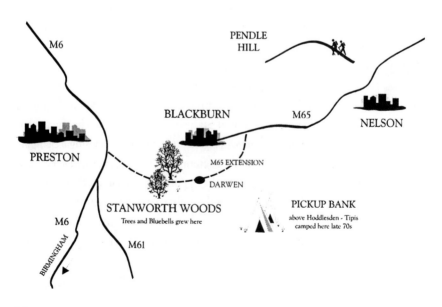

against which the protest was (partly) a reaction, not exposing themselves to the negative and threatening reactions they'd sometimes get 'down town'. But it spilled over into a cynicism about the use of processes and tools which could help and develop the protest.

Anti-politics

This was most explicit in relation to politics. Some protestors I spoke to - and argued with - were capable of lumping together all mainstream political organisations and initiatives, as 'all as bad as each other', to a degree that would trouble the most ultra ultra-leftist.

A few months after the Stanworth eviction, this was vividly illustrated by a testy exchange which took place at an Earth First ! gathering in north Lancashire, where Charles Secrett and a couple of other leading members of Friends of the Earth had come up to discuss co-operation and links. The people writing up the meeting for EF!'s *Action Update* were clearly toning things down when they said, 'there was mixed feeling as to whether FoE and EF! shared common ground ... while FoE are basically moderates, EF! is based on a principle of "no compromise" and encourages radical direct action ... it is not about reform'. Whilst some EF!ers apparently expressed the 'need for more allies, especially coming from groups with similar objectives', there is clearly a suspicion of mainstream politics on the part of some of the most committed DIY activists, which extends to organisations which it seems barmy not to see other than as absolutely necessary allies.[3]

P art of this suspicion of people who are not, now, doing exactly what the most radical DIY activists are currently involved in mirrors a lack self-consciousness about the roots and background of their own politics. Anti-rationalism is expressed in a lack of interest in recent history. Yet such history could teach many lessons and raise interesting questions for exploration by DIY activists. For example, McKay's book *Senseless Acts of Beauty* looks at the DIY radical politics and cultural interventions of the anarcho-punks Crass in the early 1980s, and suggests sideways connections between them and the hippies whom many of their fans would have despised. There are in existence histories to our counter-cultures which deserve to be restored to those currently up the trees and on the freedom trails ... today's 'in your face' activists might find the tales and

---

3. 'Earth First Gathering', *Earth First ! Action Update*, Bristol, October 1995.

reflections of people who are ten years or so older useful and empowering.

Disabling and paranoid beliefs about conspiracies, traitors in waiting, and the mainstream news media being merely establishment propaganda, are perhaps other 'subjective factors' (as old Leninists used to call them) which people in the DIY scene might seek to work on. During the eviction days at Stanworth, our house was open to people who'd been up in the trees for months but couldn't go back there now. Between meals and baths and sleeps on the floor and the sofa, the TV news was turned up. People were absolutely amazed to find that the eviction was not only being covered as a top item on national and regional bulletins, but was being presented pretty fairly and sometimes even with a feeling of sympathy to the 'tree people'. Up at the site, they'd taken fewer chances than they were offered to speak on camera, regarding press crews with suspicion. But there were good chats down in the house about the need to win allies everywhere, and to get the message across wherever you could. Basic stuff for those who've long got their head round sophisticated theories about the struggle for hegemony, but needing to be learned again by young oppositionists in every generation.

The most worrying aspect of the political identity of a few of those living up in the woods was a type of arrogant and exclusive posturing, fed by the kind of self-righteous sectarianism I recognise only too well from a few years spent as a student Trot. However familiar and understood this phenomenon is on the left, it's still tolerated in the DIY scene. The codes of conduct and organisational disciplines which attempt to keep such types in check in more settled groupings haven't yet developed - and there's some reluctance to develop them, because of suspicion of *all* hierarchies, and a liberal lack of discrimination about which contributions and styles of involvement and leadership are most useful. So some of the most bossy and over-confident types were far too often allowed to shout their orders without direct challenge.

Fittingly, there was a discussion sparked by gender politics in the Stanworth camp which drew out debate and understanding around this issue, and isolated one or two of the sectarians. Some of the women living in the trees were creating space for themselves to meet and talk, and responded positively to an opportunity for a series of women's self-defence sessions to be run in quiet clearings in the woods. These went well and were enjoyed by all who joined in - but were the object of suspicion and anger by some of Stanworth's self-appointed spokesmen. Attempts were made to marginalise the women who were central to the sessions - including one whose status temporarily changed in these men's discourse from being a respected and highly supportive 'local' to being an 'outsider'. Accusations flew around that the women-only sessions were divisive - why couldn't self-defence sessions be run for everybody, as everybody would be targetted by security and police when eviction was attempted. The angry men didn't seem to be listening to the explanation (offered by men as well as women) that these sessions were about harnessing and developing the particular skills and confidence of women - and that women in the protest camp, as well as in wider society, perhaps needed their own space within which to assert their needs and prepare to defend themselves against put-downs and more serious attacks. Such talk sometimes opened out into limited discussion about the divisions of labour that you could find in the camp. Here, in the front line of radical eco-politics, you'd sometimes see women cooking the stew whilst the men were up the trees with hammers and nails and rope.

Positive choices

At Stanworth, the need to develop interest and awareness around questions of oppression presented itself particularly in relation to gender politics. A few people got into discussions about the resonances between feminist and eco-politics, but these were quite abstract. Dealing with issues raised in day-to-day camp life seemed trickier and more unsettling. And issues of race and belonging are perhaps deserving of further interrogation and discussion. For example, the activists who initially called the national DIY directory *The White Book* and were then surprised that black organisations didn't send in entries, indicate the need to spend some time learning about the politics of ethnicity. The rather sarcastic description of the process which led to the directory being renamed simply *The Book*, which appears in recent editions, only underlines this point.[4] There have also been warnings of the way that fascists can seek to rework radical environmental agendas so as to steer them towards their own concerns.[5]

But the big question raised for me concerned the ways in which strands of left thinking with which I'm familiar might link with or at least relate to the different

4. *The Book: formerly known as the White Book, futurely known as the Stella Pages : directory of active groups in the UK*, On the Fiddle Publications, PO Box 2600, Brighton, September 1995.
5. See, for example, M. Kalman and J. Murray, 'New-age Nazism', *New Statesman and Society*, 23 June 1995.

agendas raised by this kind of protest. There's overlap already. But there are tensions too. And these need exploring rather than denying. Those who simply celebrate the DIY scene are kidding themselves if they believe this will somehow rejuvenate their fundamentally old-fashioned projects, which have lacked vitality and force for some time. Suggestions that traditional left strategies simply need reviving to defend the anti-road protestors and 'new age travellers' against government attacks and media slanders are not only wishful thinking. They deny the extent to which the new radicalism needs admiring and needs to be allowed to teach and - in its own way - lead the way. At the same time, much of what's been learned on the left as it has struggled through Thatcherism and sought the road to renewal is 'transferable learning'. Ways need to be found to connect with the DIY activists and their groups and publications, and to develop dialogue and proposals around the insights and questions which result. This is surely an important task as people in the DIY movement look beyond the defensive struggles at Stanworth and Newbury, and towards influencing the positive choices that people may make about transport and work and lifestyle and values into the next millenium. Or have people on the left lost self-confidence to the point that they really feel they can offer nothing to a living radical movement of change and protest, apart from being a bystander, able to provide applause, a bath and access to the nine o'clock news?

What kind of New Labour?

David Donnison

Socialism has contributed more to human progress than any other political movement. It fulfils many of the functions which used to be performed by religions. Like them, it has to pass through a reformation when changes come about in the economic and social conditions which inspired its birth and shaped its early years. This is such a time - a time when we should identify and adhere to basic principles of the faith but learn to deploy them in new ways.

Scoundrel time

This is a scoundrel time that we live in. While millions of people are out of work - far more than official figures claim - and one third of our children are growing up in poverty, while pensions fall further and further behind wages and more cuts are made in services on which the most vulnerable depend, while class sizes in the schools increase and more children are excluded from school as unmanageable, while homeless people camp out begging in the streets, politicians in both our main parties try to bribe the voters with promises of tax reductions and compete for favour by attacking foreigners, refugees, lone parents and poverty-stricken youngsters. I have often disagreed with political leaders before; but never since Suez have I felt so ashamed of my country. The Suez adventure was over in days. This just goes on and on.

With Government back-benchers abandoning ship and the British voting for almost anyone who might help to get the present regime out, this ought to be a great time for reformers. It's when you ask who *they* might be that you realise it is not going to be that simple. What traditions do we have to draw on which might inspire a coherent resistance movement? As in most Western countries, other than the United States, our progressive politics are strongly marked by socialism. For many, that's still what 'the Left' means. Meanwhile others regard the whole movement as tainted by dreadful memories of Stalin. Which helps to explain the confusion among their opponents that has helped to keep the Conservatives in power for so long, and may do so yet again.

A progressive tradition

In so far as human progress is due to politics, democratic socialism has contributed more to that progress than any other system of ideas. In the countries of Western Europe and Australasia, where this tradition has been strongest, it brought working-class people into political movements and positions of power on a scale never achieved in North America, Ireland or other societies lacking a strong socialist tradition. It built for them a stronger welfare state and came closer, for longer, to achieving full employment. At a time when so many write it off, it is important to recall those achievements. Socialism served the purposes of a religion (I say that with respect, not derision), explaining human suffering, providing moral principles and a guide to conduct, presenting us with a cast of saints and sinners upon whom to model our behaviour, bringing people together in comradeship to rededicate themselves, and promising them hope of a better future. (Economics, as a discipline, has many of the same functions, but for a different church - coming complete with a priesthood, schisms, arcane symbols, and most of the other trappings of a religion.)

From time to time, every system of beliefs passes through a crisis which compels a reformation of some kind. Old gods and the principles they stand for are jettisoned as new times call for new ones. (Karen Armstrong, in *A History of God*, tells the Christian version of this story.[1]) Socialism is now going through such a crisis. Its founders were the first political thinkers who squarely asserted that morality, law and culture are a product of a society's economic

---

1. Karen Armstrong, *A History of God*, Heinemann, London 1993.

and social structure, and can only be changed by changing that structure. Their successors, faced with ill-comprehended changes in economic and social conditions, are uncertain how to respond to a situation for which their own intellectual training should have prepared them better than most. Some stand their ideological ground and tell their comrades they should be preaching the old faith louder. (Brecht's comment on the East German regime's response to popular uprisings exactly describes their stance: they decided that they needed not a new programme but a new electorate.) Others engage in supermarket politics: finding out what their opponents are selling, they offer their own brand, better and cheaper. In between stand a lot of honest, bewildered socialists; wanting a fairer, more equal society, but not convinced that either wing of

'From time to time every system of beliefs passes through a crisis which compels a reformation of some kind'

the movement can achieve that. It took four successive defeats at the polls and sixteen years of opposition to persuade these tendencies to hold together, but that precarious alliance will not survive another defeat. If we pause to reflect on the origins of socialism we may reach a clearer understanding of the things which can be jettisoned and those which must be retained, and thereby create a sounder, stronger movement.

'The origins of Socialism': how far back should that take us? To John Balle? ... the prophet Amos? I think it more helpful to focus on the years in which its programmes took shape - which in Britain means the first four decades of the twentieth century. Those years built three assumptions into the culture of our movement.

(1) *Social class relations shape the main conflicts in capitalist societies* and create the institutions which manage these conflicts. The rhetoric of the movement focused on conflict with the bosses: the top-hatted, stripe-panted fat cats of the cartoons in every left-wing leaflet. But for most people the principal frontier in the class war ran between manual and non-manual workers. So many other things were divided, roughly speaking, by this boundary. By the 1940s it distinguished those who hoped to buy a house one day from those who expected always to rent one, those who hoped to buy a car from those who waited in the bus queues, those who hoped to have an occupational pension of some sort from those who had to rely on the state for an income in retirement, and those who expected to pay

something for education and hoped their children would go to college from those who relied on the state to provide and hoped their children would get an apprenticeship.

These patterns, we can now see, arose from an accidental and temporary convergence. While they lasted, they created growing solidarity within the working class, and a growing conviction that the workers, being a majority, would ultimately win - a conviction strengthened in the course of two world wars which reminded leaders of the regime that it would not survive unless they could persuade millions of working people to endure great hardships and risk their lives in its defence.

The world-wide turbulence of this period imposed constraints on the behaviour of bosses, political, industrial and commercial. This turbulence continued right up to the fall of the Berlin wall in 1989. Starting with strikes and threatened revolution in the early years of the century, it extended through two world wars, with the Russian revolution and the looming threat of Fascism lying between them, and then the cold war which marshalled millions of armed men on the far side of the iron curtain. Leaders of capitalist regimes knew there was always an alternative available if their citizens became sufficiently alienated. Since the fall of the wall, capitalism has not 'won': rising unemployment, pollution and crime show that it is tottering towards disaster. But there is no longer any readily available alternative. And that has given leaders of the regime a brutal confidence which has led to the attack on trade unions, and encouraged the driving down of wages and working conditions at the lower end of the labour market, the greedy inflation of bosses' incomes, the reintroduction of selective secondary education, the erosion of the rights of the homeless, and much else.

(2) *The nation state was assumed to be the principal arena for political action*, and the main stages on which the action took place were in London, and particularly in Parliament. London and the nation state likewise provided the central arenas for industrial and commercial decision-making, and for literary, artistic, religious and other activity. There was an empire which provided a world-wide framework for this economy, but it was, in a sense, London's empire - the main decisions about investment, the management of colonies and the despatch of troops being taken there.

Some people would contest this picture, arguing that the main arenas for political action were in the workplace in industrial cities all over the country. But although some of the struggles which went on there had a heroic and seminal character, these battles were essentially tactical. Strategic victories had to be won in Parliament, and were partly due to influences operating on a larger scale - like major wars or depressions. The 1915 rent strikes in Glasgow were a classic example, leading to legislation which still affects us eighty years later. Led initially by women, they were made politically significant when these women involved their men and the unions at a time when the Government desperately needed shells for the western front. Only in Ireland did a grass-roots movement 'create facts' on the ground which had to be recognised by the imperial Parliament.

(3) *The public service professions were to be the reformers' civilising force*, made accountable through Parliament and local councils. They would provide solutions for a wide range of social and economic problems, in the nationalised industries as much as the public services. The British version of radical politics reaches back into the early years of the nineteenth century, owing a lot to Bentham, Chadwick and the utilitarians. They were succeeded by people like the Webbs, Beveridge, Keynes, Tawney and the whole Fabian tradition - highly educated, mainly London-based, male and middle-class. A growing array of specialists were trained to perform defined functions in the services they helped to create, and organised both in appropriate bureaucratic hierarchies, and in professional associations which maintained standards of skill and conduct. Together, it was assumed, they would gradually oust the squirearchy, the philanthropic gentry, the jobbery, the profit motive and other 'archaic' forms of governance. The Webbs' battle with Charles Loch and the Charity Organisation Society over the reform of the poor laws was a classic assertion of what became, for seventy years, the winning, 'professional' culture.

Royal Commissions and Committees of Inquiry and the queues of expert witnesses who appeared before them, the Royal Colleges of medicine (with whom Bevan had to negotiate at such length before setting up the NHS), the churches and their bishops (with whom Butler had to negotiate before drafting the 1944 Education Act), the Oxbridge senior common rooms, the Reform Club, the BMA, the NUT and many other professional associations - all were parts of the London-centred, professional power structure through which every reform had to be negotiated. In time, it was assumed, this power structure would provide for the working class things hitherto reserved for the middle class: security of employment, adequate wages, decent housing and health care, college education, generous pensions, legal aid and so on.

'Socialists assumed that the needs of the poorest people would be met through the development of universal services'

On both sides of the manual/non-manual frontier, the class system was of course far more complex than this account suggests. The needs of the poorest people were discussed in philanthropic circles and among the liberal establishment (in the Charity Organisation Society, the Eugenics Society, the LSE...) but they were not central to socialist thought. Socialists assumed that these needs would be met - indeed, until Peter Townsend and Brian Abel Smith blew away their complacency in the mid-1960s, they were convinced they *had* been met - through the development of universal services which benefited everyone.[2] Special services for the poor, they believed (and with reason) tended to become poor services.

When the first majority Labour government of 1945 and its successors began to develop and consolidate a moderate form of socialism, this system, which had its counterparts in many other western countries, depended for its progress on near-full employment, a steadily expanding tax base as inflation brought more and more people into the tax net, and confidence in continuing growth - growth of population and wealth, and growth of towns and their public services. In the early 1970s that progress faltered. The 'oil shocks' turned terms of trade sharply against countries producing no oil. Unemployment began to rise. Pre-tax, pre-benefit incomes which had, over the longer term, tended to become more equal, started - slowly at first - to grow more unequal. Commitments entered into by Governments for the expansion of public services - pensions, universities, hospitals and much else - began to outpace the growth of tax revenues. Tax thresholds hit bottom as nearly everyone was brought into the net. Henceforth, increased public expenditure would call for higher tax rates. Soon Crosland was telling Labour activists that 'the party's over'. Barbara Castle, in her *In Place of Strife* initiative, failed to persuade the unions that they had to collaborate more closely with government in managing the economy and restraining

---

2. Brian Abel Smith and Peter Townsend, *The Poor and the Poorest*, Codicote Press, 1965.

their members' demands for rising incomes. Galloping inflation and mounting international trade deficits followed, leading to the 'winter of discontent' and Margaret Thatcher's first Government.

Forgetting their own confused abandonment of earlier aspirations - or dismissing this as due to temporary failures of nerve under pressure from the IMF and the City - many socialists at first believed the Conservatives' own rhetoric. A new and reactionary regime had come to power, rolling back the frontiers of the state, privatising public services and attacking the working class and its institutions. To oppose it, a more robust socialism was required. The country, as we know, did not accept that.

Gaining a clearer view

We need a more realistic grasp of this history if we are to respond more effectively to it. The three assumptions on which socialism was built have become increasingly obsolete. I will say something about each in turn.

(1) Urban industrial society and its class system have changed. Class conflicts remain a central feature of social and political life (our television sitcoms have made an industry out of them) but they no longer run mainly along the boundary dividing manual from non-manual workers. It would now be closer to the truth to describe our country, as Will Hutton does, as a 30/30/40 society: 30 per cent struggling to survive; 30 per cent precarious; 40 per cent reasonably secure.[3] The percentage split varies from one city and region to another. As cities have become more deeply divided into rich and poor quarters, there are large neighbourhoods - and their schools - which accommodate people drawn almost entirely from one of these three groups.

The middle 30 per cent are the politically crucial group in this system. No party can gain power without a large share of their votes. Mrs Thatcher offered them access to share ownership, home ownership, private pensions and much else. But they found that all these promises became liabilities once the essential foundation of secure employment and rising wages was withdrawn. Many, feeling their jobs, mortgages and pensions are threatened and their children's opportunities very uncertain, are now hostile towards the Tories, but equally towards

---

3. Will Hutton, *The State We're In*, Jonathan Cape, London 1995.

their fellow citizens in the bottom 30 per cent whom they are unwilling to help if that means higher taxes.

Meanwhile the institutional framework of class is changing. The average manual worker's family are home owners, car owners, telephone owners, and drink their beer at home, not in the pub. Michael Young's and Peter Willmott's account of *Family and Kinship in East London*, written in the 1950s, would seem as exotic to them as a description of African bush people.[4] Fewer people belong to trade unions. Among those who do, most did not vote Labour in recent elections. And the meaning of a union has changed: Equity has more members than the National Union of Mineworkers; union officials are more likely to be talking to their members about insurance policies than strikes. In England (but not yet in Scotland) a non-political trade union system is developing - it would scarcely be right to call it a 'movement' any more - increasingly like that of the Americans. When the TUC tried to mount nation-wide demonstrations about cuts in social security benefits in 1980 they flopped. (The French unions have been doing better, but for how much longer?)

(2) Economic and political changes are dissolving the nation state. More power is drifting outwards to multi-national enterprises, upwards to international agencies, and - in most western countries other than Britain - downwards to regions, cities and neighbourhood levels of action. Voluntary organisations like Greenpeace, and many groups within the women's movements, have been quicker than the political parties to recognise the power to be won in these arenas. Giant enterprises like Shell can be stopped in their tracks by the petrol consumers of the world. The United Nations has only to announce some future conference on poverty or the environment and the faxes and E-mails begin to hum, mobilising an army of voluntary activists who will come to the larger, and frequently livelier, 'alternative' conference which will accompany the main event.

In more conventional political spheres, the growth of networks like those mobilised in the AMA's Anti-Poverty Unit, the National Local Government Forum Against Poverty and the Consortium of Local Authorities working with the Local Government Centre at the Warwick Business School shows that

---

4. Michael Young and Peter Willmott, *Family and Kinship in East London*, Routledge and Kegan Paul, London 1957.

significant numbers of civic leaders are going back to an earlier radical tradition which saw the local, not the national, arena as the place where you have to start if you want to make the world a better place. Their initiatives also assert a need to work more closely with colleagues in other authorities.

(3) Thatcherite governments did not roll back the state or privatise much of it. They ended up with a state as large as before, and far more centralised. The big change which they achieved was the dethronement of the public service professions. Kenneth Clark, bringing about the biggest reform of the NHS since 1948, neither consulted nor informed the BMA. He then publicly insulted them before they had even opened their collective mouths - asserting on television that they had always opposed every reform of the health services and would doubtless continue to do so. Nick Timmins' recent book, *The Five Giants*, vividly tells the story.[5] The universities, the school teachers, the lawyers, the town planners and many less prestigious professions have been treated as roughly.

They had it coming to them, we can say with hindsight, if we look at the way many of these professions treated the public. They achieved marvellous things, enabling many families to transform their lives. Neil Kinnock spoke for millions in his famous speech telling how the first Kinnock got a university education. But we have also alienated from education a higher proportion of youngsters than almost any other country at a comparable stage of development, turning many of them out into the world barely employable. Nissan had to educate British workers to somewhere near the standards expected of Japanese manual workers before it could set up a factory in Sunderland. We have built some marvellous public housing - and so neglected and mismanaged other parts of it that no-one would willingly live there. After much misery, thousands of flats are being demolished. The Warner Report, following scandalous abuse in children's homes, showed that local authority homes were in general worse than voluntary homes. The NHS does marvellous things for us, but in some of the back wards it has been a different story. If the professions had treated the users of their services with greater respect and listened more carefully to them, these things would have been less likely to happen. The defects of the manual services were as disturbing - as anyone who worked among

---

5.   Nicholas Timmins, *The Five Giants. A Biography of the Welfare State*, Harper Collins, London 1995.

the bin men in London's refuse collection services would confirm. Stein Ringen's review of research on welfare states around the western world showed that, wherever the outputs resulting from their massive growth have been measured, the gains made by their staff have been more obvious than those made by their users.[6]

When demonstrators marched against Thatcher's 'cuts', the banners were carried by union members. Which was a proper thing for them to do. But the patients, the pupils, the council tenants, the social workers' clients and the general body of citizens did not march at their side; and the Government drew its own conclusions from their absence. It was not because people had lost the capacity to march: the poll tax and the calves on their way to veal crates brought them out in thousands.

Since then, the descendants of the gentry dethroned by the Webbs and their Fabian allies early in this century have struck back: managers and accountants now, many of them are brutal and bureaucratic in their own ways. Some of the reforms which were fed straight into legislation from think-tank back rooms, without consulting those most directly affected or the professions working with them, have been disastrous. The poll tax is the classic case. But much that has been done in the public services and the nationalised industries was overdue. Could the Labour Party have done the job more constructively?

It would be nice to think so - but I fear not. Look

'In the most deprived neighbourhoods, people are opting out of the statistically known world'

no further for a reason than the numbers of UNISON members among the candidates for the Party's National Executive. When the Supplementary Benefits Commission tried to set up local liaison groups at each social security office to represent some of the poorest people in the country, they were defeated not by reactionary politicians, nor by bureaucratic officials, but by staff unions. (*The Politics of Poverty*[7] tells the story.) When Labour councillors in Islington tried to decentralise their services to small neighbourhood offices where they would work in closer consultation with their users they were held up for years - not by a wicked Tory government but by NALGO.

---

6. Stein Ringen, *The Possibility of Politics*, Oxford University Press, Oxford 1987.
7. David Donnison, *The Politics of Poverty*, Martin Robertson, London 1982.

Looking ahead

What should reformers make of all this? Idealists would expect them to be particularly concerned about the poorest people. Realists would add that those who want to change things must first win a majority. These conflicting demands lead straight into the Labour Party's dilemmas. The most excluded 30 per cent of the population have suffered the harshest effects of recent years - victims both of economic changes which are making many of them redundant or highly exploitable in the labour market, and of political changes which place them on the losing, minority, side of class conflicts that increasingly separate them from the rest of society. When unemployed workers have tried to form local groups to provide advice, recreation and advocacy for people out of work, they have often had to start by overcoming the hostility of the local trade unions.

The most deprived neighbourhoods, in which many of the poorest are increasingly concentrated, have the lowest rates of enumeration in the Census, the smallest proportions of their enumerated population appearing on the electoral registers, and the lowest proportions of those registered turning out to vote. They are opting out of the statistically known world. These wards, which ought to be fiefdoms of any party claiming to speak for the underdogs, are where Labour and (in Northern Ireland) SDLP candidates are most likely to be defeated by the parties of anger: Militant, the BNP, Sinn Fein, and some pretty odd Liberals. Their candidates may be impractical, racist, violent... but they are usually authentic local people who live in the area and speak for their neighbours. Labour was always ill-equipped to help the poorest people, having neither tried to listen to them nor developed a fully thought-out politics of poverty.

I suggest five closely related points to watch for which will identify those who recognise the need for a new kind of Labour Party but who have not abandoned the principles which brought the best of their forebears into the movement - points which distinguish them from Brechtian fundamentalists on the one hand and salesmen of the political supermarket on the other. They are not a manifesto or a political programme: there are many other things which would appear in such documents. But together they tap the heart of a political philosophy and show the character of the life blood flowing there.

1. Social class These people - let's call them socialists for short - have not forgotten that people's opportunities in an urban, industrial society, and their relationships with the rest of that society, depend greatly on their economic status - the level and security of their incomes, the jobs they do and their relationship to the means of production. Specially talented or fortunate individuals can always break through these constraints. But for people in large numbers that is impossible.

Socialists know, for example, that the poorest people will, on average, live shorter lives than richer people. The King's Fund Report on *The Nation's Health* showed that in Britain the children of unskilled parents will, on average, die about ten years sooner than the children of professional and managerial parents - a difference amounting to more than 10 per cent of the average life span.[8] Likewise, they know that if (for example) you put large numbers of unemployed lone parents and their children into blocks of flats which are impossible to heat to a tolerable standard with the income support payments they have to live on, there will in that district be higher levels of social security fraud, more shop lifting, more electricity meters illicitly by-passed, more drug dealing - or some combination of these criminal patterns. Since so many of the friends upon whom these young women depend have to resort to such survival tactics, none of them can afford to be seen willingly speaking to police officers or other representatives of authority. So a subculture develops. It is not one which has abandoned morality: these are courageous, generous, resourceful women. But in such neighbourhoods morality *becomes* whatever behaviour keeps you and your child alive and healthy, and your friends understand that code very well.

If you want to change the patterns which produce early death or a criminal subculture, socialists recognise that you must start by getting to know the people concerned and listening to them; then, with their help, changing the opportunities open to them. This is not just ideology: it is social science - with powerful ideological implications. Priests and doctors have the privilege of telling people to be good and healthy. Politicians have the harder task of creating a world in which it is easier for people to be good and healthy - and harder to be bad and unhealthy.

Socialists know, however, that the simpler class divisions and conflicts of fifty years ago have given way to more complex patterns which exclude and exploit

---

8. Alwyn Smith and Bobbie Jacobson, *The Nation's Health. A Strategy for the 1990s*, King's Fund and Oxford University Press, Oxford 1988.

people in - roughly - the poorest third of the population. Conflicts between their interests and those of the people in the next third have for many purposes become the dominant ones. They cannot be resolved without changing the opportunities, the security and the morale of both groups.

2. Those things cannot be changed simply by handing out larger social benefits. Nor could the state afford to provide them. Therefore, **a return to high levels of employment**, giving opportunities for decent work to all who can support themselves, is for socialists a first priority. High levels of unemployment impose a massive financial cost, arising from social benefits for the unemployed and their families, and the loss of taxes which they no longer pay. This cost amounted to about £24bn - half the Government's deficit - when that deficit was it its peak of £50bn a few years ago. Such costs make Chancellors of the Exchequer, no matter what their party, enemies of any social reform which costs money. Unemployment, by threatening the jobs, the wage levels and working conditions of workers throughout the lower reaches of the labour market, damages a far larger swathe of people than those who are out of work. It corrodes a whole society. It makes it harder to encourage less successful youngsters to pursue their education to a point at which it qualifies them for interesting jobs: if there are to be no jobs at the end of it, why bother? It turns every good trade unionist into an enemy of reforms which might threaten the jobs of union members: more flexible retirement ages for the elderly, more opportunities for people with disabilities to find work, and for prisoners to earn money to recompense their victims and support their families - all must be viewed with suspicion. High levels of unemployment destroy a whole society's hopes for the future. Meanwhile long term unemployment imposes terrible human costs as figures for suicides clearly demonstrate.

3. Getting large numbers of people back into work is going to be a slow and difficult task which cannot be successfully tackled **unless public sector initiatives make that possible.** This is not the place to describe the programmes required. The point to stress is that private sector employers are reducing their demands for labour as often as increasing them, and in the present state of the labour market have no interest whatsoever in the million and a quarter people who have been out of work for more than a year. There are plenty of others with more recent experience of work who are available for the jobs. To bring those people back into work, the state will have to employ them or pay others to do so. Although it will eventually save a great deal of public expenditure and increase tax revenues, that must at first cost money. Anyone who claims that they will simultaneously bring about dramatic reductions in unemployment and in taxes is lying. The problems which party leaders cannot confront while in opposition destroy them when they win power.

4. Socialists will be working **to create a more open, accountable, responsive, community-oriented array of public services.** 'Community' notoriously means whatever the speaker wants to make the word say. Its essential features for these purposes are that the people who experience a problem or have a need gain a hearing and win some power in shaping the way their society responds to their situation. Conversely, it means that people whose job is to solve social problems and meet human needs recognise that it would be incompetent and unprofessional to neglect the evidence which can be offered by those who actually experience these needs and problems. Where it works, such a regime dissolves social hierarchies and helps to ensure that everyone is treated with the respect every human being deserves. It also leads to the development of more creative services and projects than previous regimes ever envisaged.

This kind of thing is not achieved only - or even mainly - through representation in committees and similar formal procedures, useful though they may sometimes be. Public service workers must be placed in settings where they get to know the people they serve, and are known by them and exposed to their comments. They must also work in close collaboration with colleagues in other agencies who serve the same areas and populations. The public will not tidily confine their demands to the narrow brief or the particular patch of the map that a bureaucracy happened to give to specialised departments and their staff. The organisation of all this - the systems of neighbourhood offices, neighbourhood forums, issue-based forums, open Council meetings and the devolution of powers to community-based groups of various kinds - will vary from place to place. There is no space here to go into further detail, but the human realities of the strategy should be clear. We shall not get the unemployed young people who are now hanging about the housing estates back into the electoral registers and the polling booths unless we start listening to them and responding to what they say. Why *should* they show any interest in the political agenda they are being offered? Tax cuts? Sleaze in Parliament? Squeegee merchants? A royal divorce...? But training that leads to real jobs, fair social benefits for young people unable to earn their own money, housing they could afford... that would begin to mean something.

I have used the phrase 'civic leaders' rather frequently. Like 'community' it means many different things. Leaders are made by their followers, without whom they are powerless, and the followers they acquire depend on what they attempt to do and whom they play to. If, as appears to have happened in Stratford on Avon, civic leaders play to the shop-keepers and tourist services of their town centre and neglect their council estates, then they will become leaders of shop-keepers and publicans, and sooner or later someone gets murdered in their leaderless council estates.

'Anyone who claims they will simultaneously bring about dramatic reductions in unemployment and taxes is lying'

More generally, we should remember that talk about 'community' and 'giving a voice to excluded groups', though it may start from small numbers and local issues (the scale at which 'Communitarians' generally assume it will stay) must also extend to larger scales if it is to make much impact. The argument must lead to city-wide and nation-wide action on training and jobs, on income distribution, on comprehensive education and many other programmes which enable excluded groups to find a way back into the mainstream of their society.

5. While much that a socialist government will have to do - about employment, social security, taxation and so on - will call for action on national and international scales, it **must also give greater attention to smaller scales of action, and particularly to the civic or municipal scale.** If we are to recreate a sense of shared citizenship and concern for our fellows, if we are to rebuild the credibility of public service and the professions responsible for it, if we are to help people who have been out of work for a long time to find a way back into the economy, if we are to help people in the precarious middle third of our social structure to feel a responsibility for those in the excluded lower third, that will mainly have to be achieved at urban and neighbourhood scales. This will call for much more than rhetoric - and particularly for the creation of a local

government financial system which gives civic leaders more responsibility. The task is not impossible: other European countries have managed it. That question is not essentially technical but political: do Westminster politicians and their civil servants really want to give civic leaders more power? And are civic leaders and their citizens prepared to find ways of taking back the power which they have lost?

In conclusion

This, I must stress again, is not a manifesto for a Labour Government. That would deal with many other things not touched on here. It may, however, suggest how a socialist would interpret such a manifesto. The interpretation would start from a recognition that, where the fate of large numbers of people is at stake, their status in the economy goes far to determine what they can do and how they will behave. If they are to do more or to behave better, the opportunities open to them must be enlarged and improved. Until they are, preaching and whip-cracking are insulting and counter-productive. The most important opportunities of all are those which enable people to support themselves and their families, and to contribute something to their society. Every study shows that this is what most people want most. For that, skills and decent jobs are basic. No matter how successful private enterprises become, they will never, unaided, extend those opportunities to the people now most profoundly excluded from them. The state, funded by all of us, has to give a lead. There has to be a new relationship between the public and the professions supposed to serve them - one which enables each to respect and learn from the other within a system that is open, responsive, accountable and democratic. Central government will have to give a lead in putting into practice these values and the priorities they point to. But it cannot do the job itself. For that, effective civic leadership will be required within a robust system of local government.

Five Poems

Putting Things Right

So simple it could be, like choosing
to stop swimming lengths and to duck
under the taut orange rope
on its red, white and blue plastic floats
into free swimming, where the boys
sleet as seals are diving to retrieve
their locker keys, waving them aloft,
and Dad in the shallow end's backing
away from me, nodding and calling
Keep kicking! Keep kicking! Well done.
but however wildly I splash
there's no disguising the fact
I can swim already and one thing's
certain - he won't like that.

Michael Laskey

The Light

At mid-morning seeing the light
in his bedroom still on, the blinds down,
I swear out loud, earmark him
for a piece of my mind. Three hours
it's been on. Three hours since he left
for school and in all that time

I haven't thought of him once.
A tug and the blind rolls up
on itself, admits the dazzle
of days when I ached with love
that I'd point his way as he began
number work, playtime, packed lunch.

Michael Laskey

Fallout
For Peter and Ursula Dronke

In a certain town (better not say its name)
It rained for a whole day, and as a consequence
All the people went mad except for one
Who'd been lying at home in a whiskey stupor.
When the rain stopped, he tottered out
Amazed at what he saw. Everyone
Was crazy. A lawyer wore a nappy
And a bib; a teacher strutted round naked;
A doctor was spitting high above him,
Exulting when he reached a window-sill.
One man, deep in thought, ripped his clothes from chin
To ankles; one was hitting nothing; one was
Shouldering the air, grunting with the effort.
One tried to make out he was the king.

They see the newcomer, yawning
And scratching his poll in puzzlement,
And they don't much like his attitude.
Thinging it's him that's off his head,
They corner him. They slap his face
And pull his neck and yank his ears,
Finally drawing blood. He apologizes
And tries to run. But they are on to him
At once, shouting and cursing. Several times
He falls under their blows and gets up again
Until finally he limps home, mud-covered
And with blacked eyes. He forces the door shut
Behind him, listening in terror as his friends
Beg for his body from the street outside.

(from the Provençal of Peire Cardenal)
Bernard O'Donoghue

What's wrong with perfection anyway?

It's spring again, time for the nation's press
to have a go at you. 'The man has won
too often; he's too good at what he does.
He never looks like missing; where's the fun
in that? An iceberg, an automaton...'
The hate-mail throws up some, I've heard it said,
who want to see you lose or see you dead.

Now, I am fond of losers - after all,
I am one - and they have their legends too.
I warm to Wallenstein and Hannibal,
Spartacus, Jimmy White, and the whole crew
of classy guys who would have made it through
with fewer late nights or a bit more nous;
who blew it all by being too like us.

That's human, and must touch a human heart.
And yet it's no less human that a man,
now and again, is master of his art
so much, that those who watch him will breathe in
with fear, because they've seen perfection.
But there's no thunderbolt; it never was
great gods, but small men, who were envious.

And I don't need you to be fallible,
any more than I'd want my money back
because the tenor in the concert hall
never hit a duff note. I can take
genius, without complaining of a lack
of tension; in fact it's all I want.
I love to watch you doing what I can't,

reaching so far, moving so fluently,
assurance glowing off you, like the light
off a snowfield. As I love to see
a handsomer face than mine in the street,
or hum a tune I don't know how to write.
Three sights to lift the heart: the northern sun;
barley under the wind; something well done.

Sheenagh Pugh

Parting Shots

'Stephen
learning to windsurf
Norfolk Broads, August 1993.'
The caption
pins our hope to his,
for an instant
lets us hold his thin body
between finger, thumb and sky
measuring how far he's come
before he wriggles free
cocooned in black rubber
making his own way.

No chance
to smooth the scowl.
He holds the pose he wants,
tense and sombre
against the flaming sail,
daring us to walk on water
daring us to fail.

Remember his face
fisting the wind,
the sudden keeling over
like a heart attack,
our throw away safety lines:
'Keep going, Hold on,
That's it, Well done!'
Each grasp at mastery
a flash back
of that first defeated struggle
to come out on top
knowing you're not.

The echoes
of what had to be endured
and won
to reach that point of balance
wash back
like secret tidings
stirring other elements to life.
The wind frets at the waves
whipping up ancient fears
of defences flooded,
being drowned in dreams...

No sudden giving up,
only a slow whittling away
of what bound us
to a common hope.
Now it is too late
he can be picked up,
held in the mind's eye
as lightweight as a snapshot
as fickle as a sigh.

'Norfolk. Summer 1994'.
Words wrap round absence
like cling film,
sealing in the hurt.
Easier to look away
or change the frame.
A yacht with a black sail
parts the mist;
a painting, or a post card
to an old school friend:
'Having a quiet and restful time
so far no rain'.

Phil Cohen

Refusing ethnic closure

*A women's therapy centre
in Bosnia-Hercegovina*

Photo-
narrative
by Cynthia
Cockburn

Zenica, Central Bosnia

Devastation in a nearby town: ethnic 'cleansing' like this has driven refugees to Zenica

The agreement they call 'Daytonski' has brought a ceasefire to Bosnia. But as 1995 ended the people of the industrial city of Zenica still felt embattled. Winter weather had taken over the blockade of central Bosnia where Serb *četniks* and Croatian *ustaše* left off.

Roads over the mountain ranges were hazardous with deep snow, tumultuous thaws, surging rivers, bridges unequal to the weight of monster military vehicles and aid convoys.

The water supply was rationed, electricity dodgy, and a curfew still prevailed. No smoke yet from the tall stacks of the steelworks that used to employ 20,000. Effort centred on the basic stuff of life - firewood, bread and cabbage.

Zenica was defended throughout the war by the Bosnian Army. It has taken in 70,000 expelled people, from places whose names are inscribed in the dark book of atrocity: Vitez, Mostar, Višegrad, Žepa.

Working with women refugees in Zenica is Medica, a women's therapy centre.

Monika Hauser, a gynaecologist from Germany, was disturbed by Western failure to respond to reports in 1992 of the mass rape of women as deliberate war strategy by the Bosnian Serb Army. She came to Zenica and made contact with Bosnian women doctors and psychologists already coping with war trauma.

Ensuring supplies during the war has involved dangerous road journeys to and from the Croatian coast. Medica's drivers use radio-equipped four-wheel drive vehicles.

The project they built together, supported by donations mainly from the German women's movement, now has 60 staff, including a gynaecology clinic with fourteen doctors and nurses, a team of seven psychotherapists and social workers, and a mobile health unit. It treats outpatients from the area and its camps, and gives longer-term therapy to around 80 severely traumatised women and children housed in its three centres.

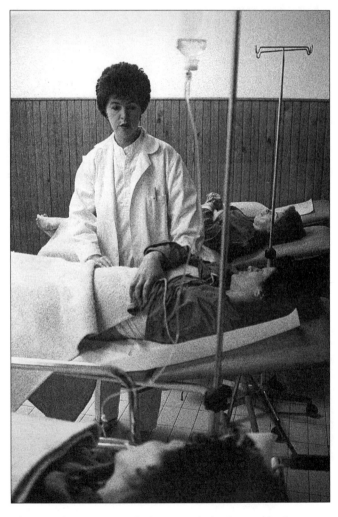

The gynaecology unit gives medical support to both refugee and local women.

The weapons used in the Bosnian war were crafted to sex-difference. For women and girls they included systematic torture-by-rape, abduction, enslavement and in some cases murder, in concentration camps and prison-houses. Involving how many women and girls? - certainly several thousands. Both the Bosnian Serb Army and the Croat HVO are implicated.

The crimes are written in the survivors. This young woman who refuses sleep at night rather than surrender to the nightmares. This one who still has choking fits. Another who's so deeply harmed that the pain is entombed in wordlessness - and must be read in her eyes. Eyes which do in fact say enough.

The women who collectively run Medica have to heal themselves and each other as well as their patients. The aggression has left no-one unhurt and many have themselves been forcibly uprooted from somewhere else.

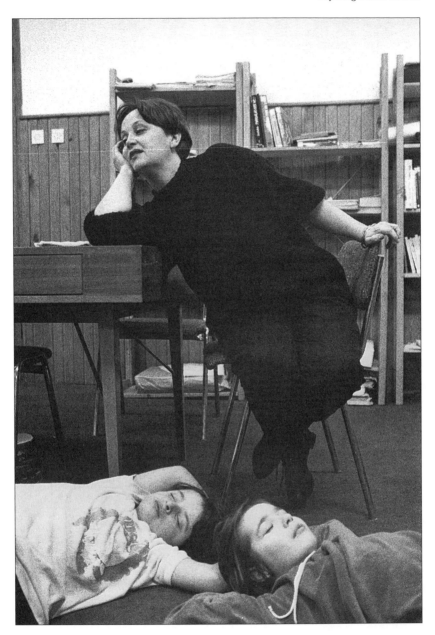

Psychotherapists work with individuals and groups of women and their children.

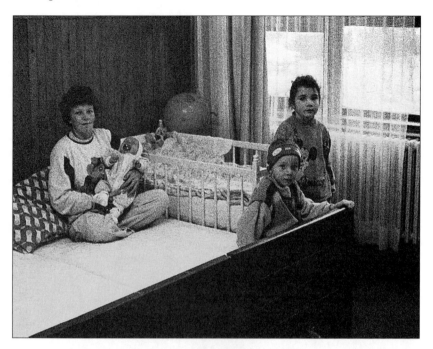

But there is a lot of love and gaiety about the place. The nursery school is bright and noisy. Solid, warm meals and log fires distance the memory of hunger and cold in the woods. Evenings knitting in front of the TV suggest old habits. One of those Balkan love songs on the radio and the young ones are up and dancing. Better still, U2 or the Pet Shop Boys.

New Year performance: Medica's children dance the Charleston

Because, contrary to the media image of the 'refugee' - scarved, weathered and confused - many of the displaced two million Bosnians are bright, educated, travelled and competent. It's just that their social and economic life has been torn in shreds. We'd all look a bit rustic if that happened to us.

The strife in Bosnia-Hercegovina is commonly represented as a war between ethnic groups. It isn't. It's a war between two ideas: the ethnic principle and the principle of mixity. Or, you could say, between fascism and democracy. We're losing.

Bosnia was the Yugoslav republic that was most 'Yugoslav', had the most mixed marriages, the most tightly-woven texture of ethnic groups. The efforts of Serbia and Croatia over the last five years have not (quite, yet) destroyed this quality.

Medica consciously keeps alive the Bosnian culture of multi-ethnicity. So while women of Muslim background are a majority, women of Serb, Croat and other ethnic groups are part of the team. Mostly, you can only tell by names: Selma will be Muslim, Duška will be Serb.

At one level co-existence is no problem: everyone wants the same kind of future. Peace, democracy, mixity. The project stops work to celebrate Muslim, Catholic and Orthodox festivals. It's done in the spirit of a gift to those whose day it is from those of other traditions.

Women of different back-grounds work together at Medica. A face reveals nothing about ethnicity. And there are numberless different ways of being a Muslim, a Serb or a Croat.

But deep down each can hurt the other by thoughtless use of words. Forever taking care now. It wasn't like that before.

And what of men? Them of the gun and the phallus. Yes. But you can't
hate them all. Not while you're longing for your own to come back safe and
sound. As with 'Serb' and 'Croat', so with men. You have to invoke a
distinction: the Good and the Evil.

The trouble is, some men are arriving back in town more than a little crazy. Government soldiers, still in combat fatigues, saw in the New Year with volleys of rifle fire and exploding grenades.

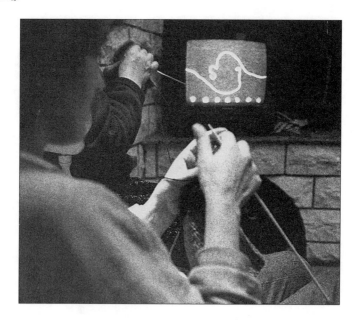

All over former Yugoslavia women's groups have found war and the aftermath of war bring more domestic violence against women. If peace comes, Medica will still have work to do. But it will be painful to acknowledge the one who may harm you is sometimes here at home, not the other side of an ethnic battle line.

Muslim graveyard and steelworks, Zenica.

This essay derives from a research project on gender and cross-communal relations in conflict zones, carried out by the author in the Centre for Research in Gender, Ethnicity and Social Change, City University. It is the second of a planned series of three photo-narratives in *Soundings*, representing women's projects in conflict zones. Thanks to the Lipman Trust, Scurrah Wainwright Charity and Womankind Worldwide for grants towards materials. And a heartfelt thank you to the women of Medica whose skill and courage have built the centre described here.

Medica is entirely dependent on donations. Correspondence: Medica, PO Box 9560, London NW5 2WF. Bank Account: Medica 0562837, Lloyds Bank London NW5 2LP, Sort Code 30-94-66.

A queer way of re-defining masculinity

Peter Tatchell

There is a correlation between male heterosexuality and crimes of violence: not all straight men are yobs, but nearly all yobs are straight. Gay men, in contrast, tend to show that being a man doesn't have to involve machismo.

The vast majority of criminals are men. Our courts and prisons are full of male offenders. The cost to the taxpayer is staggering. Since men cause crime, they should pay for it. This is the provocative thesis of Californian psychologist, June Stephenson. In her book, *Men Are Not Cost Effective: Male Crime in America* (Harper Perennial Library, 1995), she argues in favour of an annual tax surcharge on men of $100 (£63) to cover the cost of male criminality. Whether it is robbery, burglary, arson, white-collar crime, crime against children, crime against women, drug dealing, drunken driving, murder, crime in government, treason or gang violence, crime is a masculine statement, says Stephenson.

While the idea of a tax on men has an element of logic, it has one big flaw. If we look specifically at *crimes of violence* (as opposed to non-violent crime), it's not men in general who are the culprits, but a very specific type of man. As well as being mostly young, poor, uneducated and unemployed, violent criminals are overwhelmingly heterosexual. Although not all straight men are thugs, nearly all thugs are straight. It is disproportionately young male heterosexuals who revel in the machismo of violence and vandalism. They are the ones who go on the rampage terrorising women, smashing up council estates, robbing the elderly and getting into drunken fist-fights. It's almost unheard of for gay men to participate in such anti-social behaviour. Usually more gentle and less macho, most of us queers prefer to fuck men rather than fight them.

Belligerence is not, of course, an inevitable, biologically-determined feature of male heterosexuality. Rather, it is a consequence of cultural conditioning: the way many young boys grow up to think that being rough and tough is what makes a man. This leads them to despise 'sissiness'. To be soft or tender becomes associated in their minds with unmanly 'faggots' and 'poofs'. It's an attitude that begins in childhood. From an early age, traditional boys toys and boys games cultivate male assertiveness and go-getting. When combined with pressure from their contemporaries, this often evolves into domineering, competitive forms of behaviour. Subsequently, as young men grow up, many of them come to accept rivalry and aggression as 'normal'.

'Young boys grow up to think that being rough and tough is what makes a man'

This normalisation of the macho mind-set is reinforced and legitimated by cultural icons of masculinity, such as football stars like Vinny Jones and action movie heroes like Bruce Willis. These symbols of modern maleness link being a 'real man' with machismo and womanising. They encourage the idea that an icy, uncompromising masculinity is sexy and desirable, and suggest that it is part and parcel of the socially-prized state of male heterosexuality. This inevitably marginalises and devalues being gay, with its ostensible lack of 'proper' masculine values.

Broadly speaking, straight males tend to be those men who have been most successfully socialised into a harder, more aggressive form of masculinity, whereas gay men are usually the ones who have not. Queers deviate from the masculine norm in that they are generally (but not always) less fully masculinised than their straight counterparts. This queer 'perversion' is a great virtue. It is precisely our 'unmasculine' attributes and our unwillingness to 'act like a man' that, thankfully, makes many gay men less inclined to violence. The social benefits are obvious.

The contrast between hetero and homo behaviour is not, of course, absolute. What we are talking about is generalities. There are, inevitably, exceptions. While the socialisation and peer pressure experienced by many heterosexual youths predisposes them to a steely masculine personality, some end up less rugged. It's undeniable that, under the impact of feminism, more and more straight males are embracing the New Man philosophy, rejecting traditional maschismo in favour of a caring, sharing (and more queer?) notion of masculinity. Even the New Lad counter-revolution, for all its momentary robustness, is unlikely to succeed in turning the clock back to pre-feminist patterns of maleness. On the other side of the coin, although large numbers of gay men rebel against machismo, a small proportion (often straight-identified) behave just as belligerently as their heterosexual mates. Rape and violence are far from unheard of in gay relationships. Who can forget homosexual mass murderers like Jeffrey Dahmer and Dennis Nilsen?

Nevertheless, despite the existence of macho queers and non-macho straights, as a general rule hetero men tend to be the most aggressive and homo men the least aggressive. Contrary to those gays who defensively proclaim that queers are 'just the same' as straights, there is a difference and it's a difference that we gay males should proudly celebrate.

In the far distant future, since hetero and homo modes of maleness are not biologically given but culturally constructed, we may of course witness a greater convergence and blurring of straight male and gay male culture. The kinder, gentler New Man persona will perhaps, in the end, conquer male heterosexuality. As gay men grown in self-esteem and confidence - ceasing to see themselves as passive victims of homophobia and as males who have failed the test of manliness - maybe they will embrace a more assertive, strident style of masculinity. This might one day lead to a degree of male communality, where queers are just as combative as straights, and heteros are as tender as gays.

Such developments, if they ever happen, are still very far away. Here and now we have to deal with the reality of a clear correlation between young male heterosexuality and violence. This correlation seems to be linked, at least sometimes, to the formation of straight male identity. The fear of being labelled 'queer' can often be part of the reason some heterosexual men adopt an extreme form of machismo. They deliberately choose to be unruly and loud as a way of asserting their heterosexuality and distancing themselves from any taint or suspicion of queerness. Their hyper-masculinity is projected as 'proof' of hetero identity. It ostentatiously disassociates them from the perceived effeminacy of the homosexual 'other'. These insecure straights reassure themselves of their heterosexuality with the simple-minded syllogism: 'Straight men are tough. Queers are weak. I'm tough therefore I can't be queer'.

The exaltation of an exaggerated, bellicose masculinity by many young hetero males has frequently very destructive consequences. Because they come to see aggression as normal and legitimate, it weakens the restraints against violent behaviour. No wonder there is so much mugging, rape and vandalism. The whole of society suffers the terrible consequences of straight masculinity running riot. Given the human wreckage caused by super-butch hetero males, how can anyone seriously suggest that homosexuality is a 'problem'. It's true that some gay men are sissies but, unlike straight machismo, a bit of camp limp-wristedness harms no one. It can even be fun and enjoyable, as the comedian Julian Clary has proven to the delight of millions.

The social menace of male heterosexuality is all too familiar. While most people walking alone at night in a dark secluded street would feel threatened by the approach of a loud, boisterous group of young straight males, no one ever feels endangered by the sight of several obviously gay men coming towards them in similar circumstances. Likewise, the police invariably report that the big difference between gay bars and straight bars is that there are rarely any fights in homo venues but often punch-ups in hetero ones. It is also entirely exceptional for gay men to slash bus seats, riot on football terraces, burn down community centres and graffitti subway trains. Such yobbish behaviour doesn't appeal to us.

This is why the 'liberal' argument in favour of gay assimilation into straight society is so stupid. Assimilation is the process whereby a minority community integrates into the majority culture. The terms of integration are dictated by the dominant social group, and the end result is absorption and invisibilisation. For us homosexuals, assimilation means the social acceptance of queers on the condition that we conform to hetero values. However, it's daft to want gay men to act like straight men. That would result in more violence and loutishness. Instead, it is in society's interest for male heterosexuals to behave more like queers, the vast majority of whom dislike machismo and brutishness. When it comes to positive role models for young boys, gay men arguably offer the better alternative. Compared to the mindless he-man violence promoted by straight super-stars such as Arnold Schwarzenegger and Sylvester Stallone, the thoughtful artistic achievements of queers like Isaac Julien, Rupert Everett, David Hockney, Jean-Paul Gaultier, Elton John and Michael Clark seem infinitely preferable.

On the rare occasion when homosexual males get involved in gang violence, it's sometimes because they are closeted and ashamed. Unable to accept their homosexuality and fearful of being emasculated by it, their participation in hooliganism can be a desperate attempt to fit in with their straight peers, prove their 'manhood' and, perhaps, even delude themselves that they are really 'heterosexual'. They may adopt an extreme form of machismo on the fanciful assumption that behaving tough like straight men will somehow knock the queerness out of them (or at least camouflage their secret same-sex desires). When gay men get involved in yob violence, much of the time they are not acting true to their own inclinations, but responding to the social pressure to be straight by copy-catting the belligerence of the young heterosexual men around them. They join in because it's seen as the 'manly' thing to do. In other words, the thuggish gay man is usually the self-hating type who, although he has homo desires, has never fully come to terms with his homosexuality and is dominated by a macho straight mentality.

While as a general rule gay men are less aggressive, it's not impossible for us to be violent. However, patterns of queer violence tend to be different from straight ones. They are more likely to be domestic crimes of passion, rather than the anonymous, random street attacks that are more normally associated with hetero rough-necks. Of course, if pressured, threatened or provoked, we gays can lash out too. But that kind of machismo is rarely typical queer behaviour. Most of us have to make a conscious effort to overcome our reluctance to resort to violence. Unlike many straight youths who are eager to pick a fight over something trivial, the vast majority of gay men would rather avoid a punch-up, even when it is entirely justifiable self-defence. Confronted by queer-bashers, for example, most gay cruisers scatter instead of bashing back.

When we think of well-known gay celebrities like Boy George and Ru Paul it's difficult to imagine them terrorising anyone, except perhaps with their make-up. By comparison with a lot of hetero youths, queer men generally have a warmer, more emotionally-open temperament. That's why straight women often love our company. We are a pleasant relief from the dominating, bellicose behaviour of many (not all) husbands and boyfriends. The majority of women don't like all that macho nonsense, and neither do most gay men. Hence the enduring love affair between hetero girls and gay boys. Women feel safe with us, knowing that our friendship is genuine and not simply a clever ploy to get them into bed.

Gay men share a lot in common with heterosexual women. Apart from our mutual interest in men - and (perhaps) our obsession with shopping, dressing up, cooking and interior decoration - we both experience a good deal of pain as a result of the straight male mentality. It is hetero men who victimise women and queers. Their misogyny and homophobia causes us suffering. That gives women and gay men a mutual interest in challenging straight male privilege and machismo.

When we survey late twentieth century western maleness, it is impossible to avoid the conclusion that heterosexual men are often a major social liability, whereas most queers are a real social asset. Compared to straights, we're not so desperate to conform to masculine stereotypes. Less afraid to express our feelings, we tend to be more in touch with our emotions. This gives many of us a sensitivity which has enabled homosexual men to play a disproportionate role in the creative arts, and in caring professions such as teaching, nursing and counselling. Whether consciously or not, we gay men redefine what it means to be a man. We show that maleness need not involve machismo. This is not to say there aren't gay men in masculine jobs like oil-rigging, lorry-driving and coal-mining. However, even in these manly occupations, queers tend to lack the hard-edged, super-masculinity of their straight colleagues. They may do jobs that are dirty and physically demanding, but plenty can still bake a tasty quiche and run up a smart pair of curtains on a sewing machine.

Likewise, when style-conscious gay males don the macho attire of motor-bikers, soldiers and construction workers, they transform these symbols of straight masculinity by discarding their aggressive connotations. No one really feels threatened by a tough-looking gay SM leatherman (whose hobbies off the gay scene probably include gardening and opera). We all know their butchness is a pose. The masculine image of contemporary queer fashion thus embodies the eroticism of maleness without the violent menace of heterosexual machismo. It is the triumph of style over pathology.

Who can doubt that life would be infinitely more pleasant if larger numbers of straight men had the more pacific inclinations of their gay counterparts? There'd be vastly less gang warfare, wife-beating and late-night brawling. Were hetero males to embrace the less macho ambience of queers, society would end up a lot more calm and peaceful, not to mention caring and creative. The homosexualisation of male culture is, quite obviously, in the public interest. Where are the politicians with the guts to say so?

Californian sketches

Iain Chambers

Iain Chambers reflects on his travels in the sunshine state.

The following are sketches pierced by doubt and inhabited by ignorance. Whatever light they may cast upon the place called California is invariably shadowed and shaped by my experience, neuroses and obsessions... by my desire for the object.

Santa Cruz

At the corner of Water and Soquel Avenue, idling at the lights, waiting for the green, your eyes are pulled across the street until they come to rest on a group of semi-naked bodies of both sexes strenuously exercising behind glass. One presumes, given that the walls are transparent, that it is permissible to look, to bestow an inquisitive gaze on this corporeal display. After all, the perspiring participants are themselves self–conscious consenting adults, specimens under glass, life-style advertisements for the Nautilus Fitness Center, open 24 hours a day.

Yet this public exercise in bodily virtue offers a disturbing spectacle for my European eyes. While certainly more discreet than the public working out at Muscle Beach in Venice (LA) - after all, here there is a screen, an entrance fee to pay, a community to join - there is still something profoundly disquieting. Apart from the intriguing blurring of public and private space, I suspect that it involves the shock of the idea, embodied in the earnest pursuit of an abstract well-being, that there can be no pleasure without exertion, effort, expenditure. In seeking physical definition, moulding the muscles, designing and sculpturing the body, a whole series of other definitions are simultaneously being orchestrated. In the political economy of fitness, in its definitions of selfhood, it is as though you can never let yourself go. Here to waste time, that is to spend, sacrifice and consume it without regard to ultimate ends, is ritually exorcised. Bataille would not be welcomed. Here, where the body is perpetually caught in a regime - fitness, diet, vitamin - of control, pleasure has to be earned. For all this exercise is not reducible merely to a question of health: you have to work rather than, say, walk the equivalent amount of time. You have to work for, work out, moral redemption. But why does the work-out not work out? Is this still an outpost, posed on the edge of the western psyche, of the far-flung empires of righteous dissidence, those cities on a hill, forced to flee an old world that persecuted them with decadence?

'I am fatally attracted to the exoticism of the programmed pursuit of the self through play and punishment'

Is it then possible to trace on these bodies, as they fleck their physical and mental frames, and mould a libidinal economy, the ubiquitous protocols of production continuing to prescribe the terms of consumption: no pleasure without prior payment, without first earning it. If so, this expression of the body in public life is perhaps inextricably linked to its simultaneous repression elsewhere. It is thus locatable in a specific moral polity that curbs the body whenever it threatens to exit from a productive regime and enter the unchained sea of undirected pleasure. It is perhaps at this border, on this edge, that the sign of pornography is dramatically raised to police and control such traffic.

There is also a deviation here that is distinct from the diffuse moral and ascetic figuration of the body in career, of the body in public space and consumption. For body building is also a central occupation amongst America's incarcerated. Here the punitive violence, the revenge, that is inscribed on the frames of those who are invariably poor, underprivileged and often black, sentenced to 'pay the price' for their crimes, is countered in the concentration of power and physical presence, of self-management, of the only thing left to hold on to: your body. There are now noises being made to remove this 'privilege'.

All of this, of course, is also a mirror of my own neuroses. It perhaps also ignores how many women increasingly occupy and transform this overbearing male space so that the work-out is clearly working something else out. At the same time, coming from a damp island off the edge of Europe that shares some of the cues that are activated in Californian pleasures I am fatally attracted to the seeming exoticism of the programmed pursuit of the self through play and punishment (masochism?).

I both recognise myself in it and yet don't quite get the point. It is uncanny, replete with the ambiguous pleasures of losing one's self. And that, ultimately, is what most disturbs me. The truth of ambiguity has apparently no place here.

There is seemingly no room for the middle-class English habit, for example, of obfuscating, even hiding, habits of fitness: you must not be seen to be trying too hard, you are expected to play it down, to limit the display to a largely private affair. I could stretch this to a triangular observation, for I live there, and extend the frame to Italy where one is also involved in a continual exhibit of the self. But under the older, more cynical sun of Mediterranean skies I am involved in a deliberate masque, a playing out of a scene, a style, in which each shuffle of the fashion pack can reveal a variant and an ironic subscription to the narrative that allows you to decide what cards to play, which body, which 'you', to expose. As style, such a physical display reveals in the pathos of its language the knowledge of the limits that continually threatens to usurp it. Hence irony.

But then, in this rigorous Pacific heliotopia, in this allegory of the eternal summer where the last wave is postponed… forever, to be doubled by doubt and the threat of dissolution is perhaps merely to stumble over the stubborn truth of a European male melancholy obsessed with limits, with mortality?

Pirù

The floor of the valley between the two dun coloured mountain ranges is a vast citrus grove. The evening air is overpowering, heavy with the sensuous scent of orange blossom. I turn off the highway and drive up the road past the old dance hall, located near the Sunkist factory, which is boarded up and in tacky disrepair. On Center Street the police have stopped a wide bodied piece of classical Detroit styling packed with kids. There must have been at least 8 of them in the car. The oldest at the wheel looks about 14. They are all Chicanos.

My friend's house is just down the street and across from the cemetery. Here the road fittingly terminates with the sign END. He's left a note telling me to pick up the key at Sanchez's store. I go back down Center to the store. Inside in the dim light I note that everything is in Spanish. Coming out a young man on the sidewalk observes me out of the corner of his eye. I look back to let him know that I know he's checking me out. Our looks cross. He turns to face me, exposing a sharp, dark face punctuated by piercing eyes.

The gringo drives away.

Lone Pine

Under the wall of the Sierras, we suddenly find ourselves in the West. For a European California has mythically represented what lies beyond the West: the goal of utopia, the beckoning sublime on the other side of the frontier; what was gained for traversing the continent. Yet, here on Main Street is the swing-door saloon, a shop selling Western clothes, and men playing pool in straw stetsons and cowboy boots. Up the road, in the lunar landscape of the Alabama Hills, *The Lone Ranger* and countless other westerns were shot.

Jeff, a truck driver from Idaho, comes up and asks where we are from: IT-A-LEE! He spins us some home-spun philosophy about the need to be involved in your travels and not merely to look at things as you pass them by. He concludes by challenging me to a game of pool. We play a few games, me trying to remain graceful in defeat. Between shots he presses his attention on L. She deftly interrupts his approach by exercising the power of logos over the local. She tells him I write and that she feels sure I'll be putting him in one of my narratives.

San Francisco

Three studs in the ear, two rings in the nose, a silver nut and bolt through the fleshy part on the back of the neck, and a wince-inducing ring through the eyebrow: all in one body sipping coffee on Castro. I suppose to puncture, mark and signal your presence in this manner is to challenge those categories that see in the body a stable, unique and irreducible reality. It permits the 'wind from outside' (Bataille) to penetrate. The silence of the everyday physical frame, masochistically disciplined for rational and productive ends, is here interrupted in clamorous display. Using and carrying your body like this, transforming it into an unsolicited gift that shakes the limits of public exchange and conventional sense, is perhaps an unsuspected potlach that deliberately exposes the bottom line in its sensuous intimations of social sacrifice.

Here the body, generally relegated to the margins of modernity, returns to our attention. This 'reason of the body' (Nietzsche) blinds the critical gaze with the shadows that reason has persistently sought to obliterate, seeing in them only an unwelcomed elsewhere: the disruptive alterity of others—the natives, the mad, witches and shamans. But in the space of shock thinking is able to think again. Attempting to respond to the interrogation posed by such bodies my own critical narcissism comes to be undone by theirs. The utopian dream of overcoming modernity, coupled to the fear of losing one's self in the anonymity of the mass, is drawn through the punctured body into a hole in time. As a transversal slash across the unremitting pulse of reason it reveals the atopic: an elsewhere that does not respect a linearity desperately intent on completing sense. Here, among marked and modified bodies, the present is not superseded by 'progress' but rather mutates into the transitory affirmation of the erotism of excess.

Perhaps the most spectacular form of this gesture in recent years was displayed in the public, subcultural theatrics of punk. Since then, the western universe of youth has found itself inhabiting an exhausted symbolic world in which the possibility of establishing an identity based on a subculture, a relatively fixed musical and sartorial style, has evaporated into fading and fragmentary quotations, or else become so heavily indebted to localised histories, particularly those of ethnicity, as to be stripped of the possibility of conveying meanings elsewhere. Perhaps today, in reaching for the limits, the only language that truly remains open is one that only a few are willing to contemplate: the physical modelling and metaphorisation of one's very body.

L ike all languages this choice offers a subtle play of connection and disconnection to the world at large. While rational regimes seek through exercise and plastic surgery to respect and reflect conventional canons of beauty, the pierced and tattooed body interrogates and interrupts that ideology by taking it to the point where it fragments and unleashes the terrifying fascination of excess (the sublime?). Here, paradoxically, the mutability of existence (culture) encounters in the radical mutation of the body the ultimate attempt to avoid in- corporation; it becomes the last beach for the scene of a desired authenticity (nature).

I find myself asking whether, after the asexual manifestos of punk, this return to the exploration and extension of the body does not also mark an explicit return to sexuality. Perhaps. Certainly the mutation proposed in spending the body in this excessive fashion suggests sexual differences of a more polythetic nature, both in the choice of partner and of pleasure.

Signs, holes, fragments: pieces of a disavowed totality that are among the replies embodied in the signature of a tattoo and the gesture of piercing. A style of thought - one that refuses the assurance of a settled frame and the transparency of reason

- is here directly inscribed in the flesh. The enigma of being is dramatically rendered explicit, and the everyday yawns open in a flash of shock casting light on the unthought... but possible. According to Georges Bataille, in such acts of excess we encounter the unique foundation of an authentic humanity. Here, where the marginal appears at the centre (and where such spatial metaphors enter their phase of decline) the provocation of the modified, mutated and constructed body - halfway between human hybridity and the cyborg - implants the seed of a disquieting proposal.

To offer one's own body as the instance in which you consume, waste and spend your being is to invoke a supplement that threatens the idea of production that has so consistently dominated and damaged our lives. A historical violence, both repressed in ourselves and experimented on others, is here condensed in the virtual display of sovereignty exercised on one's own body. So, we might understand tattoos and piercing not merely as physical instances of minor irreverence, but as political manifestos. More modestly, I might begin to consider them among those actions which in exceeding limits contribute ultimately to the mutation of the body politic. Which is not to say that I can pretend to explain this provocation, merely to lower my glance and bend my thought to its presence - not to appropriate it but to seek in it a reply.

San Jose

The great Renaissance scholar and magician Giordano Bruno was born in the shadow of Vesuvius. He was burnt at the stake as a heretic in Rome in Campo dei Fiori in 1600. But here in downtown San Jose, amongst palm-treed streets and convertible cars, his presence is very much alive. There is here a hole in time that connects the capital of Silicon Valley directly to sixteenth-century Europe. For San Jose is also the home of the Rosicrucian Museum and the largest collection of Egyptology west of the Rockies.

The ghosts of Pharaoh Thutmosis III, Hermes Trismegistus, Bruno and others who sustained the lore of Egyptian metaphysics is discreetly fostered by the Rosicrucian Order through the display of the ancient Egyptian way of life and death. The musem itself is located in the Rosicrucian Park which occupies a whole city block. Its entrance is flanked on either side by four ram-sphinxes. In the park there is a hieroglyphic-covered red obelisk, capped in copper: 'a three-quarter size replica of the original, which stood before the House of the Sun at Heliopolis'.

Elsewhere there is the Grand Temple, a modified reproduction of the Temple of Hathor at Dendera; a statue of the falcon god Horus, associated with the sun and the heavens, son of Osiris and Isis; a statue of Thutmosis III (1505-1450 BC), the inspirational source for much of Rosicrucian thought; and the Pylon gateway, similar to the one leading to the temple of Medinet Habu (that serves as a model for the Administration Building), which is adorned by a baboon who 'sacred to Thoth — the Egyptian god of wisdom and judgement — sits atop a pair of scales balancing the ib, or heart, of a deceased person, against Maat, the feather of truth.' Inside the Museum, after wandering amongst the glass case exhibits, sarcophagi, canopic jars and a replica of the Rosetta Stone, you can descend into a tomb from Luxor - a full scale reproduction of a 4000 year old Egyptian noble's resting place.

Such appropriations are immediately susceptible to facile accusations of cultural imperialism, or, in a lighter vein, exotic kitsch. Yet, there is a deeper, more fascinating current that throws light on this scene. From the desert to the desert, from one heliocentric culture to another, from ancient, feudal Egypt to modern, multifarious California, there courses a metaphysics of the spirit, and a simulation of life, that yesterday was embodied in a pyramid and today in a silicon chip.

(All quotes are from the self-guided tour book: 'A Walking Tour of Rosicrucian Park')

Mono Hot Springs, Sierra Nevada

After the slow climb over Kaiser Pass in an overloaded car with overheated brakes we descended towards the camp site. It was on the second day, towards evening, that we met the poet. Tall, tanned and pony-tailed, he stopped us on the trail wishing to know where we came from. Santa Cruz, aah, home of that great poet Adrienne Rich. The names - Robert Duncan, Gary Synder... - fell on the mountain pasture. Italy... Fellini, the poet of cinema, segues into an anecdote invoking Anita Ekberg's arrival at the Beverley Hills Hilton in 1952, bringing the lobby to a standstill.

He is 70 and lives all summer up here in the Sierras, guiding university wives among the peaks on horseback early in the morning. Later that night, passing along the trail by his tent, we hear the measured intonations of poetry coming from a cassette player. Underneath the trees, sacks swinging from their branches safe from the bears, words in the high mountain air: the replay... the repetition... the relay...

Middletown, north of Napa valley

Went into a café for coffee. Sitting at the bar stool I was attracted by a print that I had already noticed that morning while eating breakfast at Dunsmuir under the volcano of Shasta.

I t was Edward Hopper's most noted and reproduced work: *Nighthawks* — that noirish evocation of American 'mean streets' and metropolitan angst in which the world is always 2 o'clock in the morning. I pointed this out to L and we began to speculate on a northern California bar and café genre that had adopted the Hopper 'look'. But then, staring at the print closely, I realised that the anonymous couple in the Hopper original had been transformed into Humphrey Bogart and Marilyn Monroe, that the other customer (was he there in the original? I'll have to check that) was James Dean, and that behind the counter, complete with 'El' on his shirt, was Elvis, serving coffee.

L mentioned to the woman who had served us our coffee that the painting was a 'reworking', but the waitress thought the reference was to a period piece clock on the wall advertising mineral water and replied that 'it was not working'. Meanwhile, a young man behind the bar laughingly claimed that he had painted it. Then they pointed out the other pictures hung up all round the room. Some were photo-montages, others prints of paintings; some in black and white, others in colour. In each we saw the staging of uncanny encounters in Hollywood iconography between Humph, Marilyn, Elvis, James, and sometimes Marlon: Marilyn riding pillion on Jimmy Dean's motorcycle, Marlon lounging against a post as Bogey and Monroe saunter by arm-in-arm, Elvis gunning his bike under Brooklyn Bridge. Hopper had completely slipped out of the frame into anonymity.

Back in the car we discussed this relocation of representations.

My own enjoyment of the 'reworking' of Hopper had been rudely punctuated by the fact that it was clearly not 'working' in that way for everybody. Our pleasures, although intersecting, were ultimately diverse. We even probably thought each other slightly perverse in our respective desires for the original objects. I suppose I remained shocked both by a sense of loss - the picture was now without an author and had lost the ironic ground for my speculations - and an intimation of patronising arrogance: as though the misrecognition of what I saw simply represented a universal lack, the dissipation of art in the banal flattening out of the world into parochial pockets of popular taste. But what haunts this café scene, and perhaps explains my defensive readiness to judge, is the more troubling sign of a world that refused to acknowledge my language, my culture, my point of view. In this interruption of my narrative, both I and the other actors were rendered vulnerable, for what was 'foreign', even perhaps, incommensurable, clearly operated along both sides of the incomprehension.

Sunset Boulevard, Los Angeles

To conclude on art in America.

We arrived just after nine. John Walters, the film director (*Pink Flamingos, Hairspray…* Divine), was talking on 'A Matter of Taste'. After queuing to spend a fortune on Dry Martinis we wandered out into the courtyard of this mock French renaissance hotel—Chateau Marmont—located on Sunset Boulevard.

The occasion was the Gramercy International Contemporary Art Fair. The works on display (and sale) were spread over six floors. Forty two hotel rooms occupied by galleries and individual artists. Drink in hand, I wandered from room to room observing the paintings and photographs displayed on the walls, the objects strewn across beds, overhearing the sales pitch, the prices: the art market.

In this circulation of bodies and commodities, in this city of dreams and tawdry dealings, the desire for the 'real thing', the instance of 'authenticity', hung on in the passage from one bedroom to another. Just a few blocks away and across the road is an 'original', down-home juke joint built from corrugated metal sheets. Physically uplifted and transported directly from Clarksdale, Mississippi to become the 'House of the Blues' here on Sunset, it, too, is simultaneously artificial yet intent on the 'authentic'. And then this guesting of art in the modern site of transitory experience - the hotel - probably contains little that is different from the *salon* scene in Paris of a century ago: an equal combination of artistry and artifice, equally fashionable, equally desperate.

Here in Los Angeles, as the art world prepares for digital galleries—*ArtNet's*™ proprietary *Galleries On-Line* system - and electronic art fair catalogues, the commodification of the æsthetic 'aura', the fashionable framing of momentary transcendence, reveals not merely the 'essence' of metropolitan modernity and technology but also, and still listening to Heidegger, the very essence of art as the event that discloses itself while simultaneously withdrawing from view.

Offside!

As this year's European Football Championship reaches fever pitch throughout the summer (the first international football competition to be held in this country for thirty years), an exhibition at Manchester City Art Galleries, working in collaboration with the Institute of International Visual Arts, provides an intriguing counterpoint to the competition. *Offside! Contemporary Artists and Football* presents us with thirteen international artists working in a range of media.

Colombian-born artist Freddy Contreras's installation *Stud*, a series of Vivienne Westwood fetishised stiletto shoes - *with* football studs - plays on a relation between fashion, sex and sports advertising.

© Freddie Contreras from the installation Stud, *1996.*
Shoes supplied by Vivienne Westwood

Video-still from The Footballers © *Lucy Gunning.*

Lucy Gunning's new video work *The Footballers* provides a curious combination of high art and street culture as two women mysteriously dressed in white medical coats kick a ball around an art gallery interior. Other artists in this diverse exhibition, including Crispin Jones, Rosana Fuertes, Natalie Turner, Mark Wallinger and Nick Wapplington, explore the game's cultural environment, its reflection of national aspirations and anxieties, and all the surrounding hype.

John Gill, Nick Hallam

As the gun-fire died away I saw an infantryman climb onto the parapet and into No Man's Land, beckoning others to follow. As he did so he kicked off a football; a good kick, the ball rose and travelled well towards the German line. That seemed to be the signal to attack

© *Crispin Jones, Captain Nevill, 1996.*
Nevill's football is owned by the Queen's Royal Surrey Regiment Museum.

This is one of the footballs which belonged to Captain W. P. Nevill at the battle of the Somme. Captain Nevill signalled to his men to advance by kicking a football, whereupon they attempted to dribble four footballs towards the German trenches. Nevill's reasons for his actions were complex, but in part he was displaying genuine concern for his men, who were to be in the first wave of the assault near Montauban. He was concerned as to how they would behave, for they had never taken part in an attack before. Whilst he was on leave, Nevill bought four footballs, one for each of his platoons. Back in the trenches, he offered a prize to the first platoon to kick its football up to the German trenches on the day of the attack.

Nevill did not survive the attack.

Crispin Jones

Offside! Contemporary Artists and Football, Manchester City Art Galleries, Mosley Street, Manchester, M2 3JL, 8 June - 1 September 1996. (8 June is the start of The European Championship.) The exhibition is accompanied by a fully illustrated 64 page catalogue with texts by Simon Kuper, writer for the *Financial Times* and author of the book *Football Against the Enemy*, 1994, and Richard Williams, writer for *The Guardian* and author of *The Death of Ayrton Senna*, 1995. For more information, ring 0161 236 5244.

Going global

Gilane Tawadros

Can we reconcile the gap between the local and the global in visual culture? Is this possible or even desirable? Is the 'global' just another name for Western culture calling the shots? Is the 'local' just another name for parochial narrow-mindedness or even ethnic absolutism?

The small, white labels hanging beside each artist's work at the recent Istanbul Biennial were discreet but poignant reminders of the continuous, criss-crossing movements and migrations of individuals across the globe: 'Tiong Ang, born in Surabaya, lives in Amsterdam; Yufen Qin, born in Shandong, lives in Berlin; Mohammed El Baz, born in Morocco, lives in Lille; Jyrki Siukonen, born in Tampere, lives in Leeds; Ghada Amer, born in Cairo, lives in Paris; Anish Kapoor, born in Bombay, lives in London; Alfredo Jaar, born in San Diego, lives in New York; Zvi Goldstein, born in Transylvania, lives in Jerusalem'. It is ironic, but perhaps not unexpected, that at the same time as an increasing number of individual lives are being shaped by these global displacements, calls for strengthening (and, in many cases re-inventing) the traditional values of religious and national identity are becoming louder and more vociferous.

While the organisers of the 4th International Istanbul Biennial proclaimed Istanbul to be a player on the stage of the international art world, Istanbul's municipal government, in the hands of the Islamic Welfare Party, preferred to invoke Istanbul's Ottoman past as a legacy of its continuing Islamic cultural traditions. At that moment, Istanbul seemed to exemplify the irreconcilable tension between the forces of the transcultural, progressive and modern on the one hand, and the monocultural, retrospective and anti-modern, on the other. From a liberal, Western point of view, the choice seems clear: a culture must either 'go global',

Murat Işik, Buluşma Noktasi (At the Meeting Point), *1995.*

embracing modernity, democracy and internationalism, or else sink back into a regressive and despotic fundamentalism. On the edge of the Bosphorus, with Rome to the West and Tehran to the East, the choice seemed less clear cut.

Poised between 'East' and 'West', North and South, Istanbul has occupied a unique position for the last millennium, both strategically and culturally. As the Turkish artist Murat Isik says, 'Turkey is like a decompression chamber in between the West and the East...Both the Western and the Eastern cultures (specifically the Islamic culture) are experienced to their ultimate points simultaneously'. But having been catapulted into modernity by Ataturk's comprehensive programme of modernisation in the early years of the century, Turkey is now wondering whether it threw the proverbial baby out with the bathwater in its bid to keep up with its

Western European neighbours. Consequently Suleyman the Magnificent has become the standard-bearer of national pride in a distant Islamic past. But the 'East' is not alone in invoking a continuous, national past in the face of a rapidly changing present. Even Istanbul's Western neighbours, it appears, are trying to preserve their national identity against foreign linguistic penetration, or worse, the spectre (and it does seem more illusory than real) of a swelling tide of (non-European) immigrants. But while the French Academy may contest the recent infiltration of anglophone words into the French language, conjuring up a mythically pure and unchanging cultural identity expressed in and through language, countries like Turkey are reacting against a cultural synthesis which has been part of their metropolitan experience for several hundred years.

'The "East" is not alone in invoking a continuous, national past in the face of a rapidly changing present'

This is not to say that the tension between Western and Eastern (and particularly Islamic) cultures has not been experienced before, but rather that in recent years it has been experienced in a radically different way. Rapid developments in communication technologies have dramatically altered the balance of cultural power in the eyes of ordinary people in the southern hemisphere of the globe. Global travel, mass tourism and television have been contributing factors to this shift in cultural hegemony which is now visible and tangible in a way that it has never been before in the everyday lives of Turks, Egyptians, Algerians and many others. What has become increasingly evident to them now is that 'going global' in most instances simple means 'going Western'.

Reluctant to relinquish the specificities of their cultural, religious and national identity for a so-called internationalism which too often takes the form of the West imposing its own cultural priorities on the rest of the world, a significant majority in Turkey is seeking to re-establish a continuity with its pre-Ataturk past and assert a distinctly Islamic Turkish identity.

In European countries a parallel development has been emerging with a gradual but significant shift in focus from international and even national politics to local politics on a grassroots level. In both East and West, the broader picture seems to be giving way to the specific, the global to the local, as individuals become increasingly disenchanted with their diminishing autonomy and sense of identity. But is the 'local' inevitably just another name for parochial narrow-mindedness or

Huang Yong Ping, Reptiles, 1989, in 'Magiciens de le terre', Paris.

even ethnic absolutism?

Far from being aloof from such political concerns, art is at the centre of the battle for hearts and minds in the war between the local and the global. And the battle-lines have already been drawn: global culture *v* national culture; progressive art forms *v* traditional ones; modern art *v* historical art. Into the arena have stepped a number of contemporary artists who have been making works which explore the possibility of reconciling different cultural traditions, while at the same time maintaining the specific character of an individual culture. In Murat Isik's paintings Hergé's young European adventurer Tintin encounters various aspects of Turkey's cultural past and present, united by the flat planes of colour and cartoon style of the original drawings. In one painting entitled *At the Meeting Point* (1995), Tintin meets his peer equivalent from Ottoman times on one of Turkey's beaches; in another painting called *Impossible* (1995), Tintin and Snowy express their disbelief at Turkey's Islamic heritage: 'Impossible!', exclaims Tintin, 'Turkey is part of the European Union'. Encountering Islamic culture within the European context, Tintin can only comment upon the impossibility of cultural difference.

Another artist, Huang Yong Ping (who was born in China but has lived in Paris since 1989), has tried to 'resolve' this problem of dialogue between East and

West by washing two books of Chinese and Western art histories in a washing machine. He displayed the end result of washed-out, illegible paper pulp in mounds in front of the empty washing machines which had erased all trace of cultural identity or art history from their original sources. The inevitable consequence of a crude internationalism, implies Huang Yong Ping, is the erasure of specific cultural histories and identities. Other artists like the young Bulgarian artist Pravdo and the British artist Mona Hatoum have commented on the fragility and transience of national and religious identities. Pravdo's parade of anonymous mud flags - fabric flags caked in mud which obscures their specific colours and marking - are like tragic souvenirs of war whose individual ethnic or national identities have been wiped out in a muddy battlefield. Hatoum's *Prayer-Mat* (1995), made of a bed of nickel-plated brass pins into which she has inset a small brass compass, may assist the diligent Moslem to locate the direction of Mecca, birthplace of the prophet Mohammed, but frustrates his/her capacity to pray without physical pain and discomfort. As A. Sivanandan once said, 'There is no point in finding out who I am if I do not know what to do with that knowledge'. Hatoum's point, perhaps, is that it is all very well to know the direction of Mecca but what use is that information without the essential element of intellectual critique and self-analysis which has always been a vital part of Islam. No identity, whether it be national, religious or cultural, can be painless, but where does this leave the possibility of establishing some kind of international dialogue in the cultural realm and, more specifically, in the visual arts?

Two years ago at the Tate Gallery, artists, art historians and critics from all over the world gathered to discuss this very question at a conference which marked the beginning of a new London-based organisation, the Institute of International Visual Arts, whose remit was to promote the work of artists from a plurality of cultures and cultural backgrounds and to establish a framework for dialogue and exchange between artists across all four continents. Inevitably perhaps, there were no easy answers but rather a series of questions: How do you define international and indeed how do you define the national? How can you establish a true dialogue between different cultures unless that dialogue is based on an equal understanding between cultures? And what can be done about those awkward gaps in understanding which are a productive part of cultural difference, what the art historian Sarat Maharaj calls the 'impossibility of translation'? In the end, Maharaj concludes that we have to live with the gaps, appreciate their usefulness as markers of difference and acknowledge that what we know of each other is always destined to be partial and fleeting. This is exemplified by the artist Lothar Baumgarten's installation *Imago Mundi* for the Wall to Wall exhibition at the Serpentine Gallery in 1994 which defies the viewer's desire to have a comprehensive view of different parts of the world. 'Wherever we stand', comments Sarat Maharaj, 'wherever we position ourselves, we are not able to grasp the dispersed elements of the drifting continents. However acrobatically we twist, turn and contort ourselves to bring things into view, it only serves to make us aware of the limits and blindspots of the view and viewing'.

As we approach the next millennium, the most important question - social, political and cultural - which faces us all is how we as individuals can speak from a particular place, a particular time and a particular experience but not be limited by that particularity. Like the encounter with an unfamiliar work of art, the encounter with a different culture offers one of two options: either to dismiss the artwork and turn away, or to attempt to negotiate the space between ourselves and the work to find a common point of reference - some quality in the work which triggers a memory, an experience of our own. The question of how we can hold onto the specificity of our identity, our specific location and experience and at the same time get beyond that experience to speak to other experiences, locations, identities, is the over-riding cultural and political issue of our time.

Psychoanalytic conversations

The writing of Adam Phillips

Angela McRobbie

Angela McRobbie *reviews three books by*
Adam Phillips: On Flirtation; On Kissing, Tickling
and Being Bored; *and* Terrors and Experts.
All three books are published by Faber and Faber.

These three volumes bring together a set of lectures delivered, and essays written, for a range of journals and magazines over the last few years. Their style reflects the urgency of writing alongside doing other incredibly time-consuming things, in this case being a child psychotherapist. Mostly they strike a fine balance between reflecting on clinical practice and on psychoanalysis and also reaching out to a broader audience. The praise heaped on these books by reviewers speaks not only of their inherent value, but also of a deep need in culture for the insights of psychoanalytic practice to be made more widely available. Bettelheim played this role, and to an extent Winnicott, but the gap they left behind has been filled by an array of TV psychologists, advice columnists, counsellors for everything, and an endless flow of self-improvement manuals. Anxious to separate themselves from this therapy-stuff and inevitably defensive about attacks on psychoanalysis, sometimes from high-profile figures like Jeffrey Masson - psychoanalysts who would be well placed to participate in public debate right now, about children and parents, about family values, have failed to do so. It seems as though psychoanalysis has refused the challenge of putting its expertise to the test in the public domain, and to this extent I think it has abandoned its original brief. This was, despite the need for what Phillips describes as 'assimilation' and thus respectability, a profoundly open-ended and ethical commitment to understanding how we live. This caution, and what often appears as timidity dressed up in the guise of absolute confidence about knowledge (as Phillips puts it, 'It is as if they have understood something'), inevitably rebounds, and the importance of psychoanalysis to intellectual life fades as it retreats from the challenge of, again as Phillips puts it, 'keeping itself interesting'.

The task Phillips seems to be setting himself is therefore to ruffle the feathers of the inner sanctum with intelligence, wit, and with a gentle touch. However what he is actually doing is much more radical. He brings to psychoanalytic writing a strand of common sense, which only clear headed and imaginative thinkers can do. It's the same in any discipline: sometimes to state the obvious is exactly what is needed when everybody else has been beating about the bush for so long. Thus Phillips brings into psychoanalytic language, and ruminates on and around them, themes which are the currency of everyday life. The meaning and significance of the time we spend worrying, for example; the role in the child's life of being bored; the place of fear in the process of growing up; and the social rituals of kissing and flirtation. If the writing is occasionally uneven, if the reader requires more substance, more debate and if one sometimes wishes that Phillips would bring to bear on his interests more of the interdisciplinarity which he admired in psychoanalysis before it was boxed into a singularly professional corner, then he does at least make real efforts in these directions. His voice is understated and refuses the kind of authority of interpretation which has made psychoanalysis so often exclusive, forceful and reductionist. It's castration, and that's all there is to it!

This low key voice which speaks continually in favour of ambivalence and uncertainty is presumably a more subtle strategy to bring to psychoanalysis the language of post-structuralism. While many would argue that, through Lacan, this has already happened, the fact is that the only public intellectual face of Lacanian, post-structuralist, psychoanalysis (gasp) exists in the very esoteric fields of linguistics, literary theory and film studies. It is only through Lacanian theory that psychoanalysis has been well and truly deconstructed, turned inside out indeed. But you have to work very hard with this material to be able to apply it in everyday life and to the field of social relations. This means that what Phillips is doing is all the more important. Why? Because the vocabulary of the 'anti-Es' (poststructuralism, psychoanalysis and anti-essentialism) provides us with a way of living with, and making more of, contingency and uncertainty, of living with an identity which is never adequate or fulfilled, with a sex which is never secure, and with a welter of unconscious material which shapes our conscious lives but which is never resolved, which hangs over us, disrupting the rational goals we have, providing endless deferrals and interruptions, and thus acting in opposition to dominant, normative forces which take for granted the pursuit of truth and the achievement of a true, adult self. While the work of translating this way of thinking into political terms has already begun (see for example the writing of Judith Butler, or Laclau and Mouffe) Phillips turns to his own professional field and embarks on a really difficult task, to loosen the grasp of psychoanalysis from the stake it has on speaking the truth. He encourages psychoanalysts to recognise and acknowledge that what they have always done is a kind of deconstructionist game, that they don't give answers and that they refuse to give the patients what they seem to want, that is, an answer or a solution. So of course psychoanalysts are already deeply imbricated within the post-structuralist field, but the difficulty is in getting them to make more of this: to rise to the challenge of dealing in irresolutions and complexity, and to deconstruct the cure as a thing or a state, at the same time dealing with and managing the distress of the patient. In some ways it is an impossible task, particularly in a culture which is simultaneously anti-intellectual and fiercely empirical. Psychoanalysis has to be shown to work! What Phillips envisages is psychoanalysis as a form of philosophy, a critical, probing intelligence made available to the terrified child, the bored teenager, the worried mother, the unsatisfied lover.

L et us see what this looks like in practice. In *On Flirtation* Phillips re-evaluates the act of flirtation as a form of maintaining desire. Flirting keeps boundaries open rather than letting them close. It 'puts into disarray our sense of an ending' and it 'eroticises the contingency of our lives'. In gently defending the pleasures of flirtation Phillips quietly undermines the commitment in much psychoanalysis to maturity (for want of a better word), to disavowing in oneself the wildness of desire in favour of moving to relationships or partnerships characterised by what he later describes as the 'romance of disillusionment'. In other essays in this volume Phillips re-works the anti-humanism of Lacanian psychoanalysis to suggest that, in some ways, psychoanalysis runs the danger of endorsing disappointment to the extent that both we and it 'lose the ruthless capacity for invention'. For the sake of the cure, psychoanalysis feels it has to seek an ethics of equilibrium which then replaces a more audacious way of living. Phillips maintains a commitment to the ethical project of psychoanalysis by insisting that we have to be able to think about what kind of person we want to be, and how a good or better life might be achieved, but not at the cost of complexity and uncertainty and risk taking. To translate this into Foucauldian terms, Phillips asks who is the subject of psychoanalysis. What kind of subject-making process does psychoanalysis engage in? Where Foucauldian critiques have dismissed psychoanalysis as an inspired form of subject- management and regulation, Phillips merely raises the question of what sort of outcomes it has in mind, what sort of person is the beneficiary of this practice. The best essays in *On Flirtation* extend this attempt to broaden out the language of psychoanalysis to a wilder cultural field while at the same time asking questions of psychoanalysis itself. In the piece on Erich Fromm, Phillips expresses approval for Fromm's commitment to make psychoanalysis speak with other disciplines, including anthropology, economics and philosophy. Like Fromm he understands the democratic force of psychoanalysis to reside in its commitment to pluralism rather than mastery, and to its willingness to take as important that which is frequently overlooked, ridiculed or trivialised. Phillips is well aware of the difficulty psychoanalysis has as a field of clinical practice which can only, against the authority of the medical establishment, claim to know about dreams, the unconscious and the processes of transference in the pursuit of mental health; and in this respect it shares with cultural studies that endless feeling of having to defend itself or else dress itself up in more acceptably scientific language. The scale and effort of this defence should not be forgotten. In 'Futures' Phillips reviews the work of two colleagues, Bollas and Bowie, both equally as disposed as Phillips to taking risks with psychoanalysis. This essay clarifies many of the themes running through all three volumes. It indicates the necessity for the psychoanalyst to practise and transmit the importance of complexity as a state of being. It also shows how the child emerging from the Oedipal stage is then equipped to understand that it has a mind, that the mind harbours a multiplicity of viewpoints, and that the child also realises that his or her individuality is 'one among others'.

In *On Kissing, Tickling and Being Bored*, Phillips draws more often on clinical

'Phillips envisages psychoanalysis as a form of philosophy, a critical probing intelligence'

work to demonstrate the value of imaginative thinking in psychoanalysis. Informed by broad discussions with the work of Freud himself, as well as with Winnicott, Klein, and Bion, he steers a path which remains accessible to those less familiar with this range of psychoanalytic writing. He demonstrates how, for the child, fear and panic play a role in recognising inner complexity (the spider he or she fears is the angry horrible part of the young person's own mind); and how, at the same time, fear and panic are part of the child's actually being alert to the burden and the challenge of being 'alive'. Phobias and fears do all this work; they take up such space in the conscious and unconscious landscape that they need to be taken seriously, as any parent will recognise. Likewise Phillips attempts to give more attention to the ordinariness of worrying. It too is indicative of having a stake in the future, a way of holding onto a fragmented sense of self. It's as though he is saying 'as long as I worry about my children, then I can be assured that at least I am a mother'... and therefore that I have an identity. Phillips thus fulfils his aim of making worrying ' more interesting'. The tension between parental worries and adolescent risk-taking demonstrates exactly the ways in which boundaries are endlessly tested, and that they only exist as boundaries insofar as they are in fact fluid and contestable. Phillips echoes Bettelheim when he sees the child's boredom as a developmental space. Once again it is a space which the middle-class parent in particular is concerned to fill with 'activities' and so boredom becomes a field of conflict for autonomy and separation and identity.

This notion of contested and negotiated boundaries is explored further in relation to the child's body being tickled by the adult, and to the bodily contact of kissing. It's such an obvious recurrent image in everyday life, in films, on TV, and in popular culture, the couple locked in a kiss, yet it has slipped the net of psychoanalytical criticism. Phillips suggests that this is due to adult embarrassment and that there is no popular slang for the act itself. It is interesting to note that in this respect teenage culture has in recent years de-romanticised the place of the kiss in culture by replacing it with the culture of 'snogging'. Girls magazines are now full of competitions urging girls to write in including a photograph of themselves with their boyfriends to win prizes as 'snoggers of the week'! So, despite his deep attentiveness to these processes of bodily marking as being both developmental and connected to the unconscious, the developmental stage of adolescence which has of late debunked the place of kissing, might well have an impact back on adult culture, including that of the psychoanalytic community. Phillips is perhaps a little behind, then, on how cultural innovation can also refract dream material, the unconscious and simply how we think about something. In this sense perhaps contemporary teenage culture has loosened up its parent culture.

Finally, in *Terrors and Experts*, Phillips expounds his account of the role of psychoanalysis in contemporary culture. He emphasises again the importance of making things interesting, of breathing life back into a field which may be inclined to rely on its own professional certainties. This is also where he takes on board post-structuralist accounts of language and meaning and the 'waywardness of our words'. There is no one Freud but rather, in his case, an Enlightenment Freud and a post-Enlightenment Freud (perhaps even a postmodern Freud). This recognition allows Phillips to query those processes at the heart of psychoanalysis: what is said, how the psychoanalyst comes to say it, what can be said, what boundaries are set around this exchange, what is excluded, and at what cost. What risks can the analyst take within the bounds of his or her professional work when uncertainty and contingency are brought into the heart of the psychoanalytical process? Phillips gets away with voicing these unconventional views by giving an indication every so often of how he works in practice. Some of the most illuminating parts of these volumes are when he transcribes his conversations with adult patients and with children. It is *they* who make him think.

Mad Consumers?

Tim Lang and Yiannis Gabriel

*The Sun argued that consumers were mad,
not just the cows. But in fact, scientists have been
more uncertain and consumers more rational than
politicians gave them credit for. BSE exposed
the failings of fifty years of industrialisation of
food and farming.*

The BSE crisis came as no surprise. The disease had been known about for eight years. The saga quickly entered uncharted cultural waters, following the Secretary of State for Health's announcement in March about the ten cases of Creutzfeld Jakob Disease now possibly linked to BSE. Never before has any industry or government tried to woo back a consuming public on such a scale, moreover a public which overwhelmingly distrusts its Government's handling of a food contamination affair. In the mid nineteenth century, the UK experienced two decades of adulteration scandals and in 1906 Upton Sinclair's *The Jungle* exposed the appalling conditions in the meat packing plants of Chicago. Both led to new laws. But mad cow disease was new. Whereas past crises were about the industrialisation of food manufacturing, this crisis is about the industrialisation of farming and biology itself and occurred in an era of media power, literacy and consumer knowledge.

Consumer confidence became the key factor. But whereas a culling policy might have maintained confidence if introduced in 1989, now so many 'what if' questions have been sown in the collective consumer mind, that it is hard to see what will work, except time and long-term reforms of food and farming.

Unable to face the enormity of the situation, the Ministry of Agriculture, Fisheries and Food (MAFF) resorted to familiar mechanisms - compensation, culling and collusion with the food barons. It was this alliance which proposed the culling of cows over thirty months old, as though young animals could not be incubating the disease. Retailers tried another well-worn tactic. J.Sainsbury (Europe's largest butcher) and Asda enticed back steak sales by slashing prices, as though price could compensate for any risk. Whether these desperate measures to restore long-term confidence have any impact is open to debate, but the poor understanding of the consumer by both the Government and the industry has been already exposed, and merits analysis.

Consider the issue of consultation. The crisis was two weeks old before Angela Browning, the MAFF junior minister, met the combined consumer movement in MAFF's offices in Whitehall Place, London. Meanwhile, Douglas Hogg, her boss, was desperately negotiating to get the world-wide ban on British beef exports lifted in Brussels. Twenty people representing fifteen consumer organisations, including MAFF's own Consumer Panel, were there on the invitation of MAFF's new Consumer Division head, Jill Wordley. Nothing surprising about that, except that this was weeks after MAFF knew it had a crisis on its hands. Farmers, food industrialists and retailers, meanwhile, had had many such meetings and had been haggling about compensation and culling. MAFF never even recalled its Consumer Panel, set up in the wake of the food scandals of 1988-90. Nor did it recall its quarterly meeting with heads of consumer groups, chaired by Mr Hogg. So much for consumer power?

This slight to consumer groups symbolised MAFF's policy reflex. Food and consumers come second to commerce. Whether the EU beef ban is lifted or not, too many consumers world-wide will now avoid British Beef, thereby curtailing long-term sales, which last year accounted for 20-25 per cent of UK beef production. Even if UK sales returned, the industry now has that nightmare of modern 'efficient' farming - overproduction due to loss of exports. With consumer organisations sending messages on the Internet to colleagues to watch out for dumped British beef, consumer scepticism will be high. The culture of government is itself on trial and retailers' - not just farmers'- contentment with the Conservatives has been stretched. As talk of reforming MAFF grows, consumers are now in sceptical mood.

Many have argued that the collapse of beef sales illustrated consumer irrationality. Stephen Dorrell, the Secretary of State for Health, for one, stated that he agreed with the *Sun*'s headline, that it is not the cows, but consumers who are mad. A man under pressure, he quickly regretted that remark, but he amplified obvious questions. Were consumers unreasonable? Could Government have managed them better and done as Perrier did with its contamination scare a few years ago (withdraw the product, clean up and re-launch)? McDonald's quickly withdrew British beefburgers, re-sourced and re-launched. Their problem was solved, but not British farming's.

Food companies which followed suit asserted the safety of British beef, but changed sources to satisfy consumer concerns - tacit acknowledgement of 'irrationality'? But the same businesses, the same politicians, never complained in the past about consumer irrationality. After seventeen years of extolling the efficiency of markets and consumer choice, however selfish, irrational or ill-informed, they cannot have it both ways.

> 'After seventeen years of extolling the efficiency of consumer choice, they cannot have it both ways'

The BSE story will surely enter the annals of marketing history as the first time a government has managed to devastate an industry it claims to support. And there are more lessons. The government has treated the issue as a public relations issue, rather than as a public information issue. It has addressed consumers as naive individuals, who ought to be reassured by *its* arguments. Government's PR strategy was as if people go to their butchers having to make a decision: BSE - serious threat to our family's health? Or BSE: just another food scare, a storm in a teacup? But as we have argued in our book *The Unmanageable Consumer*, consumers are more complicated and more unpredictable beings. Shopping can be conformist or whimsical, impulsive or calculated, re-assuring or unsettling. The act of consuming enables people to state their identity, conform, rebel or express a multiplicity of feelings and ideas.

W hen the government's own advisors, the Spongiform Encephalopathy Advisory Committee, expressed concerns about the CJD link in March, a public information plan was prepared with an advertising agency. When the news leaked, the public was understandably alarmed rather than assured. For eight years, consumers had been told that beef was '100 per cent safe'. Not 99 per cent. Not 99.9 per cent. 100 per cent safe. Being told that there was a risk, probably in the 1980s, however small, had a devastating effect on the government's credibility. Dorrell's formal announcement in the Commons that 10 cases of Creutzfeld Jakob's disease were possibly linked to eating beef plunged consumers into the deep well of victimhood and conspiracy.

It is said that our society has become obsessed with risk. Certainly the Government seriously underestimated the consequences of its shift from 'zero-risk' to a 'very small-risk'. The public's response to this re-evaluation of risk seems quite rational. If government scientists and politicians got the risk wrong in the first place, why should their assessment be trusted now? Why take any risk at all? Eating beef is not the same as exposing yourself to inevitable risks. You can stop eating it, if only in protest or disgust. That way, victimhood turns into empowerment. A loud and clear message went out: 'facile reassurances cannot mollify us.'

Faced with public intransigence, business found itself in a double bind. On the one hand, it ground its teeth at consumers' 'over-reaction' with barely concealed anger. On the other hand, it decided to bend to consumer fears, as Burger King's and Big Mac's advertisements showed. 'We still believe British beef is safe' and 'in response to public concern... we withdrew all beef products,' said McDonald's. Government itself was in a no less schizophrenic situation. 'Eat this food', because nannies Dorrell and Hogg say it is safe. What blissful irony, after years of attacking the nanny state!

So where was science in all this? As critics of science throughout the twentieth century have argued, science reflects but does not transcend its social context. Faced with epidemiological or environmental disasters, AIDS or Chernobyl, scientists make probabilistic judgements, on the basis of limited evidence and uncertain assumptions. Often, scientists are divided among themselves. Even more often, the public suspects that the government only listens to those scientists whose views suit its own political agenda. There has been no shortage of concerned scientists, who for years have been warning the public as well as the government of the unknown hazards of BSE. They were treated as moaning Cassandras, as if their objections to the government's own line on BSE undermined their scientific credentials. They got no grants.

But behind this sorry saga, there is a wider truth. You cannot for ever go on treating food as an industrial process. Nature is not to be raided and pillaged. This is a crisis of industrialised farming and food. The feedstuff industry and the unthinking treatment of animals lie at the heart of the matter. No wonder there was so much outrage when the public found out how little it was informed. The Consumers' Association (CA), in the past one of the most conservative consumers' groups, took an unusually proactive stance: because the risk was unquantifiable, the only course for consumers to be confident was to avoid eating beef altogether. Taking recourse to the 'Protest and Survive' strategy, hitherto the preserve of more radical groups, the CA was at last making a strong appeal to consumers as responsible citizens and potential victims; it was also answering those in the consumer movement who criticised it as having become too reformist, wrapped up in the minutiae of testing near-identical products, of little relevance in a post Fordist economy.

Could this crisis have been handled differently? **'So-called "cheap"** The government's cuddling relationship with one of **food comes with a** the country's biggest and oldest industries further **huge hidden cost'** dented its credibility, and wiped £1.6bn off key food company shares. Not for the first time in British history, food became a major political issue. Yet food rarely receives serious political debate. The love affair with efficiency and the market crosses political allegiances.

It is time for a re-think about food and farming policy. It was already in a mess. So-called 'cheap' food comes with a huge hidden cost. Bills for diet-related ill-health, pesticide residues in food and water, motorways of which the supermarkets are disproportionately high users...when one takes account of these externalised costs, food isn't cheap. And to add insult to injury, as a recent Government report admitted, one fifth of Britain cannot afford a decent diet. So current food and farming isn't a great success.

The mechanics of government require overhaul. MAFF should become a Ministry of Food, separating the function of promoting industry from that of health promotion and regulation. A separate Food Standards Agency is one option, backed by the Labour Party. A mechanism to co-ordinate national food policy, such as the Australian National Food Authority, could be better.

Government must place consumers at the heart of policy-making. Consumers have flexed their muscles in this saga. People want information about what they eat; labels don't provide it. They want food and animals to be treated as living entities rather than as inputs and outputs of arcane industrial processes. They want their representatives to be included in policy-making. They want to be heard, not patronised, seduced or controlled. The unmanageable consumer revolution has begun. As BSE has shown, governments ignore this at their peril.

Heroes and Heroines

EDITORIAL

Who dares, fails

Heroism may seem a strange theme for *Soundings* to take up in so manifestly a post-heroic age. Asked recently to name the politician in the present or recent past whom I most respected, I was embarrassed to discover that, try as I may, not a single name survived even the most casual scrutiny. Martin Luther King, Malcolm X and Nelson Mandela were as near - or as far - as I could get. I toyed briefly with Nye Bevan, before recalling those desperate weeks in the 1960s following the brief moment when the Labour Party conference was captured by an anti-bomb resolution. Bevan - my hero from the days of the Suez demonstration in Trafalgar Square in 1956, when he had put the pigeons to flight with his scathing denunciation of the nefarious Eden-French-Israeli stitch-up that had taken Britain into the most ludicrous post-imperial adventurism until the Falklands War - had responded to this triumph of CND campaigning, 'Don't send me naked into the conference chamber'. Feet of clay. End of story.

There seem to be lots of good reasons for leaving heroism where it lies. As many of our contributors remind us, it is so irrevocably a gendered and 'raced' concept as to be practically unusable in any of its old forms. There are heroines, but the very concept seems to operate on decisively masculine terrain - and not anywhere near where masculinity as he is lived is currently being interrogated. Heroes and heroines are almost always older than us, brought back into the present for a second go, and now in their second coming much more subject to our longings and desires than they were in their own time. But there is, surely, enough cultural nostalgia around for us to be deeply suspicious of giving it yet another lease of life?

Perhaps, after all, as Barbara Taylor suggests, national heroes and heroines are necessary myths. Still, one can't help feeling that one more cargo-hold of mythic freight will send the national ship of state plunging to the bottom of the Channel for good. Besides, the currency has been so thoroughly devalued - eroded by the ceaseless media exchange of instantaneous celebrity. Andy Warhol seemed to know something important when he remarked on how many people deserved their five minutes of fame. But nowadays even a minute seems to be worth endless repeats on TV, or in the 'where-are-the-celebrities-now?' features in the magazines and Sunday supplements. Retro-heroism. More apposite to the 1990s is Goethe's observation on the tragedy of being even slightly well known.

> 'One more cargo-hold of mythic freight will sink the national ship of state'

Don't heroes and heroines serve a purpose? Don't they provide our young people with figures to look up to, with role models? But every time I hear 'role models' advanced as the solution to the problems of drugs or loutishness or the decline of the black family, my first thought is of how quickly the small area of the language which the discourse of the New Managerialism has left uncorrupted has been colonised by the New Psycho-babble. Jonathan Rutherford, in a shrewd defence of male hero-worship, has the arresting thought that, for men, heroes are the sons they wish they had been. This is better than 'role-modelling'. But it also seems to be the case that heroization is the fantasy construction, by sons and daughters, of the fathers and mothers they wish they had had, but didn't. Or, to put it another way, that this kind of idealisation is part of 'the family romance' rather than the 'romance of the family'.

These days, it seems as if many of the best ideas operate, as Jacques Derrida put it, 'under erasure'. That is, with a line running through them, cancelling them in their old form, but still permitting them to go on being read, since we have no other, alternative, better concepts to put in their place, to think with. In different ways, this seems to be one thing that all our contributors to this theme are saying. They are post-heroic, or post-utopian because they are writing, so to speak, from the other side - the dark side - of heroism, idealisation and identification. Each is aware of the space in thinking and language which has to be negotiated before anything useful can be said, now, on this subject. In this sense, our contributors come on stage already well-defended, belted up. They know the doubleness, the ambivalence, which is at the heart of identification: how slippery the distinction is between 'being' and 'having'; how little role modelling has to do with someone else's actual life, and how much it has to do with our rewriting of that life, into our narratives, with auto-graphy; how little it tells us about them, how much about our desire, both for ourselves and for the other; how inextricably the merging in fantasy with is linked to the awakening of the violence of refusal and rejection from - real or imagined.

The return to the theme of heroes and heroines is part of the unending dialogue with identity and identification which has opened up in late-modern societies at the end of the twentieth century. Not the old, existential question of 'who am I', but the new question to which, in their very different ways, Foucault and Simone de Beauvoir - to name but two recent writers - have directed us. The one which breaks across the old boundaries between private and public worlds, between the subjective and the objective divide, between personal and political, which the idea of 'heroism' requires us to negotiate anew: 'What can I' - and 'How am I to' - become?

S H

An impossible heroine?

Mary Wollstonecraft and female heroism

Barbara Taylor

Barbara Taylor reflects on what Mary Wollstonecraft can tell us about heroines - and heroes.

'I wish to see women neither heroines nor brutes; but reasonable creatures.'
(*A Vindication of the Rights of Woman*, 1792)

Who needs heroes? According to Nicholas Tate, government advisor on school curriculum, we all do. Last year Dr Tate caused a brief flurry of controversy when he claimed that a properly reverent attitude toward 'our' national heroes was what was most missing from history teaching today. Taking his stand against all those newfangled historians who eschew the Great Man Theory of historical change, Dr Tate stoutly invoked the formidably unfashionable Carlylean vision of a pantheon of moral examplars: men and women whose achievements, if correctly represented to impressionable minds, would stiffen a sagging national spine. Nelson, Churchill, all those admirable royals - the list was predictable, and elicited equally predictable reactions from historians wanting to defend more recent, or at least post-Victorian, historiography. But, as Raphael Samuel pointed out in a *Guardian* article at the time, Dr Tate had a point. After all, it's not just Tory mandarins who have heroes (or, in the case of the Tory Right, a quasi-divine Heroine) but also trade unionists, socialists, feminists. Admiration for great individuals 'seems to be a cultural universal', Samuel argued, and if such heroes are mythical - 'a projection of our longings' - they are necessary myths:

> We all need, at some stage in life, mentors. We all seek out people to believe in, patterns to follow, examples to take up. We take courage from those who seem stronger or more steadfast than ourselves. We glamorise stars and worship at the feet of gurus (*Guardian*, 23.9.95).

Now at one level this is obviously true. We all idealise others, the living and the dead. But if this 'we' is divided into men and women, is it true that women create idols for themselves in exactly the same way that men do? And are women themselves objects of idealisation in the way that some men are? The questions need asking, if only because they haven't been. Virtually all discussions of heroism - whether the Great Men of Carlyle's famous essay, Weber's charismatic ideal-types, or Freud's deified father-figures - have taken male heroes as the norm. In Freudian theory, it is true, hero-worship is seen as founded on an unconscious father-worship, which presumably could be extended to mothers as well. But the idea has not been developed; and anyway it raises as many questions as it answers. For if heroes are, as Raphael Samuel suggests, 'authority figures on whom we project our fantasies of omnipotence', can women ever be such figures? Can women be imagined to wield god-like power and be loved for it?

Heroes are masculine fictions, fantasies of male power and triumph. Heroes act, lead, 'save the day'. Women, on the other hand, sacrifice and endure. Men master history; women survive it. This is a generalisation so sweeping that exceptions to it - women whose exceptional strength and achievements have been deemed heroic - immediately come to mind. On closer scrutiny, however, the deeds for which such heroines are celebrated usually prove to be grandiose versions of conventional female behaviour, while women whose exploits have taken a more transgressive form have risked transformation into viragos, Amazons, or other such man-woman freaks in the process. Heroics are what men do; but the idea of Woman, unlike the idea of Man, is inimical to such fantasies of perfect potency. 'Women...have erected no virile myth in which their projects are reflected,' Simone de Beauvoir wrote in *The Second Sex*; thus hero-worship remains a drama in which 'woman has only a secondary part'.[1] How and why this should be so are themes of this essay.

---

1. *The Second Sex* [1949], Penguin 1972, p 174.

The history of feminism provides an apt beginning-point for an exploration of these issues. After all, where is one likelier to find Great Women than in a political tradition dedicated to the enhancement of women's status? And of all the women who might lay claim to the mantle of heroine, who better fitted to wear it than the woman deemed to have inaugurated the feminist tradition? Mary Wollstonecraft may not have been the first western woman to make the case for female equality (in fact her antecedents stretch back many centuries), but she was the first to push it onto a popular political agenda. And if the mark of a heroine is personal extra-ordinariness united to historic destiny (with perhaps a dash of martyrdom), then Wollstonecraft certainly saw herself as a heroine. 'You know I am not born to tread in the beaten track -' she told her sister in 1787, five years before the publication of *A Vindication of the Rights of Woman*. 'The peculiar bent of my nature pushes me on.' Nine years later, and a year before her death, she reflected how 'all the world is a stage...':

> and few are there in it who do not play the part they have learnt by rote; and those who do not, seem marks set up to be pelted at by fortune; or rather as sign-posts, which point out the road to others, whilst forced to stand still themselves amidst the mud and dust.

In fact, whatever slings and arrows Wollstonecraft encountered - and there were plenty of them, in a life marked by insecurity and unhappiness as well as exceptional opportunities and success - she never stood still, and her personal story still easily inspires admiration. Among the two centuries' worth of feminists who have succeeded her, however, her prestige has been mingled with plenty of mud and dust. Feminist heroism has been an uneasy, perhaps an impossible, legacy.

The vicissitudes of a heroine

Shortly before World War One the American anthropologist and feminist Ruth Benedict, then a young girl, visited London's National Portrait Gallery and there saw John Opie's famous portrait of Wollstonecraft.

> I remember the child I was when I saw it first, haunted by the terror of youth before experience. I wanted so desperately to know how other women had saved their souls alive. And the woman in the little frame arrested me, this woman with the auburn hair, and the sad, steady, light-brown eyes, and the gallant poise of the head. She had saved her soul alive; it looked out from her

steady eyes unafraid. The price, too, that life had demanded of her was written ineradicably there. But to me, then, standing before her picture, even that costly payment was a guarantee, a promise. For I knew that in those days when she sat for that picture, she was content. And in the light of that content, I still spell out her life.[2]

Such a moving image - the little Ruth 'haunted by the terror of youth', searching in the face of Mary Wollstonecraft for the secret of how to grow up unafraid, how to become a woman who could 'save her soul alive'. Several decades earlier Olive Schreiner, in an unpublished introduction to Wollstonecraft's *Rights of Woman*, expressed her 'delight' in finding in Wollstonecraft the embodiment of her own radical feminine ideal[3], while to Virginia Woolf 'the high handed and hot-blooded manner in which (Wollstonecraft) cut her way to the quick of life' likewise represented an exemplary 'attempt to make human conventions conform more closely to human needs'.[4] 'The treasure of (Wollstonecraft's) soul,' Emma Goldmann wrote, 'the wisdom of her life's philosophy, the depth of her world of thought, the intensity of her battle for human emancipation and especially her indomitable struggle for the liberation of her own sex, are even today so far ahead of the average grasp that we may indeed claim for her the rare exception which nature has created but once in a century.'[5]

This adulation followed a century of denigration and disavowal. In 1798, shortly after Wollstonecraft's death, her husband William Godwin published a *Memoir* revealing his wife's unorthodox sexual history. Whatever the motives behind this disclosure, its effects were immediate. In a political climate chilly with counter-revolution, Wollstonecraft and her writings were instantly repudiated - by the wider public but also by former allies and close women friends. Soon the mere mention of her name was sufficient to evoke a style of femininity - libidinous, irresponsible, unchristian - repugnant to most nineteenth century feminists. Visiting in London in 1842 the French Socialist

---

2. Quoted in Alice Wexler, 'Emma Goldman on Mary Wollstonecraft', *Feminist Studies*, no1, 1981, p132.
3. Olive Schreiner, 'Introduction to the Life of Mary Wollstonecraft and the Rights of Woman', *History Workshop Journal*, issue 37, 1994, p189.
4. Virginia Woolf, 'Mary Wollstonecraft' [1929] reprinted in V. Woolf, *Women and Writing*, Women's Press 1979, p 103.
5. Emma Goldman, 'Mary Wollstonecraft' (see note 2) p 115.

feminist Flora Tristan, herself a free spirit in the Wollstonecraftian mould, was dismayed to find that 'even so-called progressive' women recoiled at any reference to Wollstonecraft or her most famous book. Victorian literary ladies, surveying their predecessors, either silently passed over Wollstonecraft's work or mentioned it only to derogate it; stories were even told of groups of women burning the *Rights of Woman*. Toward the end of the century attitudes began to shift, particularly in radical circles, but still many women remained hostile. When the (male) organiser of the progressive Men and Women's Club to which Olive Schreiner belonged in the 1880s proposed naming the Club after Wollstonecraft, the suggestion was strongly opposed by the women present. 'I could never reconcile myself to Mary Wollstonecraft's writings, or to whatever I heard of her,' Harriet Martineau wrote:

> Women who would improve the condition...of their sex must, I am certain, be not only affectionate and devoted, but rational and dispassionate...But Mary Wollstonecraft was, with all her powers, a poor victim of passion, with no control over her own peace, and no calmness or content except when the needs of her individual nature were satisfied. I felt...in regard to her, just what I feel now in regard to some of the most conspicuous denouncers of the wrongs of women at this day; - that their advocacy of Woman's cause becomes mere detriment, precisely in proportion to their personal reasons for unhappiness, unless they have fortitude enough...to get their own troubles under their feet, and leave them wholly out of the account in stating the state of their sex.[6]

The dilemmas of the female sex, Martineau concluded, could only be addressed politically by those untroubled women who realise that 'women, like men, can obtain, whatever they show themselves fit for' and that whatever a woman can do, 'society will be thankful to see her do, - just as if she were a man'. To Martineau and most of the activists of the Victorian women's movement, Mary Wollstonecraft had lived and spoken too much of the 'wrongs of women'.

The shift from this anxious condemnation to idealisation began at the point where the women's rights movement invented itself as a tradition, naming itself as feminism and constructing its own historical trajectory. The first histories of English feminism, published at the beginning of the twentieth century, all opened with panegyrics to Wollstonecraft as the movement's pioneer intellectual. Soon her

---

6. Harriet Martineau, *Autobiography*, vol 1 [1877], Virago 1983, p 400.

private as well as her public career was being reassessed - a development encouraged by the changing sexual perspectives of feminists in both Britain and America. 'We have had enough women sacrificed to...sentimental prating about purity,' as one American feminist argued in the 1890s, 'We have crucified the Mary Wollstonecrafts...' Millicent Garrett Fawcett's introduction to the 1891 edition of the *Rights of Woman* still referred in passing to the 'sickening' irregularities of Wollstonecraft's sexual history, but played these down in favour of a sanitised account of Wollstonecraft as a 'womanly woman' dedicated to domestic values and the stern promotion of Female Duty. Other women emphasised the deeply feminine needs and hopes Wollstonecraft had brought to her lovers: a womanliness, it was suggested, which was inherently radical in its excess, breaking through the boundaries of patriarchal sexual convention. Elizabeth Wolstenholme Elmy, who modelled her life on Wollstonecraft's, living in a free union with her lover until her suffragist friends finally persuaded her to marry, was only one of many *fin-de-siècle* women who found in Wollstonecraft the ideal heroine - a prototype New Woman - for feminism's heroic age.

But political idols lead precarious after-lives. With the demise of feminism as a mass movement in the early twentieth century, followed by its re-emergence as the Women's Liberation Movement in the 1960s and 70s, an intensely troubled relationship emerged between feminists of my generation and all our foremothers, Wollstonecraft included. Our attitude toward eighteenth/nineteenth century feminists was often condescending and judgemental, as many of us distanced ourselves from what was described as the 'bourgeois egalitarianism' of the earlier movement - that period when, in Germaine Greer's words, 'genteel middle-class ladies clamoured for reform'. 'Now ungenteel middle-class women are calling for revolution,' she wrote in 1971.[7] And although feminist historians like Sheila Rowbotham pointed out that an ungenteel middle-class revolutionary was exactly what Mary Wollstonecraft had been, most of us nonetheless accepted the assessment of Wollstonecraft as yet another 'bourgeois radical' whose politics were basically 'male-identified', locked into the needs of a patriarchal capitalist order. A new identificatory relationship had emerged, one in which Wollstonecraft appeared less perhaps as a foremother than as a certain type of formidable aunt, garbed in the ideas and manners of a former age, with whom one acknowledges a

---

7. Germaine Greer, *The Female Eunuch*, Paladin 1971, p 11.

more distant kinship, a less partial engagement.

This critical attitude toward our ancestors, extending beyond Wollstonecraft to most first-wave feminists, was part of a wider phenomenon. Late twentieth century feminism, particularly in Britain, tended to be deeply suspicious of heroines. Any feminist over forty can easily recall the fierce anti-elitism of the 1970s Women's Liberation Movement. Sisterhood, meaning a loving affinity of equals, was all. Leaders, often even spokeswomen, were forbidden. American feminism, with its 'superstars', was disparaged (although we all eagerly devoured the superstars' books). Unconscious envy of those who could think faster, speak more fluently, mobilise more resources, was common, and women possessing such advantages often learned to lie low or find themselves denounced for 'power-tripping'. This rough-and-ready levelling had real advantages, discouraging bullies and fostering an atmosphere of mutuality in which women silenced by years of male contempt or personal marginality could find confidence to speak and act for themselves. But the culture of sisterhood could also be profoundly disabling, relying as it did on an idealised communality where shared suffering became a hallmark of moral excellence: a heroics of oppression which ruled out conflict, divided allegiances or just ordinary nastiness among the oppressed. Thus when conflicts did erupt, as of course they invariably did, the effects tended to be devastating. Maintaining the heroicising myth, it turned out, was often more important than finding pragmatic resolutions to antagonisms; so instead of idealisations disintegrating under the pressure of political disagreements, their sites merely shifted and narrowed - away from all women to non 'bourgeois' women, and from there to non 'white heterosexist' women, and so on. Suddenly many activists, to their chagrin (or, more often and more damagingly, guilt) found themselves on the wrong side of an idealisation/ denigration axis. Many initiatives, and finally the Women's Liberation Movement as a whole, collapsed in the process.

Perhaps this was inevitable. As a political constituency, women-in-general could never be more than an illusion, and the antagonisms which tore feminism apart in the late 1970s can be seen as an unavoidable if harsh disillusionment. Again the vicissitudes of Wollstonecraft's reputation serve as an index. Between the mid 1980s and the two hundredth anniversary of the publication of the *Rights of Woman* in 1992, international feminist scholarship exploded. Like the young Ruth Benedict, everywhere it seemed women writers were peering into their souls and seeing Mary Wollstonecraft there. Books and articles on her poured out at such a rate that a computer search in the early 1990s produced a printout so long I could barely carry it. Sitting in some of the dozens of commemorative seminars and conferences held in 1992, I heard papers praising her educational ambitions, her romantic sensibilities, her prophetic views on commercial society, even her immersion in a semiotic *chora* (*pace* the school of *écriture feminine*) - but also others which condemned her racist attitudes, her class bigotry, her apologetics for Empire. As an Enlightenment thinker Wollstonecraft suddenly stood exposed as a defender of humanist ideals which, it was widely argued, were merely a cover for white European imperial ambitions. In the name of 'women' Wollstonecraft had launched an emancipationist project which, it was claimed, was elitist and exclusionist at its core.

The critique was important (although I think too simplistic), but behind it lay a larger dilemma. The dramatic swings in feminist attitudes to Wollstonecraft point not only to historic shifts in feminism's internal agenda and political/cultural environment, but also to the persistent tensions surrounding the figure of the Feminist herself - spokeswoman for a dissident womanhood. As a politics with Woman as both its agent and object, feminism has always been beleaguered by uncertainty about what the ideal Woman, the putative feminist heroine, should be. Actually-existing women tend to be viewed as too much Woman (as Harriet Martineau accused Wollstonecraft of being) or too little (as those who criticise Wollstonecraft for her engagement with a male-defined politics are implying). In her own day Wollstonecraft was damned by anti-feminists as a 'de-sexed Female' (even Godwin was critical of her 'Amazonian temper'), and recently one feminist critic has described her, with some justice, as a woman-hater. Yet many feminists of my generation, like Martineau earlier, recoiled from her flagrantly feminine emotional history, with its fierce insecurities and abject passions. As an exemplar of woman-in-revolt, Mary Wollstonecraft has proved far from exemplary, revealing instead a painful incoherence all too familiar to her political daughters... And it is here surely, in this encounter with a womanliness which refuses to add up to anything ideal, which fails to be anything but itself, where heroism finally expires. After all, if we can't love our own perplexities as women, how can we love Mary Wollstonecraft?

No more heroines?

Wollstonecraft had views of her own on these matters. Heroines, to her mind, were pretty much a non-existent species. Modern women, she explained in the *Rights of Woman*, were too debilitated and corrupt to produce them. 'When do we hear of women who, starting out of obscurity, boldly claim respect on account of their great abilities or daring virtues? Where are they to be found?'

> ...after surveying the history of woman, I cannot help agreeing with the severest satirist, considering the sex as the weakest as well as the most oppressed half of the species. What does history disclose but marks of inferiority, and how few women have emancipated themselves from the galling yoke of sovereign man?

Women who have achieved greatness are so rare (in England she could think of only one - the radical historian and feminist Catherine Macauley) that they barely mark the historic page. The vast majority of women have been so dehumanised by men's treatment of them, so alienated from their own intellectual and moral potential, that they entirely lack the capacity for self-transcendence on which true heroism is based, while the tiny minority who escape this fate are usually 'hunted out of society as masculine'. The picture for would-be heroines, in short, is so bleak that 'I have been led to imagine that the few extraordinary women who have rushed in eccentrical directions out of the orbit prescribed to their sex, were *male* spirits, confined by mistake in female frames' (*Vindication of the Rights of Women*, Penguin edition, pp 149, 119, 120). Heroism, like every other privilege in this unequal world, is basically a male prerogative.

By the time this gloomy assessment was being delivered, however, male heroes too were becoming pretty thin on the ground. The archetypal romantic warrior, victorious in battle and boudoir, was giving way to less vainglorious styles of manly excellence, more appropriate to a bourgeois age. The soldier-patriot was in eclipse, and many, including Wollstonecraft, mourned the change. 'The days of true heroism are over,' she complained,

> when a citizen fought for his country like a Fabricius or a Washington, and then returned to his farm to let his virtuous fervour run in a more placid, but not a less salutary, stream. No, our British heroes are oftener sent from the gaming-table than from the plough; and their passions have been rather inflamed by hanging with dumb suspense on the turn of a die, than sublimated by panting after the adventurous mark of virtue in the historic page (p 261).

The establishment of the professional army ('those wild beast warriors who butcher their fellow men and are called heroes', as one of Wollstonecraft's fellow radicals described them) had corroded the civic spirit which was the source of genuine heroism. The military had become corrupt and viciously 'effete': a perception so widespread in the eighteenth century that it led Dr Johnson to satirically propose the substitution of female soldiers for male: an idea which one feminist, 'Sophia', had earlier seriously propounded: 'It is far from being true that all *Women* want courage, strength, or conduct to lead an army to triumph; any more than it is that all *Men* are endow'd with them,' 'Sophia' stoutly claimed in 1739.[8] Anti-feminists, unsurprisingly, thought such notions ridiculous, Rousseau in particular deriding the image of the woman warrior. 'I know that, as a proof of the inferiority of the sex, Rousseau has exultingly exclaimed, How can they leave the nursery for the camp!' Wollstonecraft wrote in response to his gibes; but nonetheless, she insisted, were 'defensive wars' (the 'only justifiable' wars) once again to be fought by genuine patriots, 'the true heroism of antiquity might again animate female bosoms' - meaning that British women, like those of the classical republics, would learn to regard maternal and wifely obligations as civic duties, performed for the glory of the nation.

By the late eighteenth century such nostalgia for civic heroism was confined largely to political radicals, most British men preferring to leave military adventures to those paid to have them. 'The business of great men', as Defoe had earlier argued, was no longer to perform the sorts of deeds which are the subject of 'fables and romance', but to cultivate godly virtues: to be great was to be good.[9] With the rise of the culture of sensibility, the ideal good man also became a man of deep feeling, quick to tears and highly susceptible to poetry. Sentimental novels were crammed with heroes of this sort, engaged less in acts of public derring-do than in private odysses of personal tribulation. A heroism of emotional and moral endeavour emerged which, potentially at least, was open to women in ways that the virile escapades of traditional heroic narratives never had been. Realising this potential, however, required female protagonists to be placed in predicaments which drew on their heroic capacities - and this, as Wollstonecraft pointed out in the preface to her final unfinished novel, *Maria, or the Wrongs of Woman*, seldom happened. 'In many works of this species,' she wrote

---

8. Samuel Johnson, 'A Female Army', *The Idler*, 13 May 1758; 'Sophia, A Person of Quality', *Woman Not Inferior to Man* [1739], Brentham Press 1975, p 54.
9. Ian Watt, *The Rise of the Novel* [1957], Penguin 1977, p 86.

the hero is allowed to be mortal, and to become wise and virtuous as well as happy, by a train of events and circumstances. The heroines, on the contrary, are to be born immaculate; and to act like goddesses of wisdom, just come forth highly finished Minervas from the head of Jove (OUP edition, p 73).

Men learn heroism in engagement with the world, in historic action. But heroines have no history. The perfections for which women are praised, as Wollstonecraft observed, are not those acquired by hard labours or the exercise of extraordinary talents, but merely those assigned them as a sex. And chivalric gallants, like Burke and Rousseau, who make such a fuss of honouring women's excellences, do so not in sincere appreciation of female merit but, as Burke famously explained, merely as rhetorical 'drapery' to conceal women's real nature as 'animals...not of the highest order'.[10] The underbelly of idealisation, as Burke demonstrated so brutally and Wollstonecraft anatomised so skillfully, is contempt: 'Why are girls told they resemble angels,' she pointed out in the *Rights of Woman*, 'but to sink them below women?' In a sexually unequal world, the heroicisation of women can never be more than a hypocritical fantasy. Men create perfect women because they don't want to deal with real ones. 'I wish to see women neither heroines nor brutes; but reasonable creatures.'

But if heroines are largely a male creation, the hostility to women which underlies such fantasies is by no means a male preserve. An ambivalent attitude toward womanhood is a major component in women's subjectivity, one particularly marked among feminists. The positive valuation of femininity, like that of masculinity, is shadowed by its negation; and those most critical of the female condition are often implicitly condemnatory of femaleness *per se*. To discover a misogynist undertow in Wollstonecraft's thought, then, is not particularly surprising (which hasn't prevented some scholars from ritually denouncing her for it) - although the strength of this anti-woman sentiment in her writings is at times rather shocking. Women are, according to the *Rights of Woman*, 'vain', 'mean', 'foolish' and ever 'prey to their senses...(which) renders them *uncomfortable* themselves but *troublesome*...to others.' It is the 'desire of being always women (which) is the very consciousness which degrades the sex' she writes, and this not only in the case of fashionable ladies of low morals who neglect their children in favour of lovers and lapdogs (a favourite target of all middle-class moralists) but

---

10. Edmund Burke, *Reflections on the Revolution in France*, [1790], Hackett 1987, p 87.

even of the ordinary 'square-elbowed drudges' of Wollstonecraft's own middle class. Her fierce determination to live her own femininity in a freer mode was partly a response to the experimental spirit of the times, but also a reflection of those deeper conflicts over femaleness inherent in Everywoman's psychology, and much intensified in Wollstonecraft's case by a profoundly unhappy upbringing at the hands of a cold, ineffectual mother and drunkenly abusive father. Wollstonecraft knew how much she hated her father (she told Godwin so) but it's hard not to conclude from her writings that it was the mother who so badly failed her who was a primary focus of her rage...and her self-identity. The 'wild wish' at one point expressed in the *Rights of Woman* to 'see the distinction of sex confounded in society' can be seen then as a desire to release women's subjectivity from its current contraints, but also as Wollstonecraft's wish to defy her own femininity: to become no mere heroine but a true hero of her own life.

Rushing out of the prescribed orbit

In the Prelude to *Middlemarch*, George Eliot asks the question: 'Who that cares much to know the history of man...has not dwelt at least briefly, on the life of Saint Theresa...?' - to which the only possible answer, as the literary historian Ellen Moers points out, is lots of people.[11] Carlyle does not mention Saint Theresa (or Mary Wollstonecraft), and although 'he might well have done so had it occurred to him to refer to *any* woman as a type of heroism', the fact that it did *not* occur to Carlyle think of women as heroes was not incidental. The heroes which his essay describes are men who through force of will and imagination seized a historical moment and branded it with their visions.[12] Their life stories, as narrated reverentially by Carlyle, are tales of transcendent mastery radiating a phallic glory to which Woman can never aspire.

Yet at one point in his embarrassingly sententious yet strangely uncertain essay, Carlyle raised an awkward question: what status can heroes possibly have in a Protestant and increasingly democratic age? In a nation where 'every man (is) his own Pope' and each citizen expects to play his part on the civic stage, what role is left for 'Hero-captains' (p 277)? The answer is simple yet startling: from the Reformation onwards the reverence for heroes has gradually revealed itself in its true light, as veneration for those who eschew received opinion for the

---

11. Ellen Moers, *Literary Women* [1963], Women's Press 1980, pp 123-4.
12. Thomas Carlyle, *On Heroes, Hero-Worship, and the Heroic in History* [1840], Chapman and Hall 1892.

dictates of private judgement, whose pathways are lit by the holy 'Flame-image' of inner Truth. *Sincerity*, as Carlyle called this state of psychic communion with 'the Inner Fact of things', is indeed the chief hallmark of a Great Man, but 'a man need not be great in order to be sincere' thus 'if Hero mean (sic) *sincere man*, why may not every one of us be a Hero?'

> In all this wild revolutionary work, from Protestantism downwards, I see the blessedest result preparing itself: not abolition of Hero-worship, but...a whole World of Heroes (p 280).

At first glance, this seems an extraordinary reversal in an essay dedicated, as Carlyle himself said, to defending 'hierarchy and subordination among men'; particularly when we read that the tragedy of the French Revolution was that it replaced 'great wise men' with 'a level immensity of foolish small men'. For the radicals of Wollstonecraft's day, it seems, a truly world-shaking sincerity was not enough. But Carlyle's objection to the revolutionary democrats of the 1790s went to the heart of his argument. It was not their commitment to Liberty and Equality which troubled him, he explained, but their refusal to 'bend the knee' to greatness in others, to do obeisance to the heroic principle in them. For in refusing to acknowledge that 'there does dwell in the presence of our brother something divine... "a revelation in the Flesh"', the radicals repudiated their own portion of divinity. If no man is a hero to his valet, that is because the valet is no hero himself, that is, he lacks a soul capable of reaching toward the ideal. For it is only in doing honour to the heroic Other that the Self recognises it too is a Hero.

Heroes in other words are not Great Men but great souls, lit by divine fire. To see what all this might mean for heroines, we return - odd as it may seem - to Wollstonecraft, and in particular to the eponymous heroine of her first novel, *Mary, A Fiction* (1788). The young Mary, according to her author, is a model of sincerity, a woman of independent 'thinking powers':

> The female organs have been thought too weak for this arduous employment....(but) without arguing physically about *possibilities* - in a fiction, such a being may be allowed to exist; whose grandeur is derived from the operations of its own faculties, not subjugated to opinion; but drawn by the individual from the original source.[13]

---

13. Mary Wollstonecraft, *Mary, a Fiction* (Advertisement) [1788], OUP 1980.

Mary is passionately self-directed, willing to defy false notions of Female Duty to follow her inner path (which takes her into all sorts of trying situations). Like her creator, she is disinclined to bend her knee to anyone (this is helped by her being a wealthy heiress) - with, however, the sole exception of God. For Mary is intensely pious, although her piety, like that of her author also, is hardly of the humbling or self-immolating variety. Rather, it is in communion with her God that Mary discovers the steel in her soul, the divine self-regard which arms her against the depradations of a corrupt society. In taking God as her Hero, and recognising her own affinities to Him, this proto-feminist finds that she too has hero-potential, however little the world acknowledges it.

This religious dimension to Wollstonecraft's thought - probably its least-recognised feature - was crucial to her feminism. The 'revolution in female manners' which was called for in the *Rights of Woman* depended on women turning away from their current tinpot deities - the male sex - to rededicate themselves to God. The self-respect alien to modern women, smothered as they are under the drapery of men's chivalrous contempt, can only be attained through worship of that One who is the universal model of moral perfection. 'What can make us reverence ourselves but a reverence for that being of whom we are but a faint image?' as she wrote in her 1790 *A Vindication of the Rights of Men*. 'I FEAR GOD...(and) this fear of God makes me reverence myself.' All humanity's love of the ideal, all dreams of heroic glory, are shadowy intimations of that Divine Father whose Presence within us, men and women alike, is the foundation of true self-veneration - the sacred heroism of the soul.

Here, in Wollstonecraft as in Carlyle, was that powerfully Protestant vision, so central to western concepts of subjectivity, in which the authentic Self is ineluctably Other, an inward expression of God. Apart from its universality, what is so striking about this view of selfhood is its intensely *wishful* character. The heroic 'I' is driven by desire, by a yearning not only to love but also to *be* the idolised one: the passion which psychoanalysis describes as identification. Raphael Samuel points to this deeper aspect of hero-worship when he describes heroes as figures invested with infantile fantasies of perfection; a thesis developed by Graham Dawson in his recent Kleinian study, *Soldier-Heroes: British Adventure, Empire and the Imagining of Masculinities* (Routledge 1994). Dawson shows very clearly how the idealising identifications on which heroes are based derive from imaginary versions of our parents: every child's personal gods. The modelling of the ego on the parental deities of early life is a universal feature of personal development - the religious illusion, we might say, at the core of every psyche. The worship of super-human heroes is part of what makes us fully human.

How does gender figure in this psychic drama? The 'I' moulded in the image of its heroic Others occupies a body which is biologically sexed. Psychological gender, however - the lived sense of being male or female - is not inborn like physical sex but acquired: a trickier business altogether. The fantasies which give birth to the ego are a conflux of masculine/feminine identifications whose outcome is never Man or Woman in some absolute sense, but a sexual identity which is always partial, defensive, wishful. We feel ourselves to belong to one sex because of our fantasies about what it would feel like to belong to the other: imaginings which pull us to and fro along the gender axis. The psyche, in other words, like the Christian soul, has no intrinsic sex: a point from which recent feminist theory has made much, but which earlier feminists were also keen to emphasise. 'It be not philosophical to think of sex when the soul is mentioned,' as Wollstonecraft wrote. The ambiguities of sexual identity which Christian and particularly Protestant tradition encoded in the distinction between the sacred and profane aspects of the self, with the 'distinction of sex' firmly consigned to the latter, gave license to feminism's most subversive idea: that in essence Woman and Man are one; or as Carlyle might have put it, in hero-potential there is no sexual difference. 'A wild wish has just flown from my heart to my head...' Wollstonecraft wrote in the *Rights of Woman.* 'I do earnestly wish to see the distinction of sex confounded in society' - a wish which could only be formulated once sexual difference was removed from the plane of the eternal to the contingent and historical. 'I wish to show that the first object of laudable ambition is to obtain a character as a human being, regardless of the distinction of sex' (p 82).

Yet the God who sanctions these aspirations in Wollstonecraft's case is discernibly masculine, an image of paternal perfection. Like her description of heroines as 'male spirits', ultimately Wollstonecraft can only imagine greatness as phallic. Why? Certainly there was nothing in her own history to suggest that men are finer beings than women; yet identification with an image of the Great Woman is as absent in her thought as it is in the wider culture. And the level of ambivalence surrounding the figure of Wollstonecraft herself points to similar difficulties among other women with feminine idealisations. To 'rush out of the orbit prescribed to their sex', as Wollstonecraft described heroines, may be a grand thing in men; but for women to be extra-ordinary in this way apparently stimulates at least as much hostility as admiration. Why are heroines such a peculiarly difficult proposition?

We all, men and women alike, have an investment in maintaining gender boundaries, even if we are inclined to engage in border skirmishes. The very precariousness of sexual identities makes us less inclined to abrogate them. And we all, at one point in our lives at least, absolutely require a woman to be as ordinary as possible: an ordinary mother. Mothers, however, are in fact the most powerful figures in fantasy life; so powerful indeed that it seems likely that devotion to heroic fathers, or Gods, is primarily a defence against the fearful adoration aroused by maternal power. The figure of Woman is, one might say, over-burdened with heroic stature from the start; small wonder there is resistance - in women as well as in men - to allowing Her more.

If heroines are to be allowed, then, it must be in their guise as suffering, self-sacrificing nurturers, not as possessors of the uncompromising valour characteristic of male heroism. As Mothers, Wives and Lovers, women give their all to their children, their men, and their gods. Female saints, whether of the holy or secular variety, adore and perish; patriot mothers deliver up their heart's blood to military crusades; all those Dorothea Causabons of the intellectual world devote themselves to wiping male pens; and even the suffragettes insistently presented themselves not as feminist warriors but as agonised martyrs to the female Cause. The Lady of the Lamp, probably the best-known British heroine, prompts baby memories as she moves across battlefields to succour and heal. But the Iron Lady of more recent British history was never Mother to the nation, only its castrating Nanny or Leaderene with bigger balls than any of the sorry little men around her.[14] We may admire virile women, but most of us find it hard to love them and harder still to *be* them - and without that loving identification no heroine can survive.

Feminism, with its intense love/hate relationship with its foremothers, throws these issues into sharp relief. As feminists, we yearn for extra-ordinary women with whom to identify; but creating such women, we then repudiate them. We

14. See Jacqueline Rose's analysis of Thatcher's heroinism for the provocative suggestion that 'perhaps it is only a woman leader today who can claim so literally to embody the phallus.' ('Margaret Thatcher and Ruth Ellis', in J Rose, *Why War?* Blackwell 1993, p 72).

assign to Wollstonecraft all those heroic virtues so patently lacking in ourselves, then decry her for being too masculine; or, identifying with her feminine predicaments, deny her heroic status. As the symbolic founder of a politics centering on Woman, we endow her with our ongoing conflicts over what Woman has been, is, can be. 'Only the concept of a subjectivity at odds with itself,' Jacqueline Rose has written, 'gives back to women the right to an impasse at the point of sexual identity'[15]: the impasse which can be heard both in Wollstonecraft's own feminism and in her complex legacy to her political daughters. But perhaps finally it's here, in the pain and confusion as well as the courage which Wollstonecraft brought to the impossibilities of femininity, that her real heroism (and ours) is to be found.

---

15. Jacqueline Rose, 'Feminism and the Psychic' in *Sexuality in the Field of Vision*, Verso 1986, p 15. Of course being at odds with oneself is hardly confined to women, as many recent studies of masculine identity emphasise. The fantasy of the Hero underlines the problem. Machismo heroics are usually as alien and oppressive to men as to women, while real courage - as Pat Barker shows in her magnificent fictional exploration of masculinity in wartime (*Regeneration, The Eye In The Door, The Ghost Road*) - tends to draw on similar sources in both sexes. Officers in WW1 were moved to acts of extraordinary courage and self-sacrifice by feelings of devotion to 'their' men which, Barker suggests, were powerfully maternal in character.

Heroes and mother's boys

Jonathan Rutherford

Jonathan Rutherford argues that men's hero worship of other men has been part of their struggle to separate themselves from their mothers, and to secure themselves an identity.

You bought a racehorse
In your barrister days
And called it after me-
Mother's Boy.
It was a chestnut colt
And I recall dark days
Of delight in the 1950s
Bringing water to the red horse.

It won nothing
And cost you money-
Like me.
If you could live your life again
Which would you choose,
Your racehorse or me?
    Paul Durcan, 'Mother's Boy'[1]

In this poem to his father, Paul Durcan declares for the racehorse: 'you'd choose your racehorse/And so would I'. For men, heroes are the sons they wish they had

---

1. 'Mother's Boy', Paul Durcan, in *Daddy, Daddy*, The Blackstaff Press, 1990.

been; they are loved by their fathers.

Manly heroes have been central to our notions of England and its empire. Warriors, achievers, extraordinary men, who have been noted and admired for their physical courage and endurance. In their pursuit of fame, virtue and glory they escaped the mundanity of ordinary life, the world of women, mothers and domesticity. They provided the nation with its sense of purpose and destiny. With the rise of mass culture every man who met a violent death in war was accorded his heroic virtue. There was no more arresting emblem of nationalism than the cenotaph to the Unknown Soldier. The concept of sacrificing one's life for one's country transformed meaningless, catastrophic death into an eternal heroism, a surrender to the transcendental symbols of race and nation. The hero was submerged in something greater than himself, his short life transformed into immortality. The nation glides out of an immemorial past and sails majestically into a limitless future carrying her sons forward with the promise of her eternal gratitude for their sacrifice.

Take the tourist trail across central London. Begin at Victoria Station and work your way through Belgravia to Hyde Park, down to Buckingham Palace and then along The Mall to St James's Square. The public face of our national culture is overwhelmingly imperial and royal; grandiose and triumphal commemorations of military victories, self-sacrifice and violent death. There are no monuments dedicated to civic culture or intellectual life; there are no statues of philosophers or writers as there are scattered throughout Paris. It is only when you reach the club land of St James's Square that you will find a few statues of men not directly related to militarism or war. They are the explorers, the other face of empire. They too were celebrated in premature death: Franklin, who lost his life in the search for the North West Passage and Robert Falcon Scott who died in his bid to reach the South Pole. At the base of Scott's statue is an inscription, taken from a letter he addressed to the British public, written in the last hours of his life. He apologises for his failure. He knows he is going to die, but bows to the will of providence. 'Had we lived', he wrote, 'I should have had a tale to tell of the hardihood, endurance and courage of my companions which would have stirred the heart of every Englishman. These rough notes and our dead bodies must tell the tale.' The year was 1911. The long Victorian age was soon to end with the outbreak of the First World War. But it seems, walking across central London, as if it is still with us. All the dead bodies are still speaking from their graves, their tale of self-sacrifice and heroism fuelling the belief that England is the greatest nation on earth and the Englishman its most noble warrior.

The imaginary Englishman with his stiff upper lip and masterly control over world affairs was invented in the years between 1870 and the outbreak of the First World War. Each Christmas hundreds of boys' adventure stories appeared, eulogising Britain's empire builders. Life for the fictitious imperial hero was a series of opportunities to exercise his prowess and demonstrate his supremacy over foreigners and the working classes. Nothing he encountered was **'The public face of our national culture is overwhelmingly imperial and royal'** beyond his knowledge, there were no surprises and no mysteries. Whatever the odds stacked against him, he was imbued with a boundless optimism and good cheer. It was a world in which the instrumental white, male body radiated Teutonic splendour. Hundreds of thousands of boys could lose themselves in daydreams of heroic endeavour, projecting themselves out to far-flung corners of the empire without any fear of being lost or abandoned. Yet there is a frisson of unease in these insistent representations of heroic endeavour. In a final letter to his wife before he died, Scott wrote about his concern for his son's manliness; 'Above all, he must guard and you must guard him against indolence. Make him a strenuous man. I had to force myself into being strenuous, as you know - had always an inclination to be idle'. He ends his letter: ' What lots and lots I could tell you of this journey. How much better has it been than lounging in too great a comfort at home.' The strenuous exertions of the imperial hero, his refusal to contemplate, to think or to pause, suggest that his adventures involved a compulsion to escape the idleness and comfort of domesticity. Perhaps all those heroic dead bodies harbour a secret. Perhaps the icy wastes of the Antarctic proved easier to confront than a deeper fear, closer to home.

The hero is a figment of adolescence, he stands beyond the adolescent's immediate life, a shining contrast to the ordinary, a symbol of desire and the future. He is the subject of daydreams. Typically he is presented as the figure who saves the dreamer from peril. But his significance lies in another scenario; it is the dreamer who rescues his hero. In his gratitude, the hero looks at the dreamer and in his gaze the dreamer recognises that his hero knows and understands and loves him. In 'The Interpretation of Dreams', Freud wrote: 'By picturing our wishes as fulfilled, dreams are after all leading us into the future.' Dreams, wishes, desires contain the idiom of our lives. They lead us into relationships with others and into ways of being with ourselves. The pleasure of the imaginary hero is that he truly knows us. It is the pleasure of loving and being loved, a part of the transition into adult maturity and sexuality. When the hero has been used, when he no longer has that aura of wonder around his life, he is left behind, an illusion created by childish longing and youthful desire. Our lives hold a detritus of heroes; each has occupied a particular theatre of our imagination in which we have enacted our future selves. As we grow they become part of the archaeology of our desire, what inspired us and gave us hope in our passage to adulthood: a formative influence on political and personal empathies.

The liberation of individuals from the authority of their parents is a necessary part of human development. For the boy, it involves an intense, ambivalent struggle to separate himself from his mother. In his relationship with her lies the language of emotion; expressions of need, pleasure, pain. In contrast, the public world of fathers appears distant and peripheral. In this family drama , society and culture demand that the male infant must deny and repress the maternal idiom of sensuality and feeling in order to acquire the instrumental language of masculinity. The mother is lost as an object of love. 'One feels,' writes Freud in his essay, 'Mourning and Melancholia', 'a loss... has occurred, but one cannot see clearly what it is that has been lost.' Nobody has actually died but something inside feels on the point of death. The problem of mourning becomes a central preoccupation in the boy's developing psyche. But patriarchal culture prohibits the expression of this loss in language. It is known, but cannot be spoken of, and therefore cannot always be resolved. There can be no end to the mother's dying; and the need to keep her alive in order to safeguard their own sense of well-being holds men prisoner. Misogyny and childish emotions alternate in a man's attempts to be free of this burden. His liberation from the shadow of his parents is continuously postponed and he remains something of a perpetual adolescence.

'The imperial hero pursued glory in the hope that he would discover the father he longed to become'

Trapped in such a predicament the boy turns inside himself and manufactures a dream-world of omnipotence, independence and risk. Risk-taking is an integral part of an adolescent's struggle against parental authority. But if the transition to adulthood is continuously postponed it becomes an end in itself. The heroic figure who continuously risks his life for a cause greater than himself personifies the eternal adolescent. The story of the Empire is full of such men, real and fictional: mother's boys, repressed, sentimental, loving boys in general because it was a way of loving the boyishness in themselves. Arrested in his capacity to love another, such a man can only aspire to complete autonomy; a quest for an ultimate self, freed of social relations. On his own, he imagines himself freed of emotional dependency, able to act without compliance to the wishes of another. As a child, solitude created anxiety: in heroism it becomes a positive virtue. The hero develops his own autarchic emotional economy. He has bequeathed his love to his mother in order to sustain her life inside himself. But even as he pays her homage, each feat of strength, each mission accomplished is a blow against her and a triumph of his freedom from her.

Out of guilt at this imaginary destruction of the mother, the hero develops a masochistic desire to suffer for her. Under her gaze, he turns his violence upon himself. The image of the suffering hero is of a masculinity under assault, a son unable to renounce his mother. It is a masochistic body, driven to excess, which cries out for pity, for the love and the care of the mother, and in the same instant rejects such a need in a fit of manly prowess. The hero defies all odds in his struggle to assert himself against the hold she has on him. Even as he is wounded in battle, he struggles to fight on, his prostrate body publicly signifying an aggression against the self; his weapon destined not so much for the enemy, as for the siren call of his mother's love. The price of winning is his life, which he willingly gives, because in that moment of victory he will finally be freed of his need for her. In truth he never left the maternal home he strove to be free of. What he feared more than the enemy, more than his own death, was women and their sexual desire. He may well have been willing to die for his mother country, but he was incapable of living with his mother.

Fated, driven by the seduction of death and the need to subjugate his body, the imperial hero pursued glory in the vain hope that he would discover the father he longed to become. It is this heroic drama of a boy's struggle for self-becoming and his anxieties and fantasies about the power and influence of his mother which are central to Freud's psychoanalytic writings. Freud claimed that his oedipus complex was universal, but it is principally a description of the boy's acquisition of gender identity and sexuality. The father intrudes upon the infant-mother relationship, initiating the oedipus complex and sexual differentiation. He brings language, individuation and access to culture. At the same time his rivalry with his son for the mother produces a desire in the boy to escape his father's dominating presence. The drama resides with the father and son. Freud's emphasis on the father is a product of the demonisation and idealisation of mothers. When Freud wrote in *Civilisation and its Discontents*, ' I cannot think of any need in childhood as strong as the need for a father's protection,' he echoed the Victorian anxiety that boys needed to be protected from their mother's love. Freud reiterated the special bond between mother and son in several of his essays, but his glowing remarks do not disguise the 'terrifying impression of helplessness' he perceived in the infant's dependency on the mother. For Freud the father's role is to rescue his son from the boy's mother. It is the story of St George and the Dragon, only the distraught damsel is a youth who must be brought to sexual knowledge by an older man. The father is the boy's first idealised hero. The romance of the wounded hero in flight from women and domesticity, pursuing personal glory, is the repetition of this original plot; the desire of the son to escape his dragon/mother and gain his father's love.

In today's postmodern society, England and its imperial heroes have become risible, and a stultifying nostalgia for the lost age of empire is suspected of being promoted by an ideological interest intent on securing its political power. But postmodern scepticism has been equally disdainful of the socialism many of us espoused in the 1960s and 1970s: socialism's avowed rejection of nationalism and the bourgeois culture which manufactured the romantic hero did not stop it thriving on nineteenth century romanticism and inventing its own heroes. Instead of the unknown soldier it created the worker. It encouraged an austere self-sacrifice amongst its advocates, not in the name of national destiny but in its metaphysical claim on History as the agent of revolution. Its mythologies, its language of fraternity and earnest righteousness, reproduced an exclusively masculine culture of heroic struggle. In the 1960s and 1970s women's liberation unravelled the fabric of these identifications. Feminism invented a politics which did not rely on ascetic and dutiful sacrifice. It subverted the strenuous intensity of men's politics through its emphasis on pleasure, sexuality and the minutiae of everyday life. The struggle moved elsewhere, the dreams changed, and men weren't invited. For many men , the meteoric and passionate rise of feminism, and the pleasures women found in its solidarities, reinforced feelings of uncertainty and personal isolation. Without women the fragility of men's sense of security and belonging became apparent. The heroic myths of revolutionary struggle had been dependent upon women's everyday labours of love and domesticity. Without them the slogans sounded like... slogans.

One of the great pleasures and strengths of adolescent hero-worship is its naivety, its intense excitement and pleasure in life's possibilities. With maturity and a sceptical frame of mind we are frequently left floundering when we try to recapture that uncompromising belief in our personal destinies. We become aware of our incompleteness. The myth of idealism, the desire inherent in hero-worship, is a belief in the possibility of our own completeness. It is a dream of becoming our idealised father, escaping our mothers and our need; for some moment in the future when we will be completely present in our own mind and desire. It is the necessary corollary of adolescence. But in adulthood, when it is harder to dream about the future, it is not the heroes of our adolescence we should cling to. It is the way we used them, the belief in ourselves they helped to instil. I began with an Irish poet, and I want to end with another, Derek Mahon. It is dawn of New Year's day and Mahon has spent Christmas in St Patrick's Psychiatric Hospital in Dublin. He watches the last planes of the year pass overhead and imagines the home he will soon be returning to.

> as I chew my thumb
> and try to figure out
> what brought me to my present state-
> an 'educated man', a man of consequence, no bum
> but one who has hardly grasped what life is about,
> if anything. My children, far away,
> don't know where I am today,
>
> in a Dublin asylum
> with a paper whistle and a mince pie,
> my bits and pieces making home from home.
> I pray to the rain-clouds that they never come
> where their lost father lies; that their mother thrives;
> and that I
> may measure up to them
> before I die.[2]

---

2. 'Dawn at St Patrick's', Derek Mahon, in *Selected Poems*, Penguin, 1990.

Mahon's modest wish for personal integrity, to be a good father and to be able to love, does not add up to a blueprint for a future utopia. It has none of the panache and verve and excitement of the adolescent's romantic heroism. But that is for dreaming. Mahon's sentiment is for living.

Heroes of history, heroes of phantasy:

Idealisation, masculinity and the soldiers of empire

Graham Dawson

Specific heroes are worshipped in specific times and places. Graham Dawson *draws on Kleinian theories of idealisation to begin to understand hero worship as a phenomenon that is both psychic* and social.

The soldier is often thought to be the quintessential masculine hero.[1] Certainly, within Western cultural traditions since the time of the Ancient Greeks, military virtues such as aggression, strength, courage and endurance have repeatedly been defined as the natural and inherent qualities of manhood itself. If the apogee of manly virtue is thus attainable only in battle, the ideal masculinity represented by the soldier hero has served as an inspiration, a guide to living for men and boys living humdrum lives far from any war zone. As an understanding of what men essentially are, it has also served a series of reactionary politics, ranging in our own times from Enoch Powell's discourse on 'the essential specialisation of the two sexes of our race' ('One is specialised ... to bear arms, specialised for all the attitudes of killing ... The other is specialised ... to the preservation and care of

---

1. The argument in this essay derives from a more detailed study in my book,
    Soldier Heroes: British Adventure, Empire and the Imagining of Masculinities,
    Routledge, 1994.

life')[2]; to the current cult of the 'warrior archetype' in the North American so-called 'Men's Movement', with its the bizarre back-to-the-woods male bonding of the 'Iron John' variety.

Against such essentialisms, it may be argued that heroes are made, not by their deeds, but by the stories that are told about them. The soldier only becomes a hero when his dangerous and daring exploits are narrated as adventures, when his triumph (even in death) is celebrated, when his qualities are recognised by an admiring public that constitutes the audience to his tale. The forms and conditions of this storytelling, as any other, are contingent on and determined by a range of factors, social, cultural and historical. The story is told within a structured relationship between storyteller and audience, in which recognition of the hero is organised according to historically variable contexts. The recognition that a working-class squaddie might expect to elicit, on returning to the intimacy of his family and community, where soldiering may be a comparatively novel experience so that the storyteller is able to occupy the exotic identity of the wanderer returned, would differ markedly from that available in his regimental 'public', among comrades who had directly participated in those experiences with him. Both family and regiment remain localised and particular publics in comparison to the national public which recognises the soldier as a national hero and construes his story in the more abstract and generalised terms of national identity.

These cultural contexts also shape the narrative conventions of the hero's story, which has been told in such variable historical forms as Greek epic, medieval and Renaissance romance, modern military biography and the war novel. From this perspective soldier heroes are cultural constructs, their ideal masculine virtues the products of history, expressions not of some universal essence of manliness but of ideological configurations of gender, class, 'race' and nation, in which versions of 'the masculine' are defined, propagated and contested. And yesterday's heroes are today's forgotten men.

Remembering and forgetting the heroes of Empire

Who now remembers, for example, Major-General Sir Henry Havelock KCB, whose commemorative statue stands beneath Lord Nelson's Column in the corner of

---

2. Enoch Powell, *Parliamentary Debates: House of Commons Official Report: Standing Committee F, the British Nationality Bill,* 17 February 1981.

Trafalgar Square abutting the Strand? Commander of a small force sent to relieve the besieged British garrisons of Cawnpore and Lucknow during the Indian Rebellion ('the Indian Mutiny') of 1857-8, Havelock was hailed by the English press as a great hero - the saviour and avenger of British India - after winning a series of victories against the rebels. The hitherto unknown name of Havelock became a 'household word' as his story took root and proliferated in newspapers, pamphlets and public meetings throughout the country.

News of his death in November 1857 'reached us when all tongues were speaking of his wonderful march, and recounting his daily battles, and when all hearts were swelling with grateful feelings to the patriot-warrior'; when, indeed, 'the nation was eagerly expecting some fresh achievements from the great hero ... one common feeling of grief pervaded the whole land, from the royal palace to the humble cottage'.[3] 'We all feel we have a lost a friend. We are all in mourning today', eulogised the Revd Reed in one of countless sermons preached in churches and chapels throughout the country on the following Sunday.[4] The memory of one 'so illustrious' would be fixed (it is imagined, for eternity) in lyrical language that transfigures suffering and loss:

> As long as the memory of great deeds, and high courage, and spotless self-devotion is cherished amongst his countrymen, so long will Havelock's lonely tomb in the grave beneath the scorching Eastern sky, hard by the vast city, the scene alike of his toil, his triumph, and his death, be regarded as one of the most holy of the many spots where [England's] patriot-soldiers lie.

This obituary, from the *Daily Telegraph*, quoted in Marshman, captures the flavour of the impulse towards heroic commemoration - in popular as well as middle-class cultural forms - which sprinkled the country with Havelock Roads and Havelock Arms, and culminated in the Trafalgar Square statue paid for by national subscription.

Soldier heroes and popular imperialism

The intense public interest and excitement generated, throughout British culture,

3. Revd W. Owen, *The Good Soldier: A Memoir of Major-General Sir Henry Havelock*, Simpkin, Marshall and Co., 1858, p 224-5; J.C. Marshman, *Memoirs of Major-General Sir Henry Havelock, KCB*, Longmans Green and Co., 1909, p 449.
4. Revd A. Reed, *A Good Soldier: A Sermon Preached on the Death of Major-General Sir Henry Havelock Bart. KCB*, Ward and Co., 1858, p 4.

by news coverage of the Rebellion made the Indian army generals like Havelock, Nicholson and Neill into a new type of popular hero. Henceforth, at least until the mass slaughter along the Western Front in the 'Great War' of 1914-18, and arguably far beyond this into the mid twentieth century, the imperial soldier hero would luxuriate at the very heart of the British national imaginary. The vast ideological edifice known as popular imperialism, whose heyday really began in the 1880s, is unthinkable without his pervasive presence.

It is rather startling to discover that, only one hundred years ago, soldiers - or more accurately, generals and other officers - occupied a position in popular culture comparable to the sports stars, rock stars, film stars and other entertainers of the 1990s. The historian of Empire, James Morris, evoking the impact of popular imperialism on succeeding generations of Victorian men and women alive at the time of Queen Victoria's Diamond Jubilee in 1897, writes that:

> the events of the past twenty-five years had swept the people into a highly enjoyable craze of Empire ... Anybody over thirty, say, at the time of the Diamond Jubilee had experienced a period of British history unexampled for excitement. What theatre! The tragedy of Islandhlwana! the thrilling defence of Rorke's Drift! Gordon martyred at Khartoum! 'Dr Livingstone I presume'! The redcoats helter-skelter from the summit of Majuba, Sir Garnet Wolseley burning the charnel-houses of Kumasi! Never a year passed without some marvellous set-piece, of triumph or of tragedy. Champions rose to glory, the flag forever flew, the Empire grew mightier yet.[5]

Those under thirty, including the children perhaps too young to understand the significance of the freshly unfolding news stories, could not help but encounter retellings of these narratives and images of their heroes, as imperial imaginings percolated into every nook and cranny of late-Victorian culture.

Compared to today's postmodern melange it was a homogenous culture, cross-class and cross-generational in a way now inconceivable, but sharply differentiated along lines of gender. In the last decades of the century and into the Edwardian period, patriotic masculinities and femininities came to be imagined and recognised increasingly predominantly in terms of their gender-specific contributions to the imperial mission. Since a 'real man' would of course be prepared to serve and, if

---

5. James Morris, *Farewell the Trumpets: the Retreat From Empire*, Penguin, 1978, p 28.

necessary, to die for his God, his Queen and his Country, the most potent and representative figure of the patriotic 'Englishman' (who might well have been Irish, Welsh or Scottish) was the soldier hero.

This popularity was made possible through the accelerating development and diversification of the culture industries from the 1870s, which was itself a part of the more general shift in capital investment into production for a popular consumer market. New products, representations and practices concerned with the Empire proliferated in many forms, ranging from the growth of the music hall and other forms of commercial entertainment to the appearance of cigarette cards and brand labelling, commemorative medals and bric-a-brac, toys, games, and other developments in children's culture. Images of imperial soldiers were pervasive across this whole range of products and representations: not only were there 'war heroes' sets of cigarette cards, but even a 'Havelock' brand of cigarettes featuring a picture of the hero before Lucknow. Indeed John MacKenzie has written of a 'hero-industry', sufficiently well organised by 1885 to cash in on the hullabaloo surrounding Gordon's martyrdom at Khartoum.[6]

Paramount among these developments was the publishing revolution, brought about from the 1880s by modern, commercial production and marketing methods, which constructed new and popular audiences for an ever-widening range of printed matter - books, magazines, newspapers and pamphlets. Stories of the colonial adventures of British soldiers, told and retold across many different narrative forms, constituted the very keystone of the hero-industry and constructed a new imperial tradition, a heroic pantheon of historical and contemporary heroes.

This was very much a tradition in the making, since new soldier heroes were regularly being produced during these decades in a lengthy sequence of colonial 'small wars' that steadily expanded the boundaries of Empire. These new adventures were eagerly featured in news reports for an increasingly fervent popular press from growing numbers of war correspondents and artists. Such reports of the latest campaign, together with eye-witness accounts and the inevitable character sketches, could be reproduced almost immediately as small books or cheap pamphlets, such as the penny collections of *Lives and Adventures of Great Soldiers in the British*

---

6. John M. MacKenzie, *Propaganda and Empire: The Manipulation of British Public Opinion 1880-1960*, Manchester University Press, 1984, pp 21-8.

Army (1885). The most famous soldiers followed earlier national heroes such as Nelson, Wellington and Havelock in becoming 'household names'. Four in particular stand out: Generals Wolseley, Roberts and Kitchener became public heroes following their famous imperial victories, won variously in Canada, West Africa, Afghanistan, Egypt and the Sudan. In the case of General Gordon, his martyrdom in the imperial service at Khartoum ensured the canonisation of an already popular, Christian soldier hero, as the most renowned of all exemplars of imperial virtue.

Exemplary lives

The figures occupying the central positions in this imperial pantheon, both historical and contemporary, embodied a distinctively Victorian form of idealised British masculinity: one characterised by a potent combination of Anglo-Saxon authority, white racial superiority and martial prowess, Protestant religious zeal, and moral righteousness. They represent a fusion between two hitherto discrete traditions, those of military patriotism on one hand, and of the evangelical 'Christian soldier' on the other, which converged originally in the 1850s to produce a new, hybrid narrative form: the exemplary life biography of the soldier hero. This set exciting military adventure to serve as the sugar-coating for the serious moral and spiritual example presented by their hero's character and achievements, so narrated as to stimulate in the reader a desire for emulation. The original audience for these biographies was adult and evangelical: within three years of Havelock's death in 1857, four full-length 'lives' had been published, all by serious Christians. But by the end of the century they had been recoded as literary fare suitable for children, particularly boys, and had become a publishing industry staple.

The emergence of a gender-differentiated, and specifically juvenile, literature enjoyed its most dramatic expansion from the late 1870s with the rise of the new imperial adventure fiction for boys, carried first in high-circulation journals typified by *Boy's Own Paper*, and from the 1880s in romances by the likes of G.A. Henty, with titles like *With Clive in India* and *With Roberts to Pretoria*. The juvenile book-market, including heroic biography and adventure fiction, was aimed primarily at adult purchasers, being designed to supply suitable birthday and Christmas presents for children, and prizes to be bestowed in schools and other improving institutions. Here, parental approval of the themes of a commercially-produced children's culture intersected with evangelical, state and civic concerns about the propagation of gender-specific moral virtues - manifested most famously in youth organisations such as the Boys' Brigade, the Girls' Patriotic League, and eventually Baden-Powell's Scouts and Guides movement. Together these various agencies worked to institute a comprehensive separation of the adventure worlds of boys and men from the domestic world of girls and women - a split inscribed not only within juvenile narrative forms, but in the wider field of gendered identities and recognitions within which texts were distributed and read.

By the end of the century the publishing houses were engaged in the systematic organisation of hero-worshipping: there were series of 'famous lives' about imperial soldiers, administrators and missionaries, past and present (as in Nelson's 'Stories of Noble Lives' series); and collections of several, highly-condensed lives within one volume (such as F.M. Holmes' *Four Heroes of India* (1892), or George Barnett Smith's *Heroes of the Nineteenth Century* in three volumes (1899-1901). The explicitly didactic motives of the genre are well expressed by Eva Hope in her *Life of General Gordon* (Walter Scott, 1885):

> And therefore his biography is a lesson. We may get from him, as from all good men and women, light to guide us in the formation of our characters, and the direction of our actions. To the young especially, who desire to make the best of their lives, an account of Gordon and his work cannot be other than useful; and if they will stop to ask what has made him great, they will be able to discover in him the qualities out of which all heroes are made.

More than mere discovery is involved here: '[Gordon's] conduct throughout is an illustration of the way in which the Christian should fall in with the designs of Him who is the ruler of the universe, and the guide of the individual' (p 362).

An earlier best-selling biographer, A. Egmont Hake, had represented Gordon in explicitly evangelical terms as a 'perfect' man, Christ-like in his 'conquest of self'.[7] Towards the end of the century this explicitly spiritual dimension of the hero tends to give way to a more forthright emphasis on patriotic self-sacrifice and imperial duty. Violet Brooke-Hunts' *Lord Roberts* (Nisbet, 1901), for example, tells an improving narrative of a soldier 'whose whole life has been devoted ungrudgingly to the service of that Empire of which he has ever had so lofty a conception'(p345). Its pages are similarly peppered with moral lessons drawn from Roberts' exemplary

---

7. A. Egmont Hake, *The Story of Chinese Gordon*, Remington and Co., 1884

conduct: 'my desire has been to give to boy readers the general idea of a career, successful in the highest degree, rich in adventure and experiences, fortunate in many respects, yet unmistakably built upon the sure foundation of honest work and single-hearted devotion to duty' (p vii). Yet despite Roberts' own Anglican piety, Christian zeal is conspicuously absent from this later narrative, being displaced by 'the thought of England's Queen and England's honour which had made men brave to suffer and to do' (p 317).

The exemplary life biographies of soldier heroes played an important role in an explicit ideological project to fashion boys into patriotic imperial subjects, as good, God-fearing Englishmen. After 1895 and particularly from 1900, this role was enhanced by the new centrality afforded to history in schools and a demand for text-books based on narratives of great men and women: pride of place went to war stories, as in the reader published in 1911 by the Cambridge University Press, in which twenty-four out of forty lives for study were military heroes (see Mackenzie, p 181). Thus were the soldier heroes of the Victorian Empire reproduced as exemplary figures in British culture after 1918 and - increasing anachronisms - into the era of decolonisation itself.

The hero as a psychic phenomenon

If the Victorian soldier hero was out of date by 1918 and seriously anachronistic by 1945, he can appear positively laughable in the cultural climate of 1990s Britain, with its redoubtable secularism, anti-authoritarianism and hedonism - not to mention its strong anti-racist currents and its profound amnesia about almost everything to do with the British Empire. But while the forms of Victorian culture may be alien, we can surely recognise, in these exemplary life biographies and the whole razzmattaz enveloping the imperial soldier hero, a cultural *process* that is deeply familiar from our own experience. This is the process we call 'hero-worship'.

A paradox at the very heart of the phenomenon of heroes and heroines can then be brought into focus. On the one hand, as I have sought to show so far in this essay, we are dealing with historical forms. On the other, we can recognise, even in heroes and heroines not our own, the effects of powerful and apparently trans-historical, perhaps universal, imaginative impulses: to value especially desirable human qualities embodied in an idealised object. How are we to conceptualise this psychic dimension of the soldier hero? Can such a perspective be pursued without collapsing properly historical analysis back into an essentialism, or undercutting it by recourse to a dubious universalism grounded in the psyche? Is it possible to develop an historical account of the imaginative idealisation that is hero-worship?

The basis for such an account can be found in the subtle theory of idealisation developed in the Kleinian tradition of psychoanalysis. In Melanie Klein's own writing, the phenomenon of hero-worship is understood to be:

> the peculiar position in the minds of people generally of idealised figures such as famous men and women, authors, athletes, adventurers, imaginary characters taken from literature - people towards whom is turned the love and admiration without which all things would take on the gloom of hate and lovelessness, a state that is felt to be dangerous to the self and to others. ... Together with the idealization of certain people goes the hatred against others, who are painted in the darkest colours. This applies especially to imaginary people, i.e. certain types of villains in films and in literature; or to real people somewhat removed from oneself, such as political leaders of the opposite party. It is safer to hate these people, who are either unreal or further removed, than to hate those nearer to one - safer for them and for oneself.[8]

This makes immediate sense of the Victorian imperial soldier hero, whose idealisation by the British national public exists in direct proportion to the hatred lavished upon the resistant colonised peoples who constitute his adversary (particularly their leaders). Sir Henry Havelock, for example, shone all the brighter in heavenly contrast to the demonised Nana Sahib, the Indian rebel leader held responsible for the notorious massacres at Cawnpore. Nana Sahib was popularly imagined back in Britain to be the 'Satanic locus of all Oriental treachery, lust and murder'.[9] The virtue of General Gordon's 'strong faith, courage and devotion to duty' is thrown into relief by Mohammed Ahmed, the 'false prophet who claimed to be the Mahdi, or Messiah, foretold long ago by Mohammed.'[10]

For Klein, heroes and villains are primarily figures of unconscious phantasy,

---

8. Melanie Klein, 'Love, Guilt and Reparation', in Melanie Klein and Joan Riviere, *Love, Hate and Reparation* , Hogarth Press/Institute of Psychoanalysis, 1937, p 97.

9. Patrick Brantlinger, *Rule of Darkness: British Literature and Imperialism, 1830-1914*, Cornell University Press, 1988, pp. 202-4.

10. *Heroic Lives: David Livingstone, H.M. Stanley, General Gordon, Lord Dundonald*, Chambers, 1894, pp. 81, 43.

who exist within the 'dynamic psychic reality' of the mind. This has 'its own laws and characteristics, different from those of the external world'.[11] Phantasy is not a wish-fulfilling alternative to, but 'a constant and unavoidable accompaniment of real experiences, constantly interacting with them'.[12] The external world 'is always perceived and related to through a screen of ... internal drives and phantasies, which may alter its impact dramatically':[13] we see the world in terms of its templates, as good versus evil or the just against the treacherous. At the same time, 'If unconscious phantasy is constantly influencing and altering the perception or interpretation of reality, the converse also holds true: reality impinges on unconscious phantasy. It is experienced, incorporated and exerts a very strong influence on unconscious phantasy itself'.[14] This opens the door to the historical determination of psychic life: it allows the possibility of theorising the gendered forms of a British imperial psyche.

Kleinian theory thus offers a powerful relational model of the psychic economy. Subjectivity is construed in terms of an 'inner world' of the imagination governed by both psychic and social determinants. This is distinct from the 'outer' world of social relationship and cultural identity, and yet complexly and variously connected to it through a spiralling circuit of psychic exchanges brought about by processes of 'projection' and 'introjection'. Projection is understood by the Kleinians to be a process whereby the 'ego' or self invests in the social world its own impulses and feelings originating within the psyche, while through 'introjection' it incorporates and internalises aspects of the social world back within the psyche, as parts of itself.

Klein conceives the inner world established through these processes as peopled by internal phantasy figures, or 'imagos'. These are imaginative constructs which mediate the psychic and the social: composite forms derived partly from identifications with the various qualities and aspects of the social world (prototypically experienced in infancy, from the parents and their bodies, as, for example, benevolent or punitive); partly from conflicting internal impulses of

11. Susan Isaacs, 'The Nature and Function of Phantasy', in *Developments in Psychoanalysis*, edited by Joan Riviere, Hogarth Press/Institute of Psychoanalysis, 1952, p 81.
12. Hanna Segal, *Introduction to the Work of Melanie Klein*, Hogarth Press, London, 1973, p 14.
13. Stephen Frosh, *The Politics of Psychoanalysis* , Macmillan, 1987, p 117.
14. Segal, *Introduction*, p 15.

aggression and libido, hate and love. The self relates to these impulses through phantasies of both beneficial and harmful interaction with its imagos - expressed, for example, in the phenomenon of hero-worship and villain-hatred.

The self as such is constituted by means of introjective identification with a multiplicity of different imagos, derived from the parents and others (of both genders) encountered in social life. The diverse and fragmentary quality of these various identifications engenders incompatibility and leads to psychic conflict. The self attempts to reconcile and resolve this conflict in an endless endeavour 'to form a whole out of these various identifications'.[15] Psychic life in the Kleinian account thus centres on a dramatic struggle for coherence, unconscious in the first instance, in which the self strives to compose a narrative phantasy capable of reconciling psychic conflict and integrating different identifications. The idealised hero, for Klein, functions as a necessary focal point or principle of psychic cohesion, 'without which all things would take on the gloom of hate and lovelessness'.

Psychic splitting and the idealised hero

But Klein also identifies a less benevolent side to idealization. This struggle for integration occurs in the face of a countervailing tendency to fragmentation, which she terms 'psychic splitting'. Chief among the factors that provoke splitting of the self and its imagos are the disintegrating effects of anxiety and the defences developed in self-protection against it. These 'ego defences' work to prevent anxiety from undermining the self by containing it within a limited zone of the psyche. 'Resistances' are established between anxiety-producing and anxiety-free imagos (the hated and idealised figures) and thus, also, between parts of the psyche. This results in 'the different identifications becoming cut off from one another': the idealised qualities remain split off from the hated.[16] The self's defences against anxiety therefore produce narrative phantasies that exacerbate the existing fragmentation of the internal world. While necessary up to a point, splitting interferes with more inclusive processes of integration, reproduces hatred and anxiety, and ensures that further psychic conflict will occur.

Klein's account therefore distinguishes between a more open, integrative mode

---

15. Melanie Klein, 'Personification in the Play of Children', in *Contributions to Psychoanalysis 1921-45* , Hogarth Press/Institute of Psychoanalysis, 1948, p 220.
16. Melanie Klein, 'On Identification', in *Our Adult World and Other Essays*, Heinemann, 1963, pp. 57-60.

of subjective composure and the more limited and defensive mode enabled by psychic splitting. In the former case, a more integrated self, open to its own contradictions and more tolerant of painful experience, confronts and strives to transform its anxieties, in efforts to reconcile the conflicting imagos. In the latter case, the self achieves a degree of coherence based on a denial of destructive and painful aspects of its own experience, and of the anxieties to which these give rise. Refusing its own conflicts, it assumes a highly defensive formation where imagos that embody these aspects, and threaten its idealised composure, are expelled beyond tightly policed borders. This fluid and complex geography of connected and separated psychic spaces established by splitting and integration constitutes the terrain on which the self struggles for narrative composure in response to its own contradictory and conflictual formation.

Heroes and villains, as described by Klein, are figures in this internal landscape, the symbolic forms of imagos which may be more or less split or integrated. If splitting is severe, a fairy-tale-like world comes into being, of benevolent knights and wish-fulfilling fairy godmothers, malevolent monsters and threatening witches, and other 'helper' and 'persecutor' figures. The self identifies itself with the idealised 'helper' imagos who can do nothing bad or harmful, and mobilises against the hostile and threatening imagos which become the bearers, through projection and disavowal, of aggressive and destructive impulses. Anxiety generated by these aggressive impulses, and the prospect that they might come to dominate or destroy the internal world, is experienced in paranoid narrative phantasies of attacking and being attacked by these terrifying, persecutory figures (and thus, by aspects of the imagined social world) ('Personification', p 219-25). The existence of these sharply-contrasting imagos produced by psychic splitting provokes 'phantasies of internal warfare', so that 'we cannot be at peace with ourselves' ('Love, Guilt and Reparation', p114); and the contours of the split internal landscape are repeatedly likened by Klein to a battlefield, in imagery strongly reminiscent of much heroic literary adventure.

Various other alignments of the self and its imagos are possible, each involving characteristic configurations of anxiety and the defensive strategies used to contain it. Triumphalist phantasies, of wreaking a deserved destruction on imagos felt to be worthless, occur where the self idealises and identifies itself with, rather than disavowing, its own aggressive impulses. Feelings of loss and mourning for what has been destroyed, and guilt at the damage it imagines has been done to others, are expelled from the triumphalist self to be projectively invested in social space. In depressive phantasies, the self internalises and identifies with this destructiveness and assumes responsibility for its consequences, exposing itself to the full brunt of guilt and loss, and experiencing its own internal world in pieces: a psychic landscape of broken ruins, mutilated bodies and other fragments from the aftermath of battle. In reparative phantasies, the self seeks to repair this damage and 'put together what has been destroyed, to create and recreate', so as to restore a sense of fullness and coherence in the internal world, and allow the self to live at peace with itself (Segal, *Introduction*, p 75).

These psychic strategies affect the investment of significance in the social world, including the way real other people are experienced. Klein's analyses explore how self-composure is always established on the basis of an imaginative positioning of others: as they are drawn into the internal psychic world, and allotted parts in the narrative phantasies that are played out within it, our sense of relatedness in social life becomes imbued with attractions and repulsions, fears and desires that neither self nor other can fully control. British readers of the atrocity stories in the news from India in 1857, for example, were titillatingly invited to imagine 'cruelties at which the heart shudders and the blood runs cold ... the ears of Christians tingle with the horrid tale'.[17] But these same cruelties 'inflamed the nation ... There is one terrible cry for revenge. The account of that dreadful military execution [by the British] at Peshawar - forty men blown all at once from the mouths of cannon, their heads, legs, arms flying in all directions - was read with delight by people who three weeks ago were against all capital punishment'.[18]

The hero-worship of Havelock in the autumn of 1857 was determined at the psychic level by this complex melange of phantasies, in which his idealisation can be read as at once a defence against the massive national trauma of the Rebellion, a disavowal of the internal rage, hatred and impulses to cruelty provoked by the atrocity-stories, and a gratifyingly triumphalist reassertion of British imperial virility. For, as the popular Sunday newspaper, *Lloyd's Weekly*, put it:

---

17. James P. Grant, *The Christian Soldier: Memories of Major-General Havelock KCB*, J. A. Berger, London, 1858, pp 26-7.
18. Thomas Macaulay, quoted in Francis G. Hutchins, *The Illusion of Permanence: British Imperialism in India*, Princeton University Press, 1967, p. 85.

In the midst of the blood, and outrage, and disaster - in the worst darkness of the storm, towering as a giant above all other fighting men, stands gallant Havelock! His cheering voice, his keen sword, his dashing generalship, make up, for us, a figure of radiant hope. His name becomes a 'household word'. Men who have lost sons; mothers who have children and husbands to mourn; and those broken-hearted men and women who live to think always of foul outrages committed upon their own flesh and blood - all hail the name of Havelock (4 October 1857).

From psychic imagos to cultural imaginaries

Thus can repercussions of psychic conflict be traced throughout social life. But the example of the Indian Rebellion news stories also allows us to see how phantasy assumes a public, cultural form in specific cultural conditions. Havelock the hero depended not only on psychic idealisation, but on the mid-nineteenth-century communications revolution that was speeding up the transmission of news and expanding the public audiences for news stories.

It depended too, of course, on the historical conflict of the Indian Rebellion itself. The really radical potential of Kleinian theory lies in its conception of the reciprocal contingency of psychic life upon social contradictions. Anxieties and fears originate not only in the internal world, but in social conflicts that impact on psychic splitting and integration, and are carried of necessity into the depths of the psyche, by introjective processes that must use whatever is available from social life as resources for composure. By holding onto the sense of Havelock the hero as a cultural form encoding exemplary qualities of middle-class, Christian, imperialist masculinity, it becomes possible to see how the full range of complex, conflictual social relations - of imperialism, class, religion, gender - exist in dynamic interaction with the struggle for greater psychic wholeness and integrity.

This potential is not always realised in the Kleinians' own writing. This tends to conceive of the social domain, at best, in narrowly interpersonal terms, at the expense of a more sophisticated understanding of complexly structured social relations; at worst, it regards the social as a mere locus of internally derived phantasies. The dangers inherent in this analysis are tellingly evident in Melanie Klein's own argument about the psychic significance of heroic exploration. Here, the example of 'explorers who set out for new discoveries, undergoing the greatest deprivations and encountering grave dangers and perhaps death in the attempt', are used to illustrate how impulses and interests originally derived from the infantile relationship to the mother may be transferred to other scenarios. 'Phantasies of exploring the mother's body, which arise out of the child's aggressive sexual desire, greed, curiosity and love, contribute to the man's interest in exploring new countries'. Far-off lands function 'in the explorer's unconscious mind' as metaphorical substitutes for the lost mother, expressing a reparative wish 'to re-create her and to find her again in whatever he undertakes'. As such, the conflicting impulses of the original ambivalent relationship - an aggressive drive to possess and rob her of her riches and a countervailing drive to restore and make good the damage caused thereby - are reproduced in the new context, merging into 'the later drive to explore' ('Love, Guilt and Reparation', pp 102-5).

Klein wants to demonstrate how the early triumph of reparative over aggressive wishes in relation to the mother underpins creative and constructive activity in later life. But her insistence on the reparative component of the drive to exploration leads, in effect, to an extraordinary complacency about colonialism and genocide.

> These wishes to make good merge into the later drive to explore, for by finding new land the explorer gives something to the world at large and to a number of people in particular. In his pursuit the explorer actually gives expression to both aggression and the drive to reparation. We know that in discovering a new country aggression is made use of in the struggle with the elements, and in overcoming difficulties of all kinds. But sometimes aggression is shown more openly; especially was this so in former times when ruthless cruelty against native populations was displayed by people who not only explored, but conquered and colonised. Some of the early phantasised attacks against the imaginary babies in the mother's body, and actual hatred against new-born brothers and sisters, were here expressed in reality by the attitude towards the natives. The wished-for restoration, however, found full expression in repopulating the country with people of their own nationality (p 105).

Here, the sense that national actions fuelled by unconscious phantasy colonise actual social spaces inhabited by real others, is subordinated to a concern for the inner drama, to the point where the native populations of colonised countries are rendered entirely dispensable. Nor does Klein offer any suggestion of how the real relations of dominance and subordination established in the colonial encounter might have impacted upon, or indeed helped to constitute, phantasies of this kind.

By failing to relate these phantasies to their current (rather than original) social context, Klein casts colonialism firmly in the past, effectively justifies it in colonialist terms, and renders invisible the native experience of colonisation.

Striking, too, is the absence of any developed interest in culture, language or representation in Klein's argument. Interest in exploration cannot be related exclusively to 'the unconscious of the explorer', but is organised by the cultural narratives - the adventure stories - of a collective grouping or national community. Through representation, the explorer him or herself (Klein's discussion is curiously unconscious about gender) becomes a hero, even a soldier hero, one of those 'idealised figures' who focus the projective identifications of a wide public audience (p 97). These narratives are not only shaped by imaginative investments derived from the psyche; they are also forms of representation, socially and culturally determined. Their analysis must involve a double movement: following their traces inwards along the 'psychic pathways' that traverse the landscape of the internal world; and outwards into the cultural imaginaries - those vast networks of interlinked discursive associations, themes, images, motifs and narrative forms which map the social world, invest it with imaginative significance, and represent the identities of those who inhabit it.

Following Klein's own argument about the necessary inter-relation between projective and introjective processes, these two dimensions of analysis need to be grasped. Projected imagos from the internal world sediment into the forms of a cultural imaginary, which is, as it were, 'in-formed' by phantasy. Through introjection, these cultural forms in turn inform phantasy and structure its imagos. Heroes and villains may well be psychic requirements, but they assume particular forms with specific cultural values and qualities attached to them: bold explorers and treacherous natives, for instance, or the English Christian soldier and 'the Mahomedan [who] is a ferocious animal, and made so by his creed'. The introjection of cultural forms can be seen as a crucial missing link in Klein's argument about the impact of the social world upon unconscious phantasy. For, if projection is how the self gets into culture, introjection is how culture gets into the self. Grasping this double movement, we will be in a position to write a history of men and heroes - from the soldiers of the Victorian Empire through to the Linford Christies and Jarvis Cockers, the Philip Lawrences and Sir Michael Roses of our own day - as heroes of history, *and* of phantasy.

Heroines: black skin, blue Eyes and muslin

Becky Hall

Becky Hall *reflects on literary heroines, race and identification.*

Courage, suffering, passion, loneliness, resilience, hunger, disappointment, difference. These are the words that spring to mind when I think of the literary heroines of my imagination. Jane Eyre, Maggie Tulliver, Margaret Hale, Tess Durbeyfield, Catherine Earnshaw, Elizabeth Bennet. When I dress myself up as the heroine of my own narrative it is always in the borrowed language of literature. It is always with a particular framework of reference. To speak of myself is often to echo the familiar stories etched into my imagination, the stories which have made it a comforting place to inhabit. It is almost impossible to revisit the psychic worlds of my most adored heroines without producing at the same moment the whisper of muslins, pale silks, organza petticoats, Indian shawls and the spectre of a Darcy, a Heathcliff or a Rochester, for until the more recent arrival of Peter Hoeg's Miss Smilla, my sites of heroic identification have been caught up with my own troubled romance with the literature of nineteenth century England.

Wedged into a small, private corner of my memory there is an image of a little girl with brown skin and horribly short curls. She is secretly studying a bright illustration to a fairy tale, Snow White and Rose Red. She is anxious and furious and quietly ashamed. Waged in an unforgiving war she is desperately trying to decide which of the two little girls is prettier, which looks more like herself. Only one of the sisters can be the heroine; there is after all only one Prince Charming.

Fear of discovery heightens the urgency behind the decision. A flood of shame as she watches herself gripped by her preoccupation. She grimly settles for the ebony hair and crimson lips of Rose Red. There is a momentary glimpse of triumph at having the courage to reject this particular fantasy of femininity - the flaxen locks, peachy mouth and blue, blue eyes that constitute the unbearable desirability of Snow White. Yet it is with a deep sense of resignation and disbelief and insurmountable rage that she quietly slips the book back into its place and climbs up the stairs heavy with the awful knowledge that in the social world she inhabits she will never look like she does in her dreams.

Romantic love and physical beauty - 'probably the most destructive ideas in the history of human thought'.[1] Perhaps nobody looks like their heroines. Perhaps the most wonderful thing about the imagination is that we can shake off the physical, social and cultural limits of our own bodies and travel the unknown shores of others. But as I write this I am reminded of Frantz Fanon's poignant essay *The Fact of Blackness*, in which he speaks of the 'dark and unarguable' visibility of colour inscribed upon the body.[2] Black skin as the signifier that is seen and 'read' as racial difference. And I am reminded of Pecola Breedlove, the little black girl of Toni Morrison's first novel who prays for nothing more than a pair of new, blue eyes.

'Look a Negro!...Mamma, see the Negro!' (Fanon, p 112). The moment Fanon describes is that in which he confronts the image of his own blackness through the frightened eyes of a child. 'I am overdetermined from without' he writes, 'the slave... of my own appearance'(p 116). Fanon imagines the sight of his own blackness to materialise out of the system of representation governing the colonial imagination. The image of the Negro 'battered down by tom-toms, cannibalism, intellectual deficiency, fetishism, racial defects, slave ships'(p 112). Pecola Breedlove wears her ugliness with a devastating conviction. The world around her offers nothing to contradict the 'knowledge' that she is only what she sees herself to be in the eyes of other people, a poor, black, ugly little girl. She sees the 'vacuum where curiosity ought to lodge', the distaste, the separateness, the 'total absence of human recognition' as a glance hangs suspended before her face (*Bluest Eye*, p 47). Despite the movement of her mind, Pecola knows her blackness to be 'static

1. Toni Morrison, *The Bluest Eye*, Grafton Books, 1983, p 113.
2. Frantz Fanon, 'The Fact of Blackness' in *Black Skin ,White Masks*, Pluto Press, 1986, p117.

and dread'; like Fanon she is fixed, the slave of her appearance. Pecola's friend Claudia learns that the best place to hide her rage and shame is in fraudulent love. Unable to grasp the nature of the secret magic possessed by little white girls, repulsed by the disinterested nature of her violent dismemberment of blue-eyed, yellow-haired pink-skinned dolls, she learns to worship Shirley Temple. Pecola simply prays for the miracle that will bring her beauty and love. She prays for blue eyes.

Both Fanon and Morrison address the production of visibility as an exercise of power. Each interrogates the cultural systems of representation within which blackness is produced and 'seen' and internalised as racial difference. Fanon describes the psychic trauma of recognition, Morrison the devasting paradox of being looked at and yet not seen. *The Fact of Blackness* and *The Bluest Eye* are two texts which raise critical questions about the relation of race and desire to the structures of fantasy. Fanon demands that we examine the psychic effects of colonial history. He insists that we think about the power of whiteness in the formation of colonised subjectivities. Morrison writes of a subject crippled by the aching gap between social reality and fantasy. A subject shattered by the limits inscribed upon her body. We leave Pecola lost in the hopeless impossibility of her dreams, intent on the 'blue void' which she cannot reach or see, but which fills the valleys of her mind. Both Fanon and Morrison remind us that the desire to inhabit a white body carries with it the long and complex history of race and representation. Their work reminds us that fantasies of whiteness lend a problematic historical inflection to those identifications which cross the material boundaries of skin colour. This is not to invest all race-ed identifications of the imagination with the desire to *be* white, but to recognise the difficulty of addressing fantasies of racial transgression. Fanon is primarily concerned with the masculine subject of the colonial moment, Morrison writes across the genders and generations of a black 'community' in 1940s Ohio. Both writers construct a narrative of black subjectivity which is wrestled out of a dialectic between the body, history, culture and the imagination.

For a moment *Beloved* exploded the fantasy of myself as a nineteenth century heroine.[3] The novel of slavery, memory and subjectivity hurled a shattering narrative of history into the centre of my imaginary world. There seemed no space in Jane Austen, no voice in George Eliot for the articulation of racial difference. The whiteness of my heroines told a narrative of Englishness which my

---

3.   Toni Morrison, *Beloved*, Alfred A. Knopf, 1988.

mixed-race body could only possess with a deep and unsettling ambivalence, a sense of loss. Discomfort is hard, for it demands interrogation. To re-visit the novels of nineteenth century England with the writing of Toni Morrison in mind was of course a way to imagine that literature differently. My compulsive return to those scenes of Charlotte Bronte's novel in which the snarling, snatching body of Mrs Rochester took shape required the acknowledgement that my pleasure in Jane Eyre's heroic and romantic narrative was troubled by an identification with the inhuman, unspeakable presence of the West Indian heiress. I had to learn to mourn the loss of Bertha Mason, whose language seemed suddenly intelligible to me. It spoke of difference. It spoke of Englishness. It told the narrative of England's colonial history and the systems of representation within which such discourses made themselves meaningful. *Beloved* made it possible to take my blackness and my Englishness into my imagination. It opened up a way to re-think the pleasures of identification without losing sight of the narratives of history which inform its ambivalence. My heroines remain the same. I still see myself in muslins. I still long for Mr Rochester. But the image of my fantasy has shifted. Fascinated by the materiality of black skin and the discursive production of 'race', it is through my own body that I investigate the fantasies of blackness and whiteness troubling the English cultural imagination that is also my own.

C.L.R. James
A genuine twentieth century hero?
Anna Grimshaw

C.L.R. James was born in Trinidad in 1901 and died in London in 1989. James dedicated his life to the theory and practice of revolutionary politics, and inspired many movements around the world. Among his most important writings are The Black Jacobins *and* Beyond A Boundary; *a representative sample may be found in* The C.L.R. James Reader *(1992).*

On the back cover of a new collection of critical essays, *Rethinking C.L.R. James*, James is described as 'a genuine twentieth century hero'.[1] At first it seems easy enough to agree with such a statement, given James's long and remarkable life, the rich legacy of his writings, his passionate commitment to fundamental social change, his integrity and humanism; and perhaps, above all, his fundamental vision of people in general as the universal force animating history.

Moreover, as a physical presence, speaking publicly or in private conversation, James was unforgettable. Almost fifty years after she first listened to his lecture in a Los Angeles church, Constance Webb could recall with striking clarity the effect James had on an audience:

---

1. G. Farred (ed), *Rethinking C.L.R. James*, Blackwell, 1996.

He was over six feet two inches; slim, but not thin, with long legs. He walked easily, with his shoulders level. His head appeared to be on a stalk, held high with the chin tilted forward and up, which made it seem that his body was led by a long neck — curved forward like that of a racehorse in the slip. Shoulders, chest and legs were powerful and he moved decisively. But, as with highly trained athletes, the tension was concentrated and tuned, so that he gave the impression of enormous ease. He was without self-consciousness, simply himself, which showed in the way he moved, and one recognized a special quality. [2]

But beneath our easy ability to ascribe heroic status to particular individuals, as a familiar strategy for focusing our own aspirations, lies a range of more complex and interesting questions. What is a (genuine) hero? What might be the distinctive characteristics of a *twentieth century* hero? These questions in turn lead us to ask others: about the nature of the self; the relationship between the self and society; and the role of subjects in history. For, in conferring heroic status on James we have to recognise that we are placing him within a certain kind of historical narrative. It is predicated on the notion of a lone subject, the classical, perhaps bourgeois, hero whose life's course constitutes a linear progress towards power and public achievement. Such a construction is, however, always precarious since, embedded within the progressive story is its opposite, thesis and antithesis. The conventional hero belongs to what might be called the tradition of the Great White Male. The irony of situating James here seems to be immediately obvious. For his trajectory as a black man, colonial subject and revolutionary activist appears to cut across the constructions of self and society which underpin the western tradition of heroic narrative. And yet James's biography has usually been fashioned according to these very constructions, that is, an individual life organised as progressive movement through time.

I must acknowledge here that, along with several others, I have spent much time working along these lines. James's constant movement, his extraordinary productivity, his habitual casting off of papers, resulted in a trail of documents, annotated books and personal memoirs stretching across four continents.

---

2. 'The Speaker and His Charisma', in P. Buhle (ed) *C.L.R. James: His Life and Work*, Allison and Busby, 1986.

Consequently, the urgent task for students of his life seems to be to collect up these scattered fragments and to piece them together, rather like a jigsaw, until a coherent picture begins to form. Each biographer, of course, constructs their own story of James. These are distinctive in their particular emphases and interpretations; but most accounts are organised according to the conventions of heroic narrative.[3] Although this style of writing achieves a certain closure, the biographer is always aware that certain questions remain unresolved. The final pieces of the puzzle continue to elude ones grasp.

In the course of producing a number of volumes of James's work, I have discovered that part of the problem lies in the whole series of oppositions upon which conventional biography is built — public and private, individual and collective, success and failure, ideas and experience, text and discourse. I saw that disruption of these categories, the leakages between them, had the potential to generate something new and interesting. The biographer has to learn to resist the idea of life as a steady process of accumulation. Rather, the contradictory movement often manifests itself as a decisive shift from quantity to quality; or, as James says in *Notes on Dialectics*, 'LEAP, LEAP, LEAP.'[4] My own perspective on James's life and work was transformed by editing his letters to Constance Webb for publication.[5] Although his fifteen years in the United States are recognised to have been critical for the development of his thought, James's extraordinarily passionate and intense correspondence with a young American woman has until recently been regarded as a minor source supplementing the publications on politics which make up the 'official' history of the period. But, as the Webb letters strikingly reveal, James himself came to recognise that these divisions between private and public, personal and political, lay at the heart of the crisis of twentieth century civilisation. The drive to integrate the fragments of modern existence was, he believed, the creative force underlying contemporary life. He called it 'the struggle for happiness'.

Thus instead of considering the correspondence as a private counterpart to the published writings, I want to suggest that the letters James wrote to Constance Webb between 1939 and 1948 concretely express the complex drama of his New

---

3. P. Buhle, *The Artist as Revolutionary*, Verso, 1988; K.Worcester, *C.L.R.James: A Political Biography*, SUNY Press, 1995.
4. *Notes On Dialectics: Hegel, Marx, Lenin*, Allison and Busby, 1980; (written in 1948).
5. *Special Delivery: The letters of C.L.R. James to Constance Webb 1939-1948*, (ed) A. Grimshaw, Blackwell, 1996.

World experience. For here we witness his struggle as a writer to control the conflicting forces he confronted in his own life. This struggle was indeed heroic. Its scope and intensity are revealed within the writing itself, not just in the preoccupations of the letters, but in the fractured narrative, different voices and shifting perspectives which characterise the Webb correspondence. Interestingly, too, James here explicitly casts himself as a hero - at times he is the classical hero; sometimes, the romantic hero; many times, of course, he imagines himself striding the world stage as the revolutionary hero. Ultimately, however, I believe that the letters reveal him to be a tragic hero.

'We witness his struggle as a writer to control the conflicting forces he confronted in his own life'

James began writing to Constance Webb shortly after his first meeting with her in April 1939. She was part of the audience for his lecture on the race question which he gave in Los Angeles during the extensive speaking tour he undertook after arriving in the United States at the end of 1938. He had travelled from the east coast cities, through the mid-west, into California and eventually to Mexico, where he held discussions with the exiled Leon Trotsky. James's journey was the tangible expression of the feeling of freedom and expansion which he experienced on arrival in the New World.

The Webb correspondence itself documents a journey. Most simply it may be read as a story of James's American years, providing a fuller and richer account than was previously available of that period of his life which he always considered to be most creative and significant. His letters can be arranged into an historical narrative which reveals the progressive development of his ideas, the emergence of particular key questions in the Marxist movement and the process by which he (and his group, the Johnson-Forest Tendency) reached a mature position on matters of revolutionary politics. From the beginning of his correspondence with Constance Webb, James, as a writer, sought to create such a narrative. Initially he cast himself as a classic hero within the unfolding drama, a modern subject borne along by the progressive currents of world history. This conception of his own individual destiny is tangible within the writing itself. It is controlled, confident, witty, playful and yet deadly serious.

James's early letters to Constance Webb, those written between 1939 and 1940, begin to lay bare the political issues which defined his work in the United States for more than a decade. They focus on two questions: the relationship between the black struggle for equal rights and the organised movement of revolutionary Marxism; and the nature of the Soviet Union. The signing of the Hitler-Stalin pact in 1939 posed the question of whether the Soviet Union could still be considered to be a workers' state, albeit in degenerated form; and whether it should be defended under all circumstances or not. James's belief in his own historical destiny is expressed through the letters as a personal struggle to resolve fundamental problems in the theory and practice of revolutionary politics. He conceives of himself as equal to this task; but it is, he acknowledges to Webb, one which will demand tremendous commitment, sacrifice and sheer hard work.

The first real test James faced as the hero of his own story began with his decision in December 1939 to stay on illegally in the United States after the expiry of his visa. Thereafter he was forced to operate underground and to adopt a variety of pseudonyms. In many ways this marks a symbolic moment in the fracturing of his personality, a process which at first he was able to control, indeed to exploit, as an author; but, as the correspondence with Webb continues, the writing begins to reveal an increasingly desperate struggle by James to subjugate the powerful forces which threaten to fracture his sense of personal integrity. A few months after James's 'retirement', Trotsky was murdered in Mexico. Writing to Constance Webb shortly afterwards in August 1940, James commented: 'It is adversity that tests and makes people. It is easy to sail along when everything is flowing with you. But now we need courage.'

When the letters to Constance Webb resume in 1943, following a three year break, James begins to emerge in the writing as a different kind of hero from the one of the early correspondence. His sense of historical destiny has changed. He is no longer the predominantly individual or bourgeois hero of a classic narrative. James is now the revolutionary hero, the leader of a tiny political group whose ambitions are no less than world revolution. But more than this, the revolutionary hero becomes inseparable from the romantic hero. For the middle phase of the correspondence (1943-46) is distinguished not just by the sheer number of letters which James sent to Constance Webb; but by their extraordinary passion and intensity. The pursuit of love and the commitment to a cause are intertwined, each one fuelling the other, such that James begins to believe that through the sheer power of his writing he can win Constance Webb both for himself and for the revolution.

By 1943 James had gathered around him a number of close political associates.

Prominent among them were two women, Raya Dunayevskaya, a former secretary of Trotsky, and Grace Lee, a philosophy graduate. Together with James, and a handful of others, they formed the Johnson-Forest Tendency, a Trotskyist group noted for its fearless pursuit of intellectual and political clarity (Johnson was one of James's pseudonyms; Forest, the nom-de-plume of Dunayevskaya). Many of the key questions which James and his group were pursuing found expression in the middle phase of the Webb correspondence; and the writing itself conveys the excitement of discovery as the collective work of the Johnson-Forest Tendency moves towards a final consolidation.[6]

Not only does James, as an author, seek to create a progressive narrative of this political process in his letters to Webb; but it is one of manifestly heroic dimensions. The revolutionary heroes (and heroines) of his story are defined by their courage, their commitment and their personal sacrifice. But perhaps, above all, what distinguishes them is the scope and ambition of their ideas. For the tremendous momentum in James's writing is sustained by his fundamental belief in the collective destiny of his group. Despite their tiny membership, he imagines his group acting on the stage of world history, the disparity of scale being bridged not through the reduction of the world to the level of the human subject (as with the classic hero); but by the inflation of the group's ideas so that they become equal to the scale of world history itself. Such a synthesis, as James himself subsequently discovered, could only be achieved within writing and not within life.

Interwoven with this particular heroic narrative was another progressive movement, James's discovery of America. For the Webb correspondence also documents the evolution of a unique project which culminated in James's 1950 work, *American Civilization*[7]. At its very centre was Constance Webb herself. As a young, beautiful Californian woman she was for James the powerful and concrete symbol of the New World. In the letters he wrote to her between 1943 and 1946 he sought to explore the differences between them in age, gender, race and

---

6. This was expressed in the publication of a number of key political documents: *The Balance Sheet* (1947); *The Invading Socialist Society* (1947); *The Revolutionary Answer to the Negro Question* (1948); *Notes On Dialectics* (1948); *State Capitalism and World Revolution* (1950).

7. C.L.R. James, *American Civilization*, Anna Grimshaw and Keith Hart (eds), Blackwell, 1993.

backgound as the creative focus for his attempt to understand the distinctiveness of American culture. The romantic hero was undaunted by the task which faced him. He believed that through the sheer force of his writing, by his powers of persuasion as a writer, he would eventually incorporate Webb into his vision of the world. Together he imagined them embarked on a voyage of discovery, one which was entirely complementary with the political journey upon which he was also embarked with the members of the Johnson-Forest Tendency; and yet, almost from the very beginning, the letters expose a fundamental contradiction. James was certainly aware of it, once confessing to Webb that he studied Hegel by day and watched Hollywood films by night.

'His revolutionary heroes and heroines are defined by their courage, their commitment and their personal sacrifice'

The later Webb letters (1946-1948) document a different kind of story from the one James had originally attempted to create through writing. For as the revolutionary hero of his own story, James ultimately found himself pitted against James the romantic hero. He began to recognise that the model of the former was, in fact, built upon a whole series of separations between the personal and the political, individual and collective, love and revolutionary commitment. The latter, however, promised integration, synthesis. James thought that he could reconcile the two, indeed find a way to encompass all aspects of life within an expanded notion of politics; but, as his letters increasingly lay bare, it was not a problem he could solve by writing. Life itself had crashed violently into the world he sought to create and control within the text. Not least he had to confront Constance Webb herself. For almost five years she had existed only as an idea, conjured up by James in his imagination. Following her move to New York from California in the summer of 1944 she became part of his life.

Although James continued to write to Constance Webb, even after their decision to marry and live together in 1946, the progressive movement established in the earlier correspondence starts to falter. Into James's carefully constructed narrative order unruly forces erupt; the momentum of the writing is now checked by other stories which threaten to subvert the dominant movement towards political clarity and personal intimacy. Moreover, James's identity as a writer becomes less focused and coherent. At first, as the romantic hero, James enjoyed adopting different voices and identities: the playful lover, the stern teacher, the passionate movie watcher, the ferocious critic, occasionally, the willing pupil; but always, as the writer, he exercised control. In the last phase of the Webb correspondence, however, even James's textual mastery begins to slip as he struggles to overcome what he calls 'the demons' within his personality.

The dramatic turn in the Webb correspondence began with James's belated acknowledgement that Constance Webb was a real person, an independent woman who refused to play the part he had assigned to her in his dramatic story. At the same time, James knew that she offered him a different kind of life, a way of integrating the divisions which ran deeply within his personality and which two decades of revolutionary activity had exacerbated. The task of integration he had already worked out at the level of ideas; the problem was to realise it through his own life. This was indeed *the struggle for happiness*.

But the realities of James's situation began to intrude in other ways. He had been served with a deportation order and his position in the United States was no longer secure. In addition there were growing divisions within the Johnson-Forest Tendency. Although James believed in the heroic nature of their collective commitment to profound social change, he began to realise that the unrelenting political work had narrowed and distorted the personalities of his collaborators. For the dialectical counterpart to the tremendous scope of their ambition and revolutionary vision was the bickering, rivalry, jealousies and tensions which intensified within his group.

James's final test as the hero of his own story was played out against the dramatic backdrop of the Nevada desert. In 1948 he went to Reno to seek a divorce in order to make his marriage to Constance Webb legitimate. Here, while working as a gardener, he completed his great work, *Notes on Dialectics*. His letters to Webb are filled with plans for their future. He believed that a new life lay within his grasp. But what James resolved as a writer in his last letters to Webb was not realised ultimately within his own life. For greater forces overwhelmed him. By 1950 James had returned to the old political life; and his marriage to Constance Webb was foundering. After a period of internment on Ellis Island, he was deported from the United States in 1953. James never again found the conditions to complete the creative work which Constance Webb and his experience of the New World had inspired.

Ultimately James was, I believe, a tragic hero. But only we, as the present-day readers of the remarkable Webb correspondence, can place him within that distinctive tradition. Although James self-consciously played out many heroic personalities through his letters to Constance Webb, he could not cast himself within a tragic role; but, like the great figures of history and literature (Prometheus, Lear, Ahab) he was impelled to struggle with forces beyond his control. Writing about the creation of original characters in literature while imprisoned on Ellis Island in 1952, James noted:

> The great writer ... conceives of a situation in which this character is brought up against things that symbolise the old and the new. The scene is set outside the confines of civilization. What is old is established, it has existed for centuries, it is accepted. But the new will not be denied. It is not fully conscious of itself, but it is certain that it is right. A gigantic conflict is inevitable.[8]

James, the writer, conceived the drama of his situation through the Webb correspondence; but he was forced to live it out in his own life. He saw that this tremendous conflict lay at the heart of modern civilization itself. He was defeated; and yet the courage with which he faced the struggle, the struggle for happiness, inspires us today. James's importance lies as much in our understanding his limitations as in his strengths, acknowledging his blindness as much as his insight. It is his failure to realise within his own life the integration of love and politics which he imagined through his writing which makes him a genuine twentieth century hero.

---

8. C.L.R. James, *Mariners, Renegades and Castaways: The Story of Herman Melville And The World We Live In* , Allison and Busby, 1984.

Peter Wildeblood

Hero without applause

Simon Edge

For oppressed minorities, the selection of heroes and heroines can be both a liberating and a subversive act. Simon Edge argues that for, the lesbian and gay community, dependent for its structure on transitory commercialism, there is no guarantee that the right people will be venerated

Sometimes, when a man is dying, he directs that his body shall be given to the doctors, so that the causes of his suffering and death may be investigated, and the knowledge used to help others. I cannot give my body yet; only my heart and my mind, trusting that by this gift I can give some hope and courage to other men like myself, and to the rest of the world some understanding. I am a homosexual.

Looking at homosexuality in medical terms, even in the form of an analogy, usually sets the hackles rising these days; even the World Health Organisation has belatedly decided that same-sex attraction is not an illness. But these words feel different. There is a portentous tone to the opening passage of this musty book, suggesting a historic moment. 'In the last few years there has been much discussion of this question, and many authoritative men and women have given their views about the prevalence, nature, prevention, punishment and cure of homosexuality,' the writer goes on. 'There have not, I think, been any among them who could say, as I do now: "I am a homosexual."'

The book is indeed historic. The passages come from *Against the Law*, an autobiographical account by the Fleet Street journalist Peter Wildeblood of the most celebrated British homosexual trial of the 1950s.[1] The unexpected outburst of public sympathy for the convicted defendants, who included the young peer Lord Montagu of Beaulieu, set in motion the long, slow process of law reform which resulted in the limited decriminalisation of male homosexuality in 1967. Wildeblood's book, an impassioned plea for tolerance and a startlingly uninhibited personal account of the lifelong misery to which homosexuals of the day were condemned, is that exhilarating commodity in the world of letters: a heroic piece of writing that changed the world.

Today, not just in society as a whole, but also in the very community of people who no longer need to view the discovery of their sexuality as the first day of a non-appealable prison sentence, the book and its author are almost completely forgotten.

The lone lobbyist

At the time of his arrest and imprisonment in 1954, Peter Wildeblood was the diplomatic correspondent of the *Daily Mail*. The 1950s were a time of celebrated anti-homosexual purges, including the disgrace of the Tory minister Ian Harvey and the conviction of Sir John Gielgud. But the 'Montagu case' was the most vicious and notorious prosecution of the decade. Arrests of homosexuals had been steadily rising since the 1940s, and Churchill's Home Secretary Sir David Maxwell-Fyfe was determined to clamp down further. A key newspaper account of the day suggested that there was pressure from the US security agencies - mindful of the flight to Russia of the homosexual spies Guy Burgess and Donald Maclean - to weed out suspected homosexuals in public life. Prosecutions reached a peak in 1953 and 1954 after the appointment of Sir John Nott-Bower as Metropolitan Police Commissioner. Lord Montagu, whose habit of mixing beyond the confines of the aristocracy and the upper middle class appeared to irritate the establishment as much as the indecency offences with which he was charged, was convicted along with his cousin, Major Michael Pitt-Rivers, and Wildeblood. Two young servicemen had been encouraged to go into the witness box against them in return for immunity from prosecution. That some items of police evidence appeared to have been crudely doctored did not trouble the judge, who seemed more concerned at the iniquity of the three defendants in consorting with their social inferiors. Wildeblood and Pitt-

---

1. *Against the Law*, Weidenfeld & Nicolson, 1955.

Rivers were each sentenced to 18 months imprisonment; Montagu received a 12-month term.

If the government, police and judiciary had hoped to whip up anti-homosexual prejudice by making an example of Montagu and his friends, they had a surprise in store. Articles in the *Daily Sketch*, the *People*, *The Times*, the *Sunday Times*, the *Observer* and the *Daily Express* aired grave anxieties about the way the legal process had been used. The Home Secretary had already been under pressure from the Church of England Moral Welfare Council and the Howard League for Penal Reform to set up a Royal Commission to review the law on homosexuality. Now he caved in, and Sir John Wolfenden, the vice-chancellor of Reading University, was appointed to head a departmental inquiry.

As the only one of the three defendants to have agreed that he was homosexual, and with no hope of returning to his old job in the notoriously blokeish world of Fleet Street, Wildeblood had little option but to confront his experiences and his sexuality head on. The fear of prosecution was so great that few others could speak privately, let alone argue for acceptance of their homosexuality in the public domain. So it is no exaggeration to say that *Against the Law*, written within months of Wildeblood's release from prison, was the only informed piece of writing to which the Wolfenden Commission could refer.

It is self-evidently a book of its times. 'I am no more proud of my condition than I would be of having a glass eye or a hare-lip,' writes Wildeblood, in terms which would prompt howls of protest from lesbians and gay men today. But it is a passionate tract whose principal aim is to press the case for law reform, and in that, the author is utterly uncompromising.

> A homosexual who gives way to his impulses, even if he is doing no conceivable harm to anyone ... runs appalling risks. The fact that so many men do so shows that the law, however savage, is no deterrent. If, as people sometimes say, homosexuality is nothing but an affectation assumed by idle men who wish to be considered 'different', it is indeed strange that men should run the risk of life imprisonment in order to practise it.

Single-handedly, Wildeblood constituted what would now be termed the 'gay lobby'. But the book, which also included an impassioned and incontrovertible argument for prison reform, had a far deeper impact than simply influencing the ill-qualified moral arbiters who would pave the way for law reform. Wildeblood's testament broke through the vicious circle of silence and concealment which for decades had confounded any possibility of political organisation or self-defence by homosexuals themselves. Since concealment was, and is, an option, it was the most obvious reaction to oppression; but it also militated against challenging prejudice, which meant that silence itself became an instrument of oppression.

As a result of his enforced 'outing' (the incongruity of the contemporary term underlines the extent of the changes which have taken place in the last four decades), Wildeblood already had his head above the parapet. In speaking out, he probably did as much as anyone to create the modern lesbian and gay movement. As its reputation spread, his book was avidly - if often secretly - snapped up by those who knew they had an interest in the subject. In a second book published the following year, Wildeblood himself describes the response he received to *Against the Law*.[2]

> For the first few months an average of one reader in every ten was either writing to me or ringing me up, and I began to wonder whether I should ever have time to write another book... There were letters from judges, magistrates, doctors, barristers and clergymen, housewives and mothers and businessmen, and there were also a good many from other homosexuals... My telephone number was in the London directory, and for weeks the bell never seemed to stop ringing. It made quite a change when I answered the phone and found that the person at the other end was someone I knew. Most of the calls were from strangers: 'Is that Mr Wildeblood? I do hope you don't mind me ringing you up. You see, I've just read your book...'

The sense of liberation which isolated and lonely men felt from reading the book and making contact with the author and his circle leaps from the page. It is possible Wildeblood is exaggerating, but unlikely. I was gripped by the bravery, honesty and uncompromising eloquence of the book when I first read it as a proud and confident gay man in 1995; what must have been its impact in 1955?

Saints and sinners

Society tends to choose heroes and heroines who uphold its values. Such figures can often be alienating to minority communities, and it can be a subversive or

---

2. *A Way of Life*, Weidenfeld & Nicolson, 1956.

liberating act for such communities to select their own candidates for veneration. The situation is further complicated for the lesbian and gay community by the fact that there are many figures whom society deems admirable but whose homosexuality has been deliberately written out of history. The denial of sexuality currently takes its most obviously ideological form with regard to military leaders. The contention by the Ministry of Defence that homosexuality is incompatible with military service is itself scarcely compatible with the private lives of Kitchener, Mountbatten, Montgomery and Baden-Powell - not to mention those of Alexander the Great and Richard the Lionheart. There is a far longer list of historical figures - from kings and queens to great artists and writers to heart-throb stars of stage and screen - whose achievements we are expected to consider exemplary, but whose sexuality is carefully erased from the record.

Of course, the concealment of the sexuality of public figures is often as much a matter of individual choice as of ideology. The conflict between the right of the individual to remain silent and the public benefits of revealing the prevalence of homosexuality is clearly at its starkest when the individuals in question are still alive. The extent to which the right to privacy is undermined by support for anti-gay legislation or by the ostentatious upholding of a heterosexual norm has become a familiar subject of debate.

Whatever the rest of the world may think of them, the closet bishop or cabinet minister is unlikely to be the figure the lesbian and gay community chooses to venerate. But selecting our own heroes can be a tough business. The dedication to Oscar Wilde of a commemorative window in Poets' Corner in Westminster Abbey in 1995 illustrated the role of conflicting world views in the selection of candidates for beatification. For years, Wilde's criminal conviction for homosexual offences stood in the way of his elevation, but the liberal Church view eventually prevailed that the deficiencies of his personal life ought not to be allowed to obscure his literary talent. The gay community, on the other hand, considered it a great victory that Wilde should be honoured in the centenary year of his conviction; as the country's most celebrated homosexual martyr since Edward II, his greatness in lesbian and gay eyes is inextricably linked with his sexuality and its criminalisation by society. For the two camps - and two sets of guests at the ceremony - the unveiling effectively constituted two separate events.

Clashes also arise over who has the right to confer heroic status - most notably in 1991, when Ian McKellen, the actor and co-founder of Stonewall, was publicly attacked by the gay film-maker Derek Jarman for accepting a knighthood from Prime Minister John Major. For McKellen, whose name had become synonymous with the fight against the anti-gay Clause 28, the award was an unprecedented establishment nod in the direction of gay activism; for Jarman and his supporters, taking an honour from the government responsible for the vicious clause was a craven sell-out. The spat was conducted on the letters page of *The Guardian*, where a number of public figures came out as gay for the first time to declare their support for McKellen. The affair prompted the Sisters of Perpetual Indulgence - a media-hungry band of gay men clad in nun's habits who had modelled themselves on similar 'orders' in Sydney and San Francisco - to redress the balance by conducting their own 'canonisation' of Jarman. Part camp extravaganza, part serious recognition of services to the lesbian and gay community (Jarman had, among other things, financed the establishment of the direct action group OutRage), the canonisation struck a chord in the gay press. The honour of living sainthood, conferred with a punning title, rapidly became a community institution. A solicitor with a remarkable record of successfully defending gay men charged with indecency offences became St Angus of the Innocent Gaze, while an opponent of the criminalisation of sadomasochism became St Derek of Human Bondage. That the institution had become a mirror image of the national honours system was confirmed when one household-name campaigner let it be known he had turned the honour down because his activism was not for personal gain.

The gentleman vanishes

But if the maturing lesbian and gay community has begun to learn the value of honouring its own, Peter Wildeblood, arguably the greatest single contributor to the establishment of that community, has received no such recognition. Not that today's activists are ungrateful. In an amorphous and transient community which places little value on group history, his work has simply slipped out of the collective consciousness.

I first came across *Against the Law* when a friend loaned me his ageing copy. He had not heard of the work before discovering it in a second-hand shop ten years ago, but he had been instantly captivated. He suggested that Wildeblood's crisp yet passionate style might provide a useful model for a book I was considering writing, and he mailed it to me. It arrived on one of those nightmare days for the freelance journalist, when I was desperately trying to shrug off the first unmistakable symptoms of flu, knowing that it could cost days of earnings if it was not nipped in the bud. Groaning with the pain in my sinuses and a searing headache, I pulled on two t-shirts, spread an extra blanket over the duvet and crawled into bed clutching a large bottle of brandy. Looking for something to glance at as I inhaled the drink's fumes, I picked up *Against the Law* and began idly to leaf through. One hundred pages later I was still reading, utterly hooked. Although I vaguely knew of the Montagu case, I, like my friend, had never heard of the book - yet here was an epoch-making piece of writing. I was enchanted.

Another friend supplied *A Way of Life*, complete with an inscription from Wildeblood in a fading post-war hand. But this volume, too, was the result of hours spent combing the shelves of second-hand bookshops: the fact that the original owner to whom the author had offered his copperplate compliments was long gone reinforced the sense that this was a work of a bygone era and that its protagonists had slipped out of view.

I quickly found I was not alone in my ignorance of the Wildeblood. In a circle of people as committed to and active in the gay movement as anyone, no-one under 35 had heard of him, while those over that age had heard of the first book but knew nothing at all about the man. Certainly none of them could tell me whether he was alive or dead.

Beginning to feel mildly obsessive, I made inquiries further afield. If Wildeblood were still alive (he would be 72), I wanted to ask him why he had dropped out of sight and whether he resented the lack of recognition for his extraordinary contribution to gay politics and life. I wanted to know if he had ever been able to enjoy some of the more hedonistic pleasures which the lesbian and gay movement has managed to deliver since its inception in the late 1960s and early 1970s. I wanted to know whether he considered himself a hero.

The publisher Weidenfeld and Nicolson, under whose imprint the two books were first released in hardback, was unable to provide any details of where the author might be or even how many copies of the books had been sold. There was no trace of Wildeblood or his work on the computer, I was told. For all the publisher was concerned, the books might as well never have been written. Penguin, which published *Against the Law* in paperback, told the same story, and an Internet inquiry about Wildeblood's whereabouts was equally unhelpful. A message appeared suggesting I asked one of the longest-standing names in gay campaigning, the architect of the 1967 Act. Another message promptly popped up from someone else who had already thought of that and asked the man in question - but he, too, had no idea what had become of Wildeblood. Neither was consulting histories of the gay movement any more use. Gay historians writing about the period quote extensively from *Against the Law* in relation to the Montagu case, but while they give him ample credit for his influence at the time, there is no evidence that any of them has had the opportunity of speaking to him personally. Wildeblood appeared to have disappeared.

The death of consciousness

If concealment is no longer a pressing issue for growing numbers of lesbian and gay people, nor is the serious business of activism. In reality, for a burgeoning community which can muster a crowd of 200,000 at Pride, the heroes are neither Peter Wildeblood nor St So-and-So of Anything. The likes of Chris Smith and Edwina Currie are obvious exceptions, but since the locus of the community is the commercial scene, and showcase political events feature many of the same artists who draw the crowds into the big Saturday night clubs, modern lesbian and gay heroes are inevitably performers. Those who have come out and succeeded in the mainstream, yet support gay or HIV charities whenever asked, are the favourites. Thus Lily Savage, Sandi Toksvig, Julian Clary or Elton John get the thunderous applause they deserve whenever they play at lesbian and gay events. Stalwart heterosexual supporters can also secure a place on the plinth, particularly if their cultural approval rating is already high: Joanna Lumley and Kylie Minogue can rely on a frenetic reception from drag queens and disco bunnies long after they have passed their sell-by date for the rest of the population.

Unfortunately, discernment is not the community's strong point. Artists with the right product are likely to receive personal adulation from the uncritical majority even if they are indifferent or actively hostile to the gay cause. The boy bands who play the gay clubs on the way up and then forget about them until they are on the way down are borne surprisingly little ill-will. Just two years after he sued a magazine for the 'monstrous slur' of calling him gay, the ex-*Neighbours* actor Jason Donovan played the West End's biggest gay club and faced barracking only from a small minority; the club promoter who effected the rehabilitation rightly predicted he would get away with it because the young crowd at the club would either not remember or not care about the court case. Guest performers at the 1995 Equality Show, the annual fundraising event organised by Stonewall at the Royal Albert

Hall, included a black American diva who brought her grandchildren on stage with her and encouraged the audience to clap along with a fundamentalist Christian gospel song. Astonishingly, some did. The event also included a surprise appearance by the teen band East 17, whose members had previously given well-publicised interviews opposing any reduction in the gay age of consent; in a ham-fisted 'apology', the band's singer had then suggested that gay men could do what they wanted provided they stayed away from children. The handful of spectators who protested vociferously at the end of the band's Albert Hall performance were thrown out by security staff, at the request of fellow members of the audience.

At fault is a lack of collective memory, which is in turn a function of the structure of homosexual life. For ethnic groups, heredity is part of the community infrastructure; the lesbian and gay community has no such parent-child links. Rather, it is a loose-knit collection of newcomers, whose only institutions are a constantly changing set of commercial drinking venues. In a community where some of the key bonds are sexual and none are familial, social structures are generationally horizontal rather than vertical. Oral history is more a matter of bar or pillow gossip about who is gay in public life than of accounts of struggles past. The free gay papers, once the best available repository of historical experience, are trivialising themselves into oblivion as they frantically compete to offer the lowest charges and most fawning coverage to advertisers from the commercial scene. And for individuals, the growing sense that homosexuality is less a crippling oppression than an alternative lifestyle with widespread acceptance in certain social and geographical contexts has undermined the need for historical consciousness. In that sense at least, Wildeblood's drift into obscurity is a mark of his own success.

Credit restored

I found him in the end. Lord Montagu, who is now better known for the unrivalled collection of vintage cars he has assembled at Beaulieu than for his misfortune in the 1950s, responded promptly to my cautious request for assistance. He put me in touch with Wildeblood's oldest friend, another former Fleet Street journalist, who had set up home in the Moroccan city of Tangier. Between them, they told me what had happened to Peter Wildeblood.

Both agreed that Wildeblood had made the greatest single contribution to law reform. He had provided a wealth of information for the great debates in the House of Lords, where the measure to decriminalise male homosexuality was first passed in October 1965. In particular, he had enlisted the support of Lord Longford, who became one of the most energetic advocates of reform (although in 1994, the same peer was one of the architects of an unsuccessful House of Lords measure to *raise* the gay age of consent from 18 to 21). Wildeblood had then withdrawn from gay lobbying, becoming one of the most prestigious and indeed highest-paid writers and producers in television. He worked for Granada Television for a number of years, before accepting a job with the Canadian Broadcasting Corporation in the mid-1970s. After enjoying another highly successful television career in Canada, he retired to the city of Victoria, on the country's western seaboard, where he led a relatively reclusive private life.

The calm of this world was shattered two years ago, when Wildeblood suffered a terrible stroke. This left him quadriplegic and speechless: with a perfectly functioning brain but unable to move a muscle. Showing the indomitable spirit which characterised his work on gay law reform, he has regained through physiotherapy some slight movement, which has enabled him to communicate through a metallic-sounding artificial voice-box.

Wildeblood's friend in Tangier offered to forward to Canada a fax of this article, together with a short list of questions. These, he said, could be read to the paralysed man by the young care assistant who had been found to look after him. With luck, he might be induced to send back a brief response.

I duly sent the article off, with a short message asking Wildeblood if he resented the fact that later generations of gay people were not aware of the debt they owed him. A month or so later I received a fax from Morocco. Wildeblood had, it seemed, used his chin to tap Morse code into a laptop computer which had then converted the signal into letters. It was the first such communication he had been able to send his friend since his stroke. He included the following message, which our intermediary now forwarded to me, and which is a fitting conclusion to this attempt to restore him to his rightful place in lesbian and gay history: 'Please tell Simon Edge that I was exhilarated and heartened by his article and cannot possibly feel neglected when such tributes come in. Here is a quotation I have found consoling: You can achieve anything you want if you don't mind who gets the credit.'

Keyboard cowboys and dial cowgirls

Kirsten Notten

Technological heroes are usually masculine. Kirsten
Notten *is searching for ways to create microwave
amazons and dial cowgirls.*

Space. The final frontier. These are the voyages of the Starship Enterprise. Its
continuing mission: to explore strange worlds, to find new lives and new
civilisations, to boldly go where no one has gone before.

The well-known opening sentence of *Startrek, the next generation* expresses a belief
in modern science and technology. In the television series, we see the promises
that accompany this belief: technology has made it possible to cut ourselves loose
from the shackles of the limitations of the earth, with her scarcity, injustice and
inequality; the various races and species live in peace and harmony on the Starship
Enterprise; the evil only comes from the outside, from the war-hungry Romulans
or unknown creatures. The travellers themselves live, besides some cute quarrels,
in friendship, prosperity and peace. Technology appears here as a way to overcome
earthly restrictions and problems.

   The technological project emerges as one big adventure in *Startrek*. Columbus
and Captain Picard are the heroes who show us that discovering new worlds with
the aid of technological gadgets is in itself attractive and meaningful, and creates
identities. The heroism conceals the political and ethical dimension of gathering
such knowledge. Captain Picard is an explorer, not a politician or a missionary.

His task consists of avoiding responsibilities. And it is the dream of every scientist and every engineer to search for knowledge and experiment with the possibilities of technology as an adventure, while forgetting the political dimension. The popularity of *Startrek* teaches us the attraction of this dream.

Starwars is a popular science fiction movie in which other fantasies about technologies are presented. The bad guys here are the ones who use the fancy technology. The heroes disdain technology - it would corrupt their pure, masculine heroism. Harrison Ford -'Han Solo'- flies the *deux-chevaux* spaceships by fits and starts, as if they could crash any minute. And from an old hermit Luke learns to trust the power of the universe instead of technology. The authenticity of the heroes appears untouched by technological decadence. Technology is not an instrument to conquer evil but a destructive force. *Starwars* is thus a different icon of modernity from *Startrek*. Modern times do not only offer promising technologies, they have also given us Chernobyl, the greenhouse effect and experiments with embryos.

Startrek and *Starwars* represent two distinct visions about technology. In *Startrek* technology is an instrument for the salvation of the human race from the earthly. Its users are heroes. Whereas, in *Starwars*, technology appears as a devastating, demonic force. The heroes are the ones who can withstand and defeat its seduction.

Both visions, by positioning evil outside human interaction and linking it to technology, are equally apolitical. The evil is disposed of by technological progress in *Startrek*, while the evil in *Starwars* is found in technological progress. But both visions neglect the problems of human interactions accompanied by technology. Racism and sexism, for example, can not be 'solved' by technology; neither are they purely the result of technological progress. In addition, in both stories heroes are represented as autonomous subjects, clearly distinguished from the other as technology in *Starwars*, and the other as earthly restrictions in *Startrek*. These oppositions around the technological heroes are reinforced by gender. The heroes whom we encounter are men. Symbolic meanings constituting their identities, like separation and loneliness, are masculine. And hero fantasies are boys' dreams. The hero is masculine.

We learn from science fiction that our fascination for and fear of technology is linked to its power to create heroes. I love heroes. I would like to give everybody the opportunity to have the pleasure of identifying with the empowering images of technological heroes. But I do not like the apolitical, autonomous, masculine image of heroes. We need a better heroism if we want to learn to live in a technological society, to cope with contemporary technological problems and to tackle the fear of and fascination for technology.

Cyborgs as heroines (f/m)

Donna Haraway is a biologist, feminist and philosopher of science. She tells stories from the practice of high-technological scientific research in biology to offer new concepts, images and metaphors. She makes no clear distinction between science fiction and the stories of scientists, fictions of science. Both types of stories present images to understand the complex relationships between organisms and other beings in a techno-scientific society.

She tells two stories from biology about the immune system. She utilises the immune system as a metaphor to understand our relationships. In the first story, T-cells are the heroes who protect the body against strange elements which can make the body sick, and fight a fierce battle for the purity of the self. Here immunity is invulnerability and pureness. In the other story, the immune system is depicted as a complex communication system, with several centres and peripheries where ongoing negotiations take place on the boundary between self and other: 'Immunity can also be conceived in terms of the semi-permeable self able to engage with others (human and non-human, inner and outer).'[1]

Donna Haraway prefers the second story because it leaves the separation between self and other behind and offers instead a continual interaction between different elements, in which the boundaries between self and other, or between own and alien, are constructed and changed. As an alternative to the vision of the world as a battlefield, which we remember from science fiction movies, she offers a communication metaphysics. She prefers to see the world as an ongoing communication process rather than as a battlefield because the battlefield metaphysics implies a hierarchy in the separation between self and other. And this dualistic mode of thinking resulted in oppression of the ones who were marked as the other, such as women, black people and nature. The pure, autonomous self, the T-cell or Captain Picard, could act as if it had nothing to do with the consequences of its actions and could thereby ignore the oppression. On the other

---

1. Donna Haraway, *Simians, Cyborgs, and Women: The Reinvention of Nature*, Free Association Books, 1991, p255).

hand, in a communication metaphysics everybody knows that she is responsible for the boundaries which are being drawn. Everybody takes part in the practice of establishing boundaries and forming the world, so everybody is responsible for the boundaries. The meaning of heroism changes in the second story of communication metaphysics. Heroism no longer means establishing an identity by conquering the other and ignoring the consequences of these actions, but consists of taking part in the action, and being responsible in the practice of interaction and communication.

'However high-tech nappies may be, changing nappies remains as unattractive as ever'

Haraway uses the heroic status of techno-scientific practice to shift the meaning of heroism. She redraws the boundaries of high tech to incorporate women into the heroic charisma of technology. The lives of black women, who make microchips in poor working conditions in Silicon Valley, are part of our high tech world of computers. Bicycles and telephones are products of the same complex production processes as jet engines and satellites. Our usual daily environment is a high-tech world. Women's lives are as much infected with technologies as men's. Haraway disintegrates another boundary, namely the boundary of sexual difference, which is as constructed, contested and arbitrary as other boundaries. Her subjects are not women and men, but cyborgs, technological organisms. Cyborgs are her heroines (f/m).

However, this new boundary of high technology, with the heroic, attractive status of the cyborgs, also evokes a problem. The activities of cyborgs can only be valued *because of* their connection with contemporary technologies. But are women using the telephone the same cyborgs as internetsurfers? Dial cowgirls do not have the same attraction as keyboard cowboys. However high-tech nappies may be, because of the use of material sciences, chemical processes and complex distribution systems for producing them, changing nappies remains as unattractive as ever. Some connections with high tech are not as visible and open to appreciation as others. And my scepticism about the heroic status of high technology grows when I see that a lot of activities done by women are hard to describe as high-tech. Washing with a washing machine that functions by means of fuzzy logic, and text writing in WP 5.1, do not flourish as cyborg activities in the same way as tinkering with a car or building your own website. Here we have the problem of a communication metaphysics; how the boundary is drawn between thrilling high tech and plain common technology.

The loss of heroism

Cynthia Cockburn and Susan Ormrod are two sociologists who tell the story of the development of the microwave in Great Britain.[2] At first it was sold in so-called brown goods stores or electronic outlets, where it was placed next to video cameras and stereo equipment. Its users' manual, design and the accompanying sales strategies suggested that you were dealing with very complicated technology. Young, dynamic, adventurous men were supposed to buy it. It was a gadget, one of the toys for the boys.

However, the microwave went through a metamorphosis from male jewellery into a handy, boring, female cooking instrument. This metamorphosis took place because of the economic depression of the 1980s, the competition of another gadget, the camcorder, and alarming stories about microbes in badly heated meals. The microwave was thereafter praised as a fulfilling cooking instrument which was able to heat, roast and grill. From then on it was sold in whitegoods stores together with household appliances, which have the family as their target group. In general, this meant that women incorporated the microwave into their cooking practices. The users' manual and directions were made very simple, because the designers and marketeers presumed that women were afraid of technology.

Again we hear a story, not science fiction or a scientific account this time, but a story from the design, marketing and users world - another type of story which makes other aspects of the world visible and in which heroism is tarnished. The microwave user was a hero as long as the operating instructions were unreadable, its usage was frivolous and the user was masculine. The heroism of the microwave was the result of design and marketing strategies. Captain Picards are being made. As soon as the microwave was entrenched in existing cooking practices, it lost its power to create heroes. The microwave was tamed in the production and consumption processes into a cooking instrument, and women became its users.

Susan Ormrod and Cynthia Cockburn show in their story that the meaning and the function of the microwave are the results of designers, commercial people, radio waves, microbes and gender meanings. They demonstrate Haraway's communication metaphysics around the microwave, the complex

---

2. C. Cockburn & S. Ormrod, *Gender and Technology in the Making*, Sage Publications, 1993.

practice in which many actors construct the meaning of the microwave. First the microwave was created as a high-tech, heroic gadget. Later on it became a low-tech, elevated frying pan. The gender differences were an important structuring principle in this development, as well as being influenced by it. Tamed technology brings its routine connotation to the activities in which it is being used, and common activities radiate a boring meaning to the technologies in these activities. Although meanings are rearranged and boundaries were redrawn in the microwave development, the gender differences, with their higher valuation of the masculine side, remain annoyingly stable. Technological competences and caring responsibilities change in content, but not in gender, in this example of a communication metaphysics. Gender is used to construct a difference between high and low tech, in this case between a brown and a white microwave.

Haraway's project to incorporate women into the realm of high tech is a difficult task if high tech is constructed along gender lines. High tech is partly constructed precisely *by* excluding women. It is therefore necessary to rearrange the way high tech gets its meaning, in a way which might include women in the technological realm. The attraction of high tech and its power to create heroes are partly due to its masculine image. Haraway reinforces this hierarchy of values by using high tech to make women into cyborgs and heroines (f/m). To give female activities a revaluation, the boundaries between high and low tech along gender lines should be dismantled. Dial cowgirls also deserve their heroic epos.

Our fascination for and fear of technology are partly derived from its power to create heroes. If we want a better world in which heroines (f/m) can play around and take responsibility for their technological actions, we need to redraw some boundaries and arrange the world in another way. The borderlines between being a hero and taking responsibility, between high and low tech, and between feminine and masculine, need some tinkering with. Donna Haraway shows us how heroes can be responsible and how women can be cyborgs. But her project depends on the connection of high tech and masculinity. Susan Ormrod and Cynthia Cockburn show how this connection is produced in a communication metaphysics. I love heroes, especially responsible ones who are sometimes female. We need an awful lot of epics on microwave amazons and dial cowgirls no longer to be disposed of as alien by the immune system of our techno-society. Look around and see them working and playing with technology.

Heroes for our times:
Tommy Cooper

Susannah Radstone

*Susannah Radstone explores the complex ways in
which screen personas relate to the vicissitudes of
historical and psychical life, taking as her focus the
comedian Tommy Cooper and some recent film
roles played by Anthony Hopkins.*

With Tom, he had that wonderful expression - that he could look at things
and...you see, when you do...like an idiot; and I say we're all idiots because
we're making a mess of this world...and the real people I *love* are the people
who know they're idiots. It's the people who don't know they're idiots that I'm
frightened of. But *Tom:* you see if you *look* at an object - let's say I'm looking at
you - *Tom* would look [leans to the side, while looking with exaggerated
concentration]. Now that's just *that* much [repeats the movement] that
differentiates between the people who have control of everything - who just
say, like, 'when did you last see your father'... but *Tom* - [leans again]. [1]

Descriptions of our times as 'uncertain', or 'destabilised' have become ubiquitous
on the left, as has the tendency to detect dismaying portents in the signs of our
times. Eric Sykes's stumbling yet eloquent appreciation of the comedian Tommy
Cooper's performative skills bears traces of the fear which underlies many of these
contemporary forewarnings: that we (in the West) may be approaching the abyss
from which the horrors of fascism can spring. His 'when did you last see your father?'
brings to mind images of *another* father figure - not the one who gets taken away,

---

1. Eric Sykes speaking about Tommy Cooper in *Heroes of Comedy: Tommy Cooper*
   (Dir .Iain McLean, Thames Television Production, Channel 4, 13 October 1995).

the lost father, but the ghastly figure whose rule sanctions atrocities such as those to which Sykes obliquely refers.

This darting reference to the lurking risk of what can happen if we forget that 'we're all idiots' occurs towards the beginning of *Heroes of Comedy: Tommy Cooper*, an appreciation of the life and work of this British comedian-magician which follows his career from its wartime beginnings entertaining the troops. In this context, Sykes's remark brings forth from the shadows not just the abstract threat of what *might* happen, but a concrete memory of what *did* happen, and the ghostly figure which emerges here is surely that of Hitler himself. Against *this* threat, Sykes offers us the image of Tommy, shambling across the stage, playing the idiot, making sure that we see exactly how his tricks *don't* work, exposing magic's machinery to the naked eye.

In the context of renewed fears concerning the possible return from the shadows of the fascist mentality - replete with the desire for a charismatic, heroic leader - Sykes's comments start to look like something more than 'light entertainment', directing us, as they do, to appreciate and learn to build from counter-tendencies wherever they are to be found. In *Heroes of Comedy: Tommy Cooper*, an illustrious parade of admirers, including Clive James, Spike Milligan and Anthony Hopkins, bear witness to Cooper's power to captivate his audience: they were helpless before him; he could do *anything* to them; but above all they speak movingly of both their, and the wider audience's, sheer *love* for Tommy, and at points offer tantalising analyses of his capacity to elicit such powerfully benign feelings. No doubt Cooper offers countless grounds for exclusion from the 'politically correct' canon of heroes - his jokes were, after all, sometimes (though not often) at his wife's (or other women's) expense. His 'playing the fool' gets laughs by mimicking the 'intellectually challenged'. But Cooper's powers to captivate - to bring forth warmth, and even love - were inextricably tied to the audience's acknowledgement of his *flaws*. What was striking about Tommy - and what 'Comedy Heroes' underlined most forcefully - was his capacity to *hold* his audience in thrall, while systematically divesting himself of all heroic qualities: 'perfection', control, and power, the qualities that film and cultural theory align with 'heroism' in general, and that have been said to find their apogee in the fascist leader in particular.

The insights provided by such theorisations should not be under-estimated. Much valuable work has developed from psychoanalytic film theory's alignment of the fascination of cinematic heroes with infantile, narcissistic desires, and feminist psychoanalytic film theory's uncovering of classical cinema's sexual division of labour which ascribes heroic power and agency to male characters and object positions to female characters. Yet for all their value, these approaches to 'the hero' seem to ignore certain types of fascination which neither repeat nor neatly overturn the orthodox strategies by means of which heroes are constructed and through which fascination is exerted.

Cooper, for one, refuses to fit. His paradoxical performance consists in the *charismatic* divestment of the heroic—it occupies a space *between* mastery and incompetence, between the classically heroic and the classically unheroic. Standard analyses of 'the hero' focus on genres of adventure, detection, action and romance, largely ignoring comedy and *its* heroes. But perhaps comedy heroes, and Cooper in particular, offer us evidence of a continuing form of *powerful* fascination that runs counter to, but is not a straightforward reversal of, the fearsome extremes to which much writing on cultural heroes despondently points. And perhaps a closer analysis of this type of fascination might deliver a less reductive, as well as a more cheering view of our contemporary capacities, wishes, and desires: reasons to be cheerful.

Uncertain times, uncertain heroes?

In 'Comedy Heroes', one of Cooper's most ardent eulogists, the actor Anthony Hopkins, describes with lucidity those qualities which called forth his admiration: Cooper's irreverence; his capacity to make us laugh at the fool in ourselves, and his 'rare gift' of courage - the courage 'to just go and make a mess of everything'. With wry regret, Hopkins admits that he'd much rather have been a comic, but that he simply couldn't do it: that what he does is easier than what Cooper could do. Faced with Hopkins's towering recent performances - in *Silence Of The Lambs*, *Shadowlands*, and, most notably, in *Remains Of The Day* - it would be tempting to dismiss these comments as mere self-deprecation, or even as disingenuousness, but such easy dismissal risks overlooking the (admittedly credulity-stretching) *comparison*, or even the equivalence, between their work that arguably underlies Hopkins' appreciation of Cooper.

But it's no wonder that Hopkins admires Cooper's capacity to turn loss into gain, to make 'losing it', and 'mak(ing) a mess of everything' deliver us to love and laughter. In each of the aforementioned films, Hopkins's much lauded performances have detailed the sufferings of men for whom control - too much control - has been their undoing. In *Shadowlands*, Hopkins plays the Oxford don and author C.S. Lewis. The film concerns itself with Lewis' late, brief marriage to the terminally-ill American Joy Gresham. Hopkins wrests from this role a performance that bespeaks an agonised redemption grounded in pathos: the C.S. Lewis character is finally delivered from his rigid, over-controlled and cloistered life, but too late, leaving the audience crying not for what can never be, but for what comes too late.

In *Remains Of The Day*, Hopkins' enactment of the 'consummate butler', described elsewhere as the 'perfect portrayal of English repression', condenses *Shadowlands'* exposure of the individual costs of too much control with a detailing of the potentially devastating *political* costs of such excess. As in *Shadowlands*, the Hopkins character acknowledges personal desire too late, so that love can never be his. In *Remains*, however, this devastating loss is set beside the character's belated realisation that his rigid adherence to the rules of the house, and his refusal to acknowledge that which might breach those rules, had led him to collude in collaboration. He finally acknowledges what he has 'known' all along: that during World War Two, his master had been on the side of the Germans. *Remains Of The Day* connects the stealthy development of fascism 'at home' to the butler's over-rigid adherence to the rules of the house. Though *Remains* looks like a 'nostalgia film' its relation to this genre is ambiguous. For while the historical 'nostalgia film' arguably contains anxieties about the present by offering us mythical and idealised versions of the past, *Remains* exposes those myths *as* myths, forcing us to acknowledge not only darkness within the home, but also the potential darkness within each of us.[2] Nevertheless, the film's historical setting does allow some distancing, perhaps, from its work of 'bringing it all back home'.

Unlike *Remains*, *Silence Of The Lambs* - described by Lizzie Francke as 'Jonathan Demme's omen for the millenium' - locates the heart of darkness in the present, or, perhaps, in the very near future. In *Silence Of The Lambs* Hopkins plays Hannibal Lecter, a one-time eminent psychiatrist turned serial killer, entombed in the top security cell of the Baltimore Hospital for the Criminally Insane. What startles in this performance is Lecter's diabolically fascinating *charisma*.

---

2. This cursory reading of *Remains Of The Day* is indebted to a far more complex and insightful analysis given by Gillian Rose: 'The Beginning of the Day: Fascism and Representation', delivered at the 'Modernity, Culture and the Jew' conference, University of London, Friday 13 May 1994.

Lizzie Francke describes Hopkins's Lecter as 'renaissance man turned into mediaeval gargoyle':

> He draws the Duomo in Florence from memory, can distinguish which version of the *Goldberg Variations* he prefers...A reincarnation of Dracula, he personifies a self- devouring high culture *turning in on its own impeccable order*'(emphasis added).[3]

Though *Silence is* arguably concerned with 'order', or, more specifically, with an order 'turning in on itself', here the Hopkins character is both 'supremely' controlled and *in need of* control. As the above commentary pointed out, Lecter is marked out from 'ordinary man' by his mastery and his knowledge. His skills - particularly his psychoanalytic skills - appear magical, as he peers into the recesses of the Jody Foster character's mind and stuns her with his perspicacity.

In *Remains* and in *Shadowlands* redemptive affect follows from the belated acquisition of the knowledge of the human heart; and, in acknowledging the flaws and the darkness within, these characters are delivered from isolated narcissism to join the human race. In *Silence*, however, the Lecter character knows all there is to know about his darkest wishes and desires - Lecter knows it all already. His suave saunterings through the nether regions of murder, desecration and bestiality mark him out as both knowing and yet unredeemed. Instead of the compromised redemption that concludes *Shadowlands* and *Remains*, *Silence* leaves us with a terrifying vision of a world in which redemption has become impossible: while Lecter's grandiosity is fed rather than chastened by his knowledge of inner darkness, the film's millenial fantasy is of a culture still rigidly *refusing* to acknowledge that which *Lecter* so blithely acts out. Lecter must be caged up, hidden, for what he tells that world about itself; Lecter is 'the other' who cannot be acknowledged within. No wonder, then, that Lecter's eventual escape to Haiti fills the spectator with guilty relief.

Though *Shadows* and *Remains* map the stakes of psychic integration at the level of the individual and the social, their nostalgia arguably compromises their, at best partial, optimism, suggesting that even the retarded and partial redemption they offer may no longer be possible. *Silence* refuses nostalgia, offering us in its place a dystopic vision of a world within which the redemption which *Shadows*

---

3. Lizzie Francke, *Sight and Sound*, Vol 1 Issue 2, June 1991, p 62.

and *Remains* do achieve is no longer possible. Instead of an eventual and partial integration of the other within, the film details the terrible cost of disavowal: and the Hopkins part can perhaps best be understood not as a 'character' in troubled quest of integration, but as a 'part' - in the sense of a part of the self - that cannot be integrated and must therefore be projected elsewhere, caged up and punished.

Hopkins' recent roles - the butler in *Remains Of The Day*, C. S. Lewis in *Shadowlands*, and Hannibal Lecter in *Silence Of The Lambs* - cannot be straightforwardly classified as cinematic heroes. Certainly, that is, their traits and functions diverge from those of the *classical* cinematic hero. Whereas the classical hero masters the narrative by controlling action, for the butler and the C. S. Lewis character, at least, the capacity to act is severely constrained by psychical rigidity. In *Silence Of The Lambs* the film's fear of what might happen if such rigidity were to be abandoned produces Lecter, who cannot be allowed to act at all. To an extent, each of these characters arguably *critiques* the classical hero. Each of these performances occupies that 'in-between' space that belongs neither to the anti-hero, nor to the absolute hero, whose supreme *control* and *mastery* of narrative action has been said to appeal to a spectatorial narcissism which underwrites the patriarchal construction of masculinity.[4] This argument, rooted in early feminist psychoanalytic film theory, takes as its starting point cinema's capacity to return us to primitive stages of infantile development.

Heroes and fantasy

Psychoanalytic studies of the cinema suggest that, once sitting still and quiet in the darkened auditorium, the spectator is lulled into a state close to dreaming. In this state, the boundaries between the conscious and the unconscious are no longer as secure as they remain in waking life. In dreams, and at the cinema, infantile ways of thinking and fantasising come to the fore once more. Tiny infants are helpless and dependent upon their parents or carers. In order not to be overwhelmed by feelings of dependence and helplessness the child will identify, in fantasy, with the mother, and then the father, who are each perceived in turn as all-powerful. This type of fantasy belongs to the primitive infantile stage known as narcissism, and the power of larger-than-life screen heroes can be seen to stem, in part, at least, from the cinema's re-kindling of such early narcissistic fantasies.

---

4.   Laura Mulvey, 'Visual Pleasure and Narrative Cinema', *Screen*, vol 16 no 3, 1975.

Though the child's earliest fantasies of omnipotence may emerge in relation to the mother, these fantasies take hold most completely in relation to the father. According to feminist psychoanalytic theory, patriarchal culture depends upon

'These performances occupy that "in-between" space that belongs neither to the anti-hero nor the absolute hero'

maintaining, to a degree, this primitive view of the father. To this end, patriarchal constructions of 'woman' arguably disavow all knowledge of masculine dependence, need, or fallibility, by displacing them onto 'woman'.[5] On this argument, classical cinema emerges as one site upon which patriarchal subject positions are endlessly re-secured, through the captivation of spectators by screen heroes. Though this feminist critique of the mainstream screen hero has been influential, its insights do not appear to shed light on the issues raised in this article's discussion of either Tommy Cooper's performative skills or Anthony Hopkins's recent roles. These performances and roles appear neither to invite, nor simply to refuse, narcissistic identification and fantasy. Instead, they each seem to inhabit a space that falls somewhere 'in-between' the spaces of primitive narcissistic fantasy, and of the more recognisably 'adult' world of limitation, possibility and in/competence. The characters both have, and lack, control. Can psychoanalysis help us to understand the identifications and pleasures offered by such roles and performances, and can their emergence be understood as anything more than an accident of history?

Since the 1970s, film studies has been striving to overcome the apparent resistance of psychoanalysis to questions of history. Such research seeks to understand the appeal of particular types of heroes to particular audiences at particular times. If *Shadowlands*, *Remains Of The Day* and *Silence Of The Lambs* together tell a story *about* contemporary history and about contemporary fantasies, desires and identifications, how can we interpret this story, and how might we understand those 'in-between' spaces to which these stories (and Cooper's performances) take us in psychoanalytic *and* historical terms?

---

5.   This is a highly condensed summary of a range of contested positions. For a more elaborated discussion of psychoanalytic film theory see, for instance, Robert Lapsley and Michael Westlake, *Film Theory: an introduction*, Manchester University Press, Manchester 1988; entries on 'psychoanalytic film theory', 'audience and spectator', and 'scopophilia' in Annette Kuhn with Susannah Radstone (eds), *The Women's Companion To International Film*, Virago, London 1990.

Heroes, history and mourning

Eric Santner's *Stranded Objects: Mourning, Memory and Film in Postwar Germany*, offers a starting point for considering these questions concerning contemporary culture, heroes and their fascinations.[6] The helpfulness of Santner's work lies in its psychoanalytical and historical approach to questions of narcissism and the fascination of heroes. At its heart, *Stranded Objects* is concerned with advocating a culture of 'mourning-work', without which, Santner believes, our western societies risk falling back into a fascist mentality similar to that which gripped Germany so recently. Santner's thesis is of interest since his re-theorisation of fascism in relation to narcissism and 'failed mourning' sheds light on, and offers a possible psychoanalytic and historical interpretation of, the 'in-between' spaces inhabited by Cooper and the Hopkins characters.

Santner argues that the task undertaken in order to work through infantile narcissism can best be understood as a type of mourning-work that gradually enables the child to work through and eventually move beyond its fantasies of omnipotence, control and mastery. Santner theorises this mourning-work through object relations theory, and, more specifically, through D. W. Winnicott's theory of the 'good enough mother'. For Winnicott, the successful working through of narcissism depended upon the child having access to a caring and holding environment within which loss (of narcissistic fantasy) could gradually come to be tolerated. Winnicott's 'good enough mother' provides this environment and witnesses the child's struggles to come to terms with loss through its play with 'transitional objects'.[7]

Moving on from Winnicott, Santner then introduces Walter Benjamin's notion of the 'aura' and coins the term 'auratic de-auratisation' to name a particular process of mourning-work that he seeks to advocate in the postmodern West. For Benjamin, the term 'aura' referred to a particular quality of gaze or look: the quality of a returned gaze. In *Illuminations* Benjamin deploys the term in relation to his elegy for a premodern world within which varied experiences could be exchanged and

6.   Eric Santner, *Stranded Objects: Mourning, Memory and Film in Postwar Germany*, Ithaca and London.
7.   D.W. Winnicott, 'The theory of the parent-infant relationship' (1960), in D.W. Winnicott, *Maturational Processes and the Facilitating Environment*, International Universities Press, New York 1965; and 'Transitional objects and transitional phenomena' (1951), in D.W. Winnicott, *Playing and Reality*, Tavistock, London 1971.

recognised.[8] He deploys the term to describe, then, types of experience which he believes to be on the wane. For Benjamin, an awareness of the time of nature, and of death, ground the auratic exchange of experience. But Benjamin believes that, in modernity, crowds, cities and machines have destroyed those conditions in which the gaze could be returned under the sign of death. In the modern world, death remains hidden, and the cycles of natural history are masked by the progress of the machine. In premodern communities, it was this awareness of death and of natural history which grounded the exchange of experience. An awareness of that which is shared: death, and the subjection to natural history, underpins the capacity to recognise others and their different experience. Thus, here, in Santner's return to Benjamin, we find a model for forms of *recognition* within which an awareness of human limitation, death and natural history undercut narcissism's fantasies of fusion with omnipotent heroes. Santner's aim is to wed Winnicott to Benjamin. Returning to Winnicott's notion of transitional space, Santner re-theorises the activities that take place there as 'auratic de-auratisation'.

Santner's theory of auratic de-auratisation has two combined aims, each of which is pertinent to our consideration of Hopkins's and Cooper's 'in-betweenness'. Firstly, Santner's theory can help us to understand and *appreciate* these performances in relation to history and politics: more particularly in relation to the threat of fascism which, as I have already suggested, lurks implicitly within each of the Hopkins vehicles, and, as Sykes's comments suggest, behind Cooper as well.

Santner advocates a contemporary culture of mourning-work, or of 'auratic de-auratisation', to counter what he sees as a contemporary political threat in the West: the threat that unless our western cultures nurture a culture of mourning, we risk falling back into a shared pathology similar to that which arguably gripped Germany fifty years ago. Though Santner stresses the differences between those times and our own, his opening premise is that the

> postmodern destabilisation of certain fundamental cultural norms and notions, above all those dealing with self-identity and community, cannot be understood without reference to the ethical and intellectual imperatives of life after Auschwitz. For if the postmodern is, in a crucial sense, about the attempt to

---

8. Walter Benjamin, *Illuminations: Essays and Reflections*, (Hannah Arendt (ed)), Schocken Books, New York 1968.

'think difference', we take on this risk in the knowledge of what can happen if we turn away from such labours (p xiv).

Santner's understanding of the collective pathology that contemporary instabilities threaten to induce is informed by his reading of Alexander and Margarete Mitscherlich's *The Inability To Mourn: Principles Of Collective Behaviour* (Grove Press, 1975), which attempted to explain the lack of melancholy and depression that might have been expected in postwar Germany after the loss of Hitler as *Fuhrer*. His re-reading begins from Freud's distinction between melancholy and mourning.[9] This distinction rests on an understanding of the primitive nature of melancholy's relation to loss. In mourning, what has been lost is understood to have been separate from the self. In melancholy, the lost object has been perceived not as separate from the self, but as a mirror 'of one's own sense of self and power' (Santner, p 2). A predisposition towards melancholy signals, therefore, an incomplete working-through of infantile narcissism, so that the self 'lacks sufficient strength and cohesion to tolerate, much less comprehend, the reality of separateness (p 3). In melancholic grieving, what is at stake is the coming to terms with separateness and with the *limitations* and *fallibilities* of the boundaried self. For the Mitscherlichs, the German people's identification with Hitler comes to be understood in relation to secondary narcissism: unstable conditions led to the formation of an identification with a powerful, larger-than-life figure, which enabled the German people to disavow the instabilities, in the fantasised return to narcissistic fantasies of fusion and omnipotence. Otherness - the child's separateness from the mother - comes to be revised, in this pathological secondary narcissism, as the threat posed to the nation by 'othered' groups: Jews; homosexuals; gypsies....

Santner's weaving together of the Mitscherlichs, Benjamin and Winnicott produces a cultural theory alert to questions of the psychical, and to questions of social and cultural history. The Mitscherlichs emphasise the interplay between a collective psyche and historical and environmental factors; Benjamin's elegy to the aura emerges within a broader consideration of modern life and culture. Winnicott's object relations approach to infantile development replaces Freud's emphasis on innate drives with a focus on the impact of the environment and the

---

9. Sigmund Freud, 'Mourning and Melancholia', *Standard Edition of The Complete Psychological Works of Sigmund Freud*, Hogarth Press, London 1953-74, vol XIV (first published 1917).

mother in infantile development.

Taken together, these influences enable Santner to make a significant shift. Much writing on the postmodern is suffused by what Santner describes as a postmodernist 'rhetoric of mourning' (p 7). Poststructuralist and Lacanian in orientation, such writing emphasises the primary losses entailed in the entry into culture and language, turning us all into heroic 'victim-survivors'. Such writing would have it that, though such losses have *always* been attendant upon the entry into culture, poststructuralist and Lacanian theory have made them apparent.

Santner's critique of this 'rhetoric of mourning' is two-pronged. Firstly, he argues that such an abstract theory makes us *all* heroic victim-survivors of loss: what place here for historical trauma and catastrophe? Secondly, he suggests that the writers who produce and even revel in this rhetoric of mourning (Derrida's name is foregrounded here) are actually narcissistically *retreating* from particular acts of mourning-work, by producing themselves and their readers as heroic victim-survivors. Santner returns to the Mitscherlichs to explain how an identification with the victim can occur as part of a retreat to secondary narcissism. According to the Mitscherlichs, the melancholy which should have followed on from the loss of the *Fuhrer* never took place. The trauma could not be acknowledged, and in place of acknowledgement what was found was a series of defences against the acknowledgement of loss: the past was de-realised; narcissistic identification shifted suddenly from Hitler to the allies; identification shifted to the victim. Santner's critique of the postmodernist rhetoric of mourning suggests, then, that its characterisation of the human subject as a heroic victim-survivor might be likened to the narcissism which, according to the Mitscherlichs, characterised the pathology which gripped post-fascist Germany, where the narcissistic identification with the *Fuhrer* was too toxic to be gradually and carefully worked-through in mourning-work.

In place of the postmodernist rhetoric of mourning, which Santner likens to this defensive and narcissistic post-war identification with the victim, Santner advocates a fully historicised approach to culture and mourning, that differentiates between historically specific identifications and fantasies. Here the analytic task becomes that of mapping the relations between a possibly universal, though *variously negotiated*, primary loss and later historical experience. This approach can aid us in our attempt to understand the emergence and appeal of Cooper and of the cluster of Hopkins vehicles under discussion.

The second prong of Santner's critique of the postmodernist rhetoric of mourning finds its advocacy of leave-taking paradoxically 'unpostmodern', in that it uncritically accepts and works with the binaries of fusion/separation and possession/mourning. Santner's critique of this unpostmodern mobilisation of rigid binaries returns to the psychoanalytic insistence that developmental stages are only ever layered over, rather than superseded by, later and more mature ways of thinking. Moreover, he reminds us, usefully, I think, that the residues of these early identifications and fantasies fuel later and more mature processes. Thus Santner proposes that narcissistic desire - the desire to be 'gazed upon' and fused with larger-than-life figures - is never completely abandoned: 'One must, in other words, learn to recognise and even celebrate the deep core of libidinal fuel of these apparatuses' (p 125).

Santner mounts this critique before moving on to propose the urgent need for a culture that can provide spaces for auratic de-auratisation: by which he means cultural spaces analogous to the space within which the child can come to terms with its losses under the mother's good-enough gaze. But for Santner these losses are always *historically specific*, as is the quality of the environment within which they can, or cannot, be assimilated.

Santner adovates this culture of auratic de-auratisation in relation to the perceived threat posed by modernity, which 'de-stabilises the good-enough communal structures that are required for the constitution of human selfhood as well as for the performance of labours of mourning in adult life (pp 126-7). Though Santner's thesis fails to engage with the constitution of *sexually differentiated* 'selves', it is nevertheless the case that the de-stabilisations of modernity have arguably led to what some have described as a crisis in patriarchal masculinity.[10] I therefore want to conclude this essay by returning, via Santner, to my *feminist* as well as to my historical questions concerning contemporary heroes and their fascinations. The patriarchal hero is classically defined as the *agent*, rather than the *object* of history and of narrative. The hero makes things happen. The victim, on the other hand has things done to him or her - is the object, that is, rather than the agent of narrative or history. In each of the Hopkins's vehicles, the main

---

10. Elsewhere, I have addressed the question of the relation between mourning and a 'crisis in masculinity' more fully: see Susannah Radstone, '"Too straight a drive to the tollbooth": Masculinity, Mortality and Al Pacino', in Pat Kirkham and Janet Thumim (eds), *Me Jane: Masculinity, Movies and Women*, Lawrence and Wishart, London 1995.

character is neither wholly victim, nor 'classical hero'. What follows from this is that each role falls somewhere 'in between', offering itself up neither for a purely narcissistic spectator, nor for a spectator who has taken absolute leave of such positions. Each performance, then, undertakes a *degree* of mourning-work, that can be appreciated from a feminist position, as well as from a Santnerian position concerned with questions of historically specific mourning tasks and *gradations* of mourning-work (though space precludes anything but the merest sketch of the historically nuanced work undertaken by each film).

Heroes, fantasy and history

Though in 'Comedy Heroes', Hopkins stressed the difference between his skills and capacities and those of Cooper, I suggested earlier that Hopkins' fascination for Cooper might be driven by a sense of something shared. I now want to propose that these similarities and differences can best be understood in relation to varieties of 'mourning-work'.

In *Shadowlands* the C.S. Lewis character emerges as time's *victim*. Though he comes to acknowledge emotional need, dependence and self-insufficiency, love comes too late, and the film leaves us crying tears of pathos and of nostalgia for a lost moment (of love) and a lost historical period - a period that the film lovingly evokes. If identification with the victim position constitutes a defence against mourning-work, then *Shadowlands'* pathetic victimhood emerges as closer to narcissism than to its working-through. Yet the tears elicited by the film *also* acknowledge that something has been worked-through, that to an extent, the Hopkins character has moved from the rigid and heavily bounded world of cloistered self-sufficiency to a world tempered by acknowledged need. Following Santner, I would propose that the mourning-tasks undertaken by the film respond to the demands of feminism and of postmodernism. The world of science, learning and absolute knowledge is challenged, as is the citadel within which narcissistic patriarchal masculinity attempts to secure itself against chastening intrusions. Yet those worlds are evoked nostalgically here, leading me to conclude that this film's 'in-betweenness' *defends* against postmodern and patriarchal losses more than it works them through.

Earlier, I proposed that *Silence Of The Lambs* enacts a process of displacement: that difference within, or internal 'otherness' that cannot be acknowledged, becomes displaced onto a monstrous figure, Hannibal Lecter, whose literal 'cutting up' of people represents a monstrous displacement of narcissism's working-through of hallucinatory fusion. Here, once again, the film's affect is produced through an identification with the victim position, which oscillates between those at threat from Lecter, and Lecter himself. But whereas *Shadowlands'* victim-hero arguably defends against mourning-work, here the glimpses of Lecter as victim limit the film's ability to construct the entire world as victim. Here, we are allowed a glimpse of the irrational processes that have formed him, and, by extension, aspects of ourselves. And since Lecter can only be freed if 'we' take back as our own the monstrously deformed aspects of ourselves that have formed him, *this* victim-hero arguably intitiates a degree of mourning-work. Earlier, I quoted a critic who viewed *Silence* as a 'self-devouring high culture *turning in on its own impeccable order'*. What I am finally proposing, then, is that in *Silence* the 'in-betweenness' constructed by our identification with a monstrous victim-hero does lean further towards mourning than it leans towards preservation: mourning and moving beyond, rather than preserving, that is, a modern culture that, in its rigid adherence to order, risks forgetting the disorderly within.

In my introductory description of *Remains Of The Day*, I argued, following Gillian Rose, that the power of this film rests in its undoing of historical and psychical idealisations of the past. Unlike *Shadowlands* and *Silence Of The Lambs*, which solicit our identification with a victim-hero, *Remains* refuses the spectator the comfort of wallowing in pathos and victimhood. Instead the butler gradually comes to acknowledge both his own responsibility in collusion and his own previously unacknowledged desire. This acknowledgement of *responsibility* does not return us to heroic agency, but to a chastened vision - to what Gillian Rose described as 'the remains of the day' - it delivers us, that is, to a vision of what is left, and what *can* be done, once omnipotent fantasies and narcissistic control are worked through. At the same time, *Remains* does allow the spectator many of the 'auratic' pleasures of the historical nostalgia film, pleasures that call up that narcissistic longing for an impossible return to a utopian past, only to work them through. This version of auratic de-auratisation arguably offers us a new chastened 'hero' whose lineaments appear cut to the measure of feminist, postmodernist and left political desire. Yet the Hopkins character *remains* fascinating, remains a powerful figure with whom to identify. The film, and the butler character, in particular, does occupy, then, that 'in-between' space that is the basis neither for narcissistic identification, nor for an absolute leave-taking from such positions: auratic de-auratisation. And its mourning tasks are clearly related to a postmodern coming to terms with chastened masculinity and with the threat posed to culture by an environment within which absolutes, certainties and clear allegiances rule. The film's strength, it seems to me, lies in its *explicit* historical references: to fascism and to a dying order. If it has a failing, it would lie perhaps in its final vision which offers so *very* little hope. The butler is aging; his redemption has come too late and to *that extent* the traces of pathetic victimhood - and victimhood's refusal to acknowledge imperfection - remain.

As the visual track of 'Comedy Heroes' displayed shots of Tommy Cooper hitting himself on the head with the ball he was supposed to be juggling, catching his hand in his 'trick' clock and bruising himself during a 'failed' attempt at karate, Eric Sykes concluded the remarks with which this article opened: 'that's the quality of Tom - and the quality of all the comics we know and love - their vulnerability.' Yet though, in Spike Milligan's words, his face was 'a call for help', and though the audience witness his *failing*, here pathos becomes the source of laughter rather than tears, and the joke becomes, in the words of Bob Monkhouse 'that you were watching him at all'. Here, that is, the defence of 'victimhood' is challenged by the consistency with which grandiosity is undermined.

Cooper's 'victimhood', the desire for magic, and for a hero with super-human powers, is clearly grounded in narcissism, but so too perhaps is the capacity to become *helpless* with laughter, as feelings of utter dependency merge with fantasies of larger-than-life figures: as Spike Milligan said of Tommy Cooper, 'he could do *anything* to me.' To be sure, then, the comedian trades on those primitive desires for the long lost heroes of infancy. Yet, as admirer after admirer testified, Tommy had only to stand up, to have audiences *weak* with laughter, as the joke became that they were watching him at all. Though even his posture and facial expression spoke of the sheer ridiculousness of him standing there and 'us' watching him, his magic tricks elaborated the story. Though the audiences wanted magic, and though his tricks spoke to that desire, the *real* pleasure was, as one critic has already pointed out, in witnessing the magic fail:

for it was his awareness of the limitations of his magic role that produces the most brilliant comedy. You know his tricks won't work, that his sleight-of-hand will be as surreptitious as a brickie's hod - the flowers from the empty vase only pop out when he struggles with the spring mechanism, the disappearing clock-in-the-box disappears only to fall out of the back...And this was Tommy's genius: his unfaltering ability for getting his trade wrong, for showing the mechanisms and strains of his theatrical performance - then expecting to get rewarded for it.'[11]

Stuart Cosgrove's reading of Tommy Cooper foregrounds his anarchic undermining of the work ethic: 'Cooper's aesthetic form of human work, with all its wasted efforts and desperate humour, came far closer to the real futility of industrial labour than the smooth blandishments of the "proper" magician; and the response is empathy and laughter, rather than respectful applause.' While this 'workerist' reading of Cooper is illuminating, what it overlooks is that the audience's applause and laughter paradoxically acknowledged the skill with which Cooper's 'bungling' had been performed. Time after time, Cooper's admirers spoke of the sheer work and effort Cooper invested in getting 'getting it wrong' right. But even here, the emphasis is on *work*, reminding us, once more, that there *is* no such thing as magic, and that this hero had, in Spike Milligan's words, 'hands like bunches of bananas' - and feet of clay. Earlier in this article, I was trying to explore the fascination exerted by this ambiguous performance that intertwines power with powerlessness, capacity with incapacity. I am now proposing that Cooper's performances exactly enacted the process of auratic de-auratisation; but what mourning-tasks did such performances work through? In 'Heroes of Comedy', references to the British experience of the Second World War came thick and fast. War-time experience was certainly chastening, levelling and disabusing of omnipotent fantasies, particularly concerning Britain and Britishness. Yet for all that, Britain did win the war and defeat fascism. Cooper's performance, his creation of a space that is both auratic and de-auratising can best be understood, perhaps, in this context: in the context of a nation's struggle to come to terms with its losses and its gains, though the reasons for one nation's fall into fascism and another nation's defeat of fascism are clearly far more complex than this consideration of heroic qualities can admit.

Though 'Heroes of Comedy' mourned Cooper - though the programme was elegiac - here, mourning was tied not to the wished-for return of impossible idealised heroes, but to a wished-for space in which such impossible nostalgic longings become transformed into the bonds of an alliance of care - a care that even inflected

---

11. Stuart Cosgrove, *New Musical Express*, 16 August, 1986.

the tone of Cooper's critics: 'Several scores of readers told me why they disliked Tommy Cooper...What I liked about their letters was their *tolerance*. Quite a few admitted that they could be wrong. Hardly anybody wanted to have Tom shot, flogged, or strangled...'[12] This appreciation of Tommy Cooper has not been 'politically correct'. I have not attempted to read his performance in relation to difference. I have not asked how different audiences, in different places and times, might read Cooper. Instead, I am proposing that his performance provided a space in which the fear of 'difference'could be worked through—a space in which auratic de-auratisation took place, and relations between imperfect others could be forged: 'hardly anybody wanted to have Tom shot, flogged or strangled.' In *Stranded Objects*, Eric Santner argues that it was precisely this space - the space of auratic de-auratisation - that postwar Germany lacked, and that our society loses at its peril. Remember Tommy Cooper.

---

12. Peter Black, *Daily Mail*, 22 April 1986.

An exemplary life

Graham Martin

Graham Martin *reviews* Fred Inglis's *recent biography of* Raymond Williams *(Routledge, 1995)*

A shilling life will give you all the facts,
How Father beat him, how he ran away,
What were the struggles of his youth, what acts
Made him the greatest figure of his day.

W H Auden

The unslakeable contemporary thirst for biography is a considerable puzzle - what are biographies for, and why do people read them? About novelists and poets, they threaten the actual writings with a reductionist short-cut to what these are 'really about', interlaced with a secular version of that popular mediaeval *genre*, the Saint's Life. Guided by the devout narrator, we put aside the writer's works the better to contemplate the scrupulously recovered genealogy, to gaze reverently upon the childhood photographs, and wonder over the iconic record of the maturing, and then impressively adult figure. We make pilgrimage to the house sanctified by the remarkable birth, to the uncomprehending school ('little did they know that...&c.'), to the otherwise so-ordinary place of first inspiration, pressing forward to all those other locations worked into the well-known novels and poems, which the varied scenery then comes to blur and overlie: Hardy's Wessex, Lawrence's Eastwood, Yeats's Tower, Dickens's London (swept away before he died), Eliot's Burnt Norton (he visited it once). In reading such accounts, one has to keep reminding oneself that it is the art that matters, and matters because it is *not* the life, despite the complementary truth that the life can say things about the art which the art from choice or necessity has concealed.

But when it comes to 'men of ideas', what is their life-story supposed to tell you? How does the perusal of Wittgenstein's assist the reader toiling through *Philosophical Investigations*, save to draw attention to all those preoccupations he kept out of them? Is there not often the assumption that the 'work' is the product of a unitary 'mind' of which the life-story at last gives us the measure? Or are such biographies no more than attempts to satisfy friendly curiosity, meanwhile doing their best to keep their powerful siblings - the cold, competitive, intrusive, and malicious varieties - on the leash? Inglis's biography of Raymond Williams, much more influential in the role of 'man of ideas' than that of serious novelist, gives an unexpected answer to such questions. 'Love is what counts in this story' (p 2), be begins - the love, esteem, admiration, which Williams attracted from his biographer, as from so many readers of his works, from his fellows in political activity, and from his pupils, on whose behalf Inglis hopes also to speak. It is not, then, an intellectual biography, a tracing of the origins and development of Williams's; leading ideas, accompanied by discussion of their value and influence. Nor is it an account of the strategies and themes of the fiction, of its relation to the literary criticism, further complemented with analyses of the strengths and failings of Williams's; varied prose styles - discursive, meditative, polemic, autobiographical, narrative. Both kinds of book are needed, and Inglis makes incidental points about all these writings, but his over-riding interest is in the man. What were his qualities? How did they come to make him so highly regarded, indeed famous? Or if that term is now too emptied of meaning by its application to fifteen-minute nonentities, what was there in public life which responded to, may also have been elicited by, Williams's qualities? The story has then its social-historical dimension, but in the main it is personal, both commemorative and celebratory, and Inglis is admirably direct about the varied reminiscences that allow it to be so. Instead of merely foot-noting his narrative with supporting references, the text interweaves with Inglis's own voice generous quotations from the voices of interviewees drawn from every phase of Williams's

'This biography is a product not just of love, but of critical love'

life. And he is direct in a more testing way. Biographies start, or should start, as a dialogic encounter between the biographer and the subject, and can be judged by the degree to which the biographer inhabits the mind of that subject, and yet keeps a certain distance from it. Inglis both attempts this difficult task, and is open about his limited success. He provides as comprehensive an account of Williams's character and achievements as his sources and his insight make possible, and at the same time interposes his own reservations about both, leading some reviewers - expecting hagiography and stupefied by not finding it - to complain that he'd been unable to make up his mind. But as well as a narrative, the book engages in debate, briefer and more limited than one would like, sometimes confined to splutters of exasperated dissent, but debate nevertheless. It is, in a word, a product not just of love, but of critical love.

I nglis's main aim, then, has been to fill out - here and there to revise - the general shape of Williams's life as recounted in *Politics and Letters* (1979). His story is the product of admirably thorough research - seeking out interviewees surviving from his earliest years, leafing through the local Abergavenny newspapers for a particularly interesting chapter on the town's life in the 1930s, checking on Williams's student and Army journalism, surveying his adult education work in the 1950s, delving into the business correspondence with his publisher Chatto and Windus, and of course immersing himself in the more predictable primary sources: the host of books and articles, and their reviews, Williams's influence on the New Left and role in the establishment of *New Left Review*, his political involvement with colleagues such as Stuart Hall, Edward Thompson and Michael Rustin in the production of the 1967 *May Day Manifesto*, and lastly, incorporating the impressions and reflections of his one-time Cambridge students, a distinguished roster including such as Anthony Barnett, Terry Eagleton, Stephen Heath, Patrick Parrinder and Bernard Sharratt. There is some 'novelising' about the childhood days, but happily no resort to the language biographers fall back on when, short of evidence, they cook up explanatory states of mind ('he must have', 'we may suppose', 'surely'). Confronted with puzzles and vaguenesses he can't account for, Inglis says precisely this. All in all, he has done an impressively comprehensive job to which any future writer about Williams can only be indebted.

One especially striking episode is worth mentioning here - Williams's correspondence with Perry Anderson and Francis Mulhern about the after-effect of the *Politics and Letters* interviews. The one direct revelation of his subject's inner life which Inglis is able to provide, its revelatory point is that, in contrast to the characteristic aplomb with which Williams sustained his inquisitorial experience, and the self-critical honesty as well as eloquent fullness of his responses to questions probing into every aspect of his work, he nevertheless found its upshot desperately troubling. He reported to Anderson that for three or four months he had given up serious work, a condition never before experienced, and so depressing as to give him *personal* knowledge 'for the first time (of) the states out of which defeatist and reactionary ideologies have been so often built since the war' (p 261). Such an effect is surprising enough. But even more so is Williams's seeming lack of surprise. What more natural than that the experience would leave its mark? Yet this strenuous going-over of his life and achievements seems to have come upon him as a shockingly fresh experience. One is left with the disturbing thought that he had never before undertaken such searching self-criticism, difficult though this may be to believe. Inglis refrains from speculating on the event, and here one meets his main limitation. Thus, he supplies evidence of some striking contradictions in Williams's 'working' personality. His explicit commitment to

'His explicit commitment to openness of debate was coupled with a persistent refusal to respond to constructive criticism'

openness of debate was coupled with a persistent refusal to respond to constructive criticism, a closely related failure to acknowledge debts to other writers, and an indifference to those minimal disciplines of intellectual exchange - the provision of references to the books and texts he was discussing and of adequate bibliographies - as if such time-wasting chores could be left to less original minds. Inglis notes these failings with puzzled regret, but one looks in vain for the recognition that they might be directly related to Williams's artistic and intellectual creativity, both in its strength and in its shortcomings. Some such link, at any rate, would help to account for the 'almost paralysing state' (p 261) which the PL interviews brought about. By impinging upon a necessary solitude, did they bring its necessity into question, and by doing so threaten that hidden spring of positive energy which Williams is so remarkable for always having being able to tap? The many passages of murky prose that mar his discursive writing might then be the defensive carapace for his inability to envisage clearly (save perhaps in the dispiritingly sombre version sketched in *Modern Tragedy* (1966)) the route to the acceptable human future which was his never-to-be-relinquished passion.

For it is in such prose that Williams's unshakeable self-assurance reads too often as routine gesture, whereas in the novels the doubts and hesitations, the difficulties and defeats, find ample voice, and especially in those fictional self-explorations which follow the PL interviews - *Loyalties* (1985) and *The People of the Black Mountains* (1989-90). Indeed, for one self-assessment of his life's achievement, the best clue lies in the superb 'The Tale of the Measurer' (*PBM*, Vol One).

But the question to pursue here is the relevance of this survey of the 'life' to the 'work', and certainly it helps to account for some aspects of the novels. For example, their limited success in portraying a form of contemporary life representing the values Williams strove to affirm can be traced, at least in part, to the fact that, after 1945, his public life was that of a teacher, an academic, a left-wing intellectual. These roles provide notoriously meagre access to the variety of social experience which feeds into the best 'realist' novels. Think, for example, of the contrast between the social range of Angus Wilson's and of Iris Murdoch's. And as Williams himself remarks in PL, lacking face-to-face knowledge of the real movers and shakers of the modern world, he could provide no satisfactory novelistic representation of the workings of high capitalism. Then, despite his personal friendliness, his courtesy, that sustained good will to others that he so strikingly conveyed, his life was solitary, even reclusive - apart, that is, from his devotion to his wife and family - and, so it seems, by determined choice. Inglis describes a pattern of near-monastic self-discipline, a 'clenched withdrawal' (p 214) - the phrase is Eagleton's - from other than formal relationships, precisely the condition in which a man is likely to hear no other voices than his own - and it marks the novels. The monochrome interchanges which they too often offer as dialogue come to seem, in the end, a fictional mask for lonely meditation, while 'Koba', the play about Stalin illustrating the general argument of *Modern Tragedy*, is little more than an anguished internal debate, at best a draft for radio, which only talented actors could bring to 'performing' life. (Not that Williams lacked a natural ear for contemporary idiom and speech-rhythms: *The Volunteers* (1978) shows that he had, and in full measure.) Inglis also brings out the sense in which, for Williams, intellectual culture meant *books*, meant *reading*. Here was a Professor of Drama - the paradox has been noted before - who scarcely went to the theatre. He seems to have had no non-intellectual hobbies. Neither cinema nor music had a significant place in his imaginative life. Nor did travel, even in Britain. His first visit to an eighteenth century country mansion came about, not when he was writing *The Country and The City* (1973), but some years later when making a TV programme about his own life. Admirers of the books on communications and television will be interested to learn that no TV set appeared in the Williams house before 1968, when he began his reviewing stint for *The Listener*. The strenuous intellectuality of the novels would seem to be related to such causes. It is no accident that only in his *magnum opus*, *The People of the Black Mountains* (1989-90), did his fictional and poetic gifts come to fruition. Its location in the numinous scenes of his childhood and youth, its short story form, its extraordinary pre-historical range, released him from the heavy responsibility of inventing the conversations, characters, plausible situations and interesting plots, which would speak for his own time. Inglis quotes his publisher's opinion that Williams was 'no novelist' (p 292), but there are many kinds of novel, and the problem rather is that Williams only latterly discovered the kind he could do best. The 'realist' novels have fine things in them, yet overall they are too much the product of Williams's conscience, his sense of responsibility, and also his sense of fair play. The cold-eyed and angry satirist who now and again gets a showing in the Welsh trilogy might have been a more creative muse.

What then of the 'man of ideas'? Paradoxically, Inglis's biographical account is of greatest interest precisely where, on general grounds, it might be thought tangential. In the summer of 1946, after completing his Cambridge degree, Williams's immediate project was to write - kicking off with the earliest of many versions of the novel he finally published as *Border Country* (1960). But, already married, already a father, he first needed a job, and when the Oxford Delegacy for Extra-Mural Studies advertised for a Staff Tutor, he landed it. For an intending writer - the description he preferred to 'novelist' - the terms and duties were ideal: two or three weekly evening classes for six months of the year plus some summer school teaching left his mornings free for writing and class preparation, as well as considerable space in the summer months. With the crucial support of his devoted wife, he was thus able to establish the working regimen from which he was never to waver, and which underlay his astounding productivity: writing from 9 to 1, morning after morning after morning. During these years as a Staff Tutor, he was to complete *Reading and Criticism* (1950), *Drama and Society from Ibsen to Eliot* (1952), *Drama and Performance* (1954) and *Culture and Society* (1958), to assemble much of the material for *Keywords* (1976) and the literary-historical chapters for *The Long Revolution* (1961), and to draft yet more *versions* of *Border Country*. This range, in itself noteworthy, is also central to some major themes. The theoretical work on 'culture' and 'literature' developed, as he later remarked, out of his practice *as a novelist*, to which can be added, out of his practice as an adult educator, laying the groundwork for the 'idea' books by way of the courses he designed and the classes he discussed them with. His explicit dissolution of the conventional categories which sealed off one kind of discourse from another (fiction, social history, politics, culture) drew directly upon his 'actual experience' - to use that so characteristic Williams phrase. Here too is the source of the memorable interplay between literary 'text' and social-historical 'context', his radical denial of final

'No TV set appeared in the Williams house before 1968'

authority to either kind of evidence, which was crucial to the method of such later books as *Modern Tragedy*, *The English Novel from Dickens to Lawrence* (1970), and *The Country and The City*, and the theoretical foundation of what we now know as New Historicism.

But there is a deeper autobiographical presence in much of this work. Yeats claimed that the mind's contents at the age of seventeen provide the substance of all later writing, and, give or take a year or two, Williams could well have agreed. Some of the signs are explicit enough: the anecdotes drawn from his own life and that of his parents and grandparents worked into the elaborately learned argument of so many books. The celebrated essay defining culture, not as 'the acquainting ourselves with the best that has been known and said in the world' but as 'a way of life', enforces its democratic case with the tale of the obstacles which 'privilege' put in his way when, as an ordinary young man, he arrived at Hereford Cathedral to look at the mediaeval *Mappa Mundi*. A principal thesis of *Modern Tragedy*, that academic definitions of 'tragedy' incorporate a class bias, takes off from the memory of the life and death of his socialist father, implicitly celebrated as one instance amongst thousands and thousands of those who have actively contributed to the long historic and continuing action of 'revolutionary tragedy'. The opening chapter of *The Country and the City* is an even more striking case. 'This book', he wrote, 'often and necessarily follows impersonal procedures, in description and analysis, [but] there is behind it, this personal pressure and commitment' (p 3). He then recounts the complex of loyalties and linkages to the country life of his grandfather - farmworker and roadmender - and of his father - boy farmworker, then part-signalman, part-market-gardener - which he carried forward in his own personal journey from the Black Mountain country village to the city of Cambridge, and thus into the network of his educated and desk-bound life; he recounts its further reverberations, through his writing, with the cities of Rome, Moscow and New York, and, through his reading, its links with Bunyan, for whom Cambridge was a model for Vanity Fair, with *Jude the Obscure's* unattainable Christminster, and with H G Wells' sinister vision of metropolitan London.

None of this, needless to say, is decorative packaging, but neither is it only autobiography as *ad hominem* argument, as rhetoric. His own and his family's histories become the material for a sustained impersonalisation, obvious enough in the novels, but just as central in such governing ideas as 'lived experience' - that richly elusive idea whose radiations so exasperate the cultural theorist - 'structure of feeling', and 'selective tradition'. While the first of these risks the charge of head-in-the-sand individualism, as if to say 'such is my experience, and that's evidence enough for me', primarily it invokes the absolute value of each individual human life, shaped by its irreversible choices, and by the truth that, whatever social and historical determinations pressed upon its development, one life is as much as anyone has to live, and it always points, like time's arrow, in the one direction. 'Structure of feeling' generalises one aspect of such 'lived experience'. Less a theoretic concept than a potent metaphor, it focuses on the intimate inter-relationship of 'society' and 'individual', both the formation of the one by the other, and its direct opposite - what we conceptualise as 'society' exists only in the varyingly conscious experiences of 'individuals'. Where 'structure' invokes the concepts and relativities examined in sociology, economics, and history, 'feeling' appeals to the absolute ways any and all of these conditions are experienced in particular lives. By incorporating the contradiction, by insisting upon the tension between its two centrifugal terms, Williams's phrase declares the inadequacy of conceiving lives either as mere products of social 'forces', passive vectors for 'structural determinations', or as a-historic 'inner' transcendences whose material condition can be dismissed as superficial accident. As always in his work, in place of *either-or* simplicities he opts for the difficult totalising of *both-and*. One remembers from *Keywords* that the entry for 'determined' insists upon both its

> 'In place of *either-or* simplicities he opts for the difficult totalising of *both-and*'

passive and active meanings. It remains also true that Williams' deployment of the notion can present difficulties. Does 'structure of feeling' articulate both the experience of a specific novelist or playwright and that of his/her readers or audience? For the English novelists of the 1840s surveyed in *Culture and Society* there is enough evidence that it did. But in *Modern Tragedy* - discussing both European and American playwrights and novelists and in the chapters from Ibsen to Beckett spanning nearly a century - the range of distinct socio-historical 'structures' supposedly at work gets no detailed recognition, so that 'structure of feeling' begins to point to the unwitting influence of Williams's own history. The analyses and procedures can turn out less impersonal than they need to be.

'Selective tradition', perhaps the most influential of Williams's leading ideas, made its appearance in *Culture and Society*, at a time which anticipates by at least a decade its detailed application to other fields than literature, and it too generates its conceptual power from an autobiographical root, in this case not just the life, but the difficulty of writing about that life. As Inglis brings out, the final version of those seven earlier attempts at an autobiographical novel which we now know as *Border Country* was only completed after the death of Harry Williams, Raymond's father. Only then, it seems, did the novelist overcome the powerful exemplar of *Sons and Lovers*, which he read as an 'escape narrative' about the talented working-class boy climbing the educational ladder and leaving behind the formative culture of his upbringing.

Border Country enacts the reverse journey in which the academic son finally learns how to re-affirm in his own experience the values which the father lived, making possible his son's different life but for which in his own he could find no satisfactory language. Such a language, such an articulation of the father's vision, is the whole novel Williams finally completed, by explicitly confronting the disjunction between the specific idiom of the father's 'known community' and the idiom of its estranged observer, the educated son. This idea then comes to dominate his subsequent discussion of Eliot, Hardy and Lawrence in *The English Novel* ... and by successfully dislodging Leavis's selective Great Tradition, Williams demonstrates the more radical point that the construction of all such 'traditions' is a response to key moments of historical change, and that it is cultural institutions and structures that define and sustain them.

Williams and Wordsworth: as Inglis says, the resemblance has often been floated, but it does no justice to Williams's radical passion for transforming 'this pragmatical pig of a world' - the phrase is Yeats's whose alternative was, of course, 'spiritual'. For Williams the alternative was always 'material' and historical, always directed towards an achievable human future, but like Yeats's, whatever the qualifications, his best work springs from living that contradiction between the 'real' and the desired to the day of his death; and in that most honourable of senses, it remains exemplary.

Whose Heroes Does A City Remember?

Cynthia Cockburn

Cynthia Cockburn reviews The Power of Place:
Urban Landscapes as Public History by Dolores
Hayden (The MIT Press, 1995)

When I was a child and my mother took me shopping in town she'd point to the bronze statue of a stout gentleman in Victorian clothes, commanding the intersection near the local businessmen's dining club. 'That', she'd say, 'is one of your great-great-uncles.' I never learned any more about this man. But in a way I didn't need to. The presence of the statue was enough to tell us all: he counted. About the women of my family, of course, I have been able to learn even less: they didn't count.

In such ways is a place selective about its heroes and its history. The city fathers and captains of industry build monuments to men in their own image. And historians usually single out as important the buildings and areas where money has been turned to stone, neo-gothic, neo-classical or rococo.

Dolores Hayden has an alternative idea about the people and events that places could memorialise. She is an architect who moved from Massachusetts to Los Angeles in 1979. For five years she struggled to get to know and understand the city. And she had the luck, or the wit, to meet groups of working women and men of different ethnic groups who had their own take on Los Angeles and its past.

Hayden launched an initiative she called The Power of Place. It involved a small nonprofit corporation that had the purpose of 'situating women's history

219

and ethnic history in downtown, in public places, through experimental, collaborative projects by historians, designers and artists.' The book of the same name is the story, and analysis, of a series of projects that resulted.

The Power of Place asks the question: behind the self-presentation of the owners and their architects, what can we still see of the unremembered makers of this place, the great majority of its past inhabitants? Which of their landmarks are still visible, in spite of savage redevelopment? How can women and 'people of color' recover and give a pride of place to our own past?

The initiative worked with collaborative teams of historians, artists, architects, planners and local organisations to find, as Hayden puts it, 'ways to rebuild public memory in the city around different sites and buildings'. The book focuses on three exercises in what she calls 'a politics of place construction, redefining the mainstream experience' while bringing into view something formerly unseen.

One piece of historical research identifies the work and workplaces of the women, children and men who were the labour force of the city from the earliest settlements until World War Two. A practical project that arose from this involved the 'reinterpretation' of the Embassy Auditorium, a union hall used by Latina and Russian Jewish garment workers. A second exercise recovered Little Tokyo, a historic district of small businesses launched by Japanese American immigrants.

'The people you really admire in history often don't have a photograph, let alone a statue, to their name'

The third put Hayden on the trail of a woman slave known as Biddy Mason, and this project illustrates well the way artists' as well as historians' imaginations were able to redefine and re-present the heroic in an urban redevelopment.

Biddy Mason was born a slave in 1818 in the deep South of the USA, and like other slaves was forbidden to learn to read or write. But life gave her a good knowledge of herbal medicine and nursing, and she became valuable to her owners as a midwife. She was granted her freedom by a California court in 1851, at a time when Los Angeles housed no more that 1600 people, only twelve of whom were African Americans. By the 1890s, when she died, the city was three times the size, had a black population of 1200 and was on the way to becoming an industrial city.

Biddy Mason became one of the growing city's leading citizens. She reared her three daughters alone. She became famous as a midwife, delivering hundreds of babies of both the rich and the poor, white and black. She helped found the Los Angeles branch of the First African Methodist Episcopal Church, owned real estate and used her homestead to help her family into business.

The *Power of Place* project was at first demoralised to find that the site of Biddy Mason's homestead at 331 Spring Street was today an expanse of asphalt. But a redevelopment of the parking lot was due: the plan was for a ten storey garage with commercial space on the ground floor. The agency responsible for the design invited the *Power of Place* group to include some kind of commemoration of Biddy Mason.

'Perhaps they had a bronze plaque in mind', Hayden says. What they got was something more complex and more beautiful. As project director she recruited a team of artists. Susan E. King, a letterpress printer, produced a limited edition large-format book commemorating Mason, titled *HOME/Stead*. Sculptor Betye Saar transformed one corner of the pedestrian area with a photo-mural representing Biddy Mason's house and family, and an installation of a window frame with a portrait of Mason herself.

The largest and most complicated of the memorials was Sheila Levrant de Bretteville's 81-foot long wall entitled *Biddy Mason: Time and Place*. Decade by decade, the wall tells the story of the development of Los Angeles from an unimportant little Mexican town, in synchrony with Mason's own journey through time. In the plaster are impressions of Mason's obstetric instruments, the waggon wheels, her freedom papers, the homestead fence.

I like this idea that heroes can be deconstructed, that they don't need to be individualist dragon-slayers. Bronze Bertie and his kind can be knocked off their York stone perches in the middle of traffic roundabouts and replaced in the collective memory by movements, groups, and even, heaven knows, black women. It makes you realise that the people you really admire in history often don't have a photograph, let along a statue, to their name. And if you met one of these great white male heroes he'd look straight through you, and should you have the misfortune to find yourself sitting next to him at a municipal dinner you wouldn't have anything to say to him anyway.

Dolores Hayden's book makes me feel a little more patient with the continual naming and renaming of city places. I used to feel: what's the point of changing St Petersburg to Leningrad and back again? But all it is, after all, is a way of enlisting a reading of history into today's political struggles. Having Biddy Mason immortalised on a Los Angeles wall says less about Biddy herself than it does about black women in Los Angeles today. To them it says: look, this black woman was deemed significant. And everyone who looks with admiration at her marks in this place can look at you with the same eyes.

There are two formulae for the hero. There's the boring, immanent one, hero as worthy role model: see, you could do this too. And there's the transcendent one - the Jungian archetype who emerges from obscurity, overcomes obstacles, impales evil on his sword and marries the king's daughter. But a satisfactory hero doesn't have to be either of these. The best hero is simply a life lived before you that somehow affirms the potential value of your own.

Soundings

from the Editors

We said in Soundings No.1 that future issues would have 'theme' sections, usually compiled by guest editors. You have now seen *Law and Justice*, edited by Bill Bowring and *Heroes and Heroines* which we edited ourselves. Our plans for the next three issues are:

No.3 *The Public Good*, to be edited by Maureen Mackintosh
No.4 *Democracy and the Media*, to be edited by Bill Schwarz and Dave Morley
No.5 *'Young Britain'*, to be edited by Jonathan Rutherford.

(Of course, this order of things might have to be changed if there's an early election!)

The *Soundings* editors are responsible for compiling the front, more general, part of the journal. These sections will include articles by Grahame Thompson and Paul Hirst, Mike Kenny, Anne Phillips and Robin Murray. We'd be happy to have your suggestions for themes, authors and topics.

Subscriptions so far have exceeded our expectations - up by 12 per cent. We're pleased with progress, and hope you are too. If you'd like to lend a hand, you could:

- Introduce *Soundings* to friends
- Work as a volunteer in the office
- Persuade your library to take out an institutional subscription
- Interest a bookshop in taking copies

Soundings is an independent, non-profit making organisation. If you would like to make a financial contribution towards the promotion of the journal, we'd be glad to hear from you.

Stuart Hall   *Doreen Massey*   *Michael Rustin*

C/O   Lawrence & Wishart
99a Wallis Road
London E9 5LN

Soundings

Soundings is a journal of politics and culture. It is a forum for ideas which aims to explore the problems of the present and the possibilities for a future politics and society. Its intent is to encourage innovation and dialogue in progressive thought. Half of each future issue will be devoted to debating a particular theme: topics in the pipeline include: The Public Good, The Media and Democracy, 'Young Britain'.

Why not subscribe?
Make sure of your copy

Subscription rates, 1996 (3 issues)

INDIVIDUAL SUBSCRIPTIONS
UK   £35.00
Rest of the World   £45.00

INSTITUTIONAL SUBSCRIPTIONS
UK   £70.00
Rest of the World   £80.00

Please send me one year's subscription starting with Issue Number _____

I enclose payment of £ _____

I wish to become a supporting subscriber and enclose a donation of £ _____

I enclose total payment of £ _____

Name _____

Address _____

_____

_____ Postcode _____

Please return this form with cheque or money order payable to Soundings and send to:

Soundings, c/o Lawrence & Wishart, 99A Wallis Road, London E9 5LN